The Wine and Food Lover's Diet

THE WINE AND FOOD LOVER'S DIET

28 Days of Delicious Weight Loss

BY PHILLIP TIRMAN, M.D.

Photographs by Caren Alpert

CHRONICLE BOOKS

SAN FRANCISCO

ACKNOWLEDGMENTS

Library of Congress Cataloging-in-Publication Data available.

ISBN-10 0-8118-5220-2
ISBN-13 978-0-8118-5220-3

Manufactured in China.

Designed by Beverly Joel
Prop styling by Carol Hacker
Food styling by Basil Friedman
Assistant food styling by Victoria Woollard

Distributed in Canada by Raincoast Books
9050 Shaughnessy Street
Vancouver, British Columbia
V6P 6E5

10 9 8 7 6 5 4 3 2 1

Chronicle Books LLC
680 Second Street
San Francisco, California
94107

www.chroniclebooks.com

Linda Manaster has been a partner throughout and is in large part responsible for this book coming to fruition. While she doesn't have a medical degree, she was constantly questioning and challenging the medical basis behind the Wine and Food Lover's Diet and served as the chief intellectual quality control.

Bruce Falstein is as talented a writer as can be found. His talent was evident from the very first iteration of the book and he has the ability of working magic with words. I never heard him complain when a rewrite was necessary. His personality seeps into the whole text. He was able to transform pages upon pages of what must have seemed like incredibly boring medical diatribes into something digestible, cogent, and infinitely more readable.

Penelope Wisner transformed the recipes. Her knowledge is unsurpassed and her recommendations were almost uniformly accepted and appreciated. We spent a few afternoons "chewing the fat" about how certain principles should come across. Thank you.

Copy editor Judith Dunham transformed the whole book, from the beginning, and I thank her for her patience as we honed the pages down into what it is today.

Bill LeBlond, our editor at Chronicle Books, kept us all encouraged and on time and has become a real friend. I've seen him in action and watched him put the pieces together, in just the right way, on a routine basis. Bill, we now know what a "real editing process" is about. Amy Treadwell, associate editor, has done a tremendous job in keeping the wheels greased, and I thank her and Bill for always saying "well, OK, two more days, but no later than..."

Early on in the information-gathering phase of this book, my nephew Philippe Tirman, a medical student at the University of Arkansas, spent many hours doing library research. I am deeply indebted to him.

I'd like to thank my brothers and sisters (Claude, Michelle, Christine, David, and Geoffrey) for helping all along the way. Claude was a dependable recipe tester and his wife, Arlette, was enthusiastic in her comments as well. Geoff was always encouraging and helpful with suggestions. My family and I still have "inspirational" dinners together, usually at a Michelin-rated European restaurant, enjoying a true gourmet experience while staying with the Wine and Food Lover's Diet principles.

Linda's parents, Ann and Mickey, were always supportive and encouraging and her sister Susan was brimming with ideas.

Also thanks to my friends Trudy Edelson and Steve Katznelson, Demetra Wolford, Jackie Littman, and my other friends who tested recipes.

I'd like to thank my radiology partners in the National Orthopedic Imaging Associates for their support through this whole process. They were most encouraging and curious. I think it is why they are the best in the world at what they do—musculoskeletal MRI. I'd especially like to thank Betsy Holland who was very supportive early on.

I'd like to thank Chef Bernard Guillas, executive chef at the La Jolla Beach & Tennis Club, Doug Katz, chef at Fire restaurant, and Dan Baker, chef at Marché aux Fleurs, for providing recipes from their fabulous restaurants. Also I'd like to thank Dr. Clinton Pinto and Dr. Mickey Jester for their recipe contributions. I had no idea that some radiologists like to cook!

Finally I'd like to thank my Mom, the little French lady who lives in Little Rock, Arkansas, who inspired me to cook and really enjoy food and life in an epicurean way, and my late father, a brilliant radiologist, whose curiosity was insatiable and whose analytical skills were broad and far-reaching. His core principles inspired me not to accept blindly what appears to be the truth, but to search and find it instead. Finally I'd like to mention my French grandmother, Berte. When I was over-weight and was the big-shot doctor lecturing her on how she should eat less fat she looked me square in the eyes and said, "I'm 94 years old and you are going to tell me how to eat?" Touché, Mèmére.

CONTENTS

INTRODUCING THE WINE AND FOOD LOVER'S DIET

I love good food. I hate being overweight. I love to drink wine with dinner. I hate the self-deprivation of dieting. If you feel the way I do, you'll agree that it's time to change the love/hate relationship so many of us have with food.

The Wine and Food Lover's Diet celebrates our love of good food and wine. It acknowledges that for many of us, just as air and water are essential to the continuation of life, good food and a well-paired wine are essential to the enjoyment of life.

When we choose foods wisely and prepare them deliciously, we not only deliver the energy that powers every cell in the body, but also achieve the satisfaction that good food, as well as good wine, can provide. Good food is life-affirming; through it we experience both sensual delight and the gratification of personal reward.

No wonder, then, that traditional concepts of dieting fail to deliver the results we expect. How can we stay with a regimen that requires us to give up one of our primary sources of enjoyment, satisfaction, fulfillment, and fellowship? I sure couldn't.

You don't need a medical degree to know that, for millions of people who've tried them, the popular low-carb and low-fat diets don't work for the long term. Merely reducing carbohydrate or fat intake might work for a while, but once you return to your old way of eating, the extra weight will come right back. Self-deprivation is not a solution you can live with for the long term.

Losing weight helps us feel good about ourselves; eating well helps us feel good about life. A successful diet helps us do both.

Six years ago, I was an overweight, stressed-out doctor seeing overweight, stressed-out patients. Most mornings, I awoke feeling bloated and groggy. By early afternoon I was sleepy, lacking stamina and energy, and by early evening felt utterly exhausted. I drifted from one diet to the next, dropping pounds for a time, only to regain them. Years of medical training told me that there had to be a practical solution to yo-yo dieting and self-deprivation. Common sense told me that the human body itself would provide the answer.

Long before the recent low-carb diet fad raised, then dashed, the hopes of millions, I let science and common sense lead me to a diet based on low-glycemic carbohydrates in combination with protein and some fats—the Wine and Food Lover's Diet before there even was a Wine and Food Lover's Diet. Taking a few cues from my healthy, trim, and energetic ninety-four-year-old French grandmother, and burying myself in a stack of research on fats, cholesterol, and the metabolic effects of the foods we eat, I arrived at a realistic way to choose and combine foods that left me feeling more alert and energetic literally overnight. In just a few days I found that I was less focused on food, enjoying my meals more than ever, and effortlessly losing weight.

Since then, I have had no trouble sticking to the plan and keeping the weight off. Today, for me and countless others who follow this program, the Wine and Food Lover's Diet is a way of life. And now it's your turn.

This book will help you lose those extra pounds, maintain a healthy weight, increase your stamina, improve your alertness, and prevent disease for the rest of your life. All worthy goals, to be sure. But if that was all the Wine and Food Lover's Diet offered, it would probably fail. To succeed over the long term, a diet must accomplish all those things and provide a generous measure of satisfaction. If the Wine and Food Lover's Diet doesn't allow you to experience the pleasure and sense of reward that comes from good food and wine, you won't stay with it. I sure wouldn't.

The Wine and Food Lover's Diet works for all the reasons other diets don't: It depends on sound scientific principles, not gimmicks. It's based on satisfaction, not self-deprivation. It makes food your ally, not your enemy, in the fight against obesity, diabetes, and heart disease. And it offers scores of healthful, delicious meals— more than one hundred recipes ranging from simple to indulgent, many with recommendations for the ideal wine pairing—using a huge variety of foods that you actually love to eat. Unlike the quick-fix diet fads that force you to fight your metabolism, the Wine and Food Lover's Diet puts your own metabolism to work to achieve your goals. That's great news, since it isn't a fair fight: your metabolism always wins.

As a practicing physician, I can cite all the science you need to explain how you can eat rich, European-style cuisine accompanied by a glass or two of wine and achieve successful weight control. And as a certified food lover who knows his way around a kitchen, I will share the recipes that are consistent with that science, and also satisfy my need to eat well and enjoy good food and wine while improving my blood chemistry, reducing disease risk, and tapping new sources of energy.

The Wine and Food Lover's Diet is based on three fundamental truths:

- The body reacts to different foods in different ways. Understanding those reactions empowers us to control them.
- There is no short-term fix to weight control and disease prevention; the only solution is one that is sustainable over the long term.

- Food not only fuels the body; it also nourishes the soul. Meals must do both.

The Wine and Food Lover's Diet addresses all three of these truths head-on. It explains how the body responds to the chemical messages it receives from the only three food types available: fats, proteins, and carbohydrates. Every food falls into one or more of these groups, and each is essential to sustaining life and providing the calories we need for energy. Yet there are critical differences among the foods in each group. Because weight control has less to do with food quantity and everything to do with choices and combinations, it's possible to enjoy satisfying meals with moderate wine consumption and still lose weight, feel more energetic, and decrease your risk of diet-related disease. With smart food choices, we can change the messages we send our bodies from "you're tired, you're hungry, let's eat" to "burn fat, don't store it."

The Wine and Food Lover's Diet helps us change our relationship to food, so that making smart choices becomes second nature. In no time at all, you'll find that you prefer those foods that make you feel better, and avoid the ones that don't, so that a permanent lifestyle change becomes effortless.

Perhaps most important, the Wine and Food Lover's Diet will help you rediscover the simple joy of eating good food, often accompanied by a nice glass of wine, with enough quantity and variety to banish forever the misguided notion that controlling weight and lowering your risk of disease mean giving up the indulgent pleasure of eating well.

If, by chance, you are satisfied with your current weight and have already minimized your risk of diet-related disease, I urge you to keep reading. The scientific concepts underlying the Wine and Food Lover's Diet are fascinating, and the recipes are all kitchen tested and gourmet approved. So ignore the diet talk and focus on the wine and food lover's part.

Indeed, don't think of this as a diet book. Consider *The Wine and Food Lover's Diet* a cookbook supported by sound science, and let it guide you to a new relationship with the foods you eat—where food is an ally, not an enemy; where it is a means to achieve positive goals, not an obstacle to them. I hope you'll use this book to rediscover—or maybe even discover for the first time—the pure pleasure that good food and wine can provide.

The Glycemic Response

The Wine and Food Lover's Diet is the result of my successful personal experience with low-glycemic eating—the type of diet human beings lived on for tens of thousands of years, before the advent of modern industrial food processing. The word glycemic refers to the way certain foods, primarily carbohydrates, are converted to glucose (sugar) in the bloodstream. High-glycemic foods, those containing sugar or starches like potatoes and white bread, raise your blood sugar very rapidly, while low-glycemic foods have a much less pronounced effect on blood glucose. This concept, called the glycemic response, is important, because the rapid rise and fall of blood sugar play a critical role in weight control.

Yet it's not enough simply to reduce our intake of carbohydrates. If it were, there are plenty of other diets you could try (and, chances are, already have). Instead of cutting out carbs, the Wine and Food Lover's Diet asks you to choose them more wisely, in the right combinations with proteins and fats, to get more out of each meal occasion without sending your body the self-defeating metabolic messages that instruct it to make fat and store it, usually in the most unflattering places.

The Wine and Food Lover's Diet helps us manage the glycemic response, and thereby mitigate the sequence of events associated with it. That sequence is what causes us to eat too much, grow sleepy after meals, become hungry too soon after eating, and accumulate the fat that leads, inevitably, to weight gain. I've given this process a name: the Storage Cascade.

The Storage Cascade

Most people operate on the belief—mistaken, it turns out—that a healthful diet is high in carbo-hydrates and low in fats. Many of us have even taken this notion one step further, trying to eliminate dietary fat altogether.

Unfortunately, it doesn't work. The inevitable result of a high-carb, low-fat diet is this: You become heavier and hungrier. Simply put, all carbohydrates (except fiber) ultimately convert to sugar in the blood, called glucose, and certain carbohydrates—especially sugars and starches like candy, cookies, breads, potatoes, and white rice—convert more quickly than others. These are known as high-glycemic carbohydrates, because they cause a rapid rise in blood sugar, called the glycemic response. Low-glycemic carbohydrates—such as green vegetables or certain whole grains like barley and quinoa—convert to sugar much more slowly, blunting the glycemic response.

This is a critical distinction, because a rapid rise in blood sugar is like an alarm bell clanging in your bloodstream. It triggers a cascade of events, including the release of insulin into the bloodstream. Insulin is a hormone produced in the pancreas that, when secreted into the blood, instructs your cells to burn sugar for energy rather than the only other readily available energy source: fat. If you're not burning fat, chances are you're storing it. If you don't burn all the available sugar, you're going to store that, too. And if there's lots of leftover sugar, the body can actually use it to make even more fat.

I call this the Storage Cascade because one effect triggers the next: carbs turn to sugar, which signals your pancreas to release insulin, which instructs your body to burn and store sugar and store fat, most likely in places where you don't want it.

If we're going to lose weight and maintain a lower, healthier weight, we must stop the endless chain of Storage Cascades that causes us to store and produce fat.

The Enabler Theory

Everything we eat falls into one or more of the three basic types of food: fats, proteins, and carbohydrates. From these three food types we derive everything we need—and often much more than we need—to build, replenish, and power our bodies.

Meat, for instance, is both protein and fat; dairy products incorporate all three. The cells that make up every part of the body can derive energy from carbohydrates, fats, and protein, but not in the same ways. The energy in proteins, for example, must first be converted to sugar—a slow process—while the energy in carbohydrates turns into blood sugar much more rapidly.

Carbohydrates are the only energy source you need to initiate a Storage Cascade. If you consume fat without any carbohydrates, there will be no Storage Cascade and, therefore, no weight gain. Eat fat with a low-glycemic carbohydrate, such as a fibrous vegetable like broccoli or asparagus, and your blood sugar won't rise fast enough to send the metabolic message to start the Storage Cascade to any significant degree. But eat some fat and a high-glycemic carbohydrate, such as french fries, and you are setting up a doozy of a Storage Cascade: a rapid rise in blood sugar, triggering an urgent metabolic message to the pancreas to release the insulin that instructs the cells to store and even to make fat.

So high-glycemic carbohydrates that quickly raise blood sugar are, in effect, enablers of fat storage when eaten in combination with fat. If the fat is saturated fat, it is not only stored but also harms the body in the process. But if you eat a diet very high in fat and protein and extremely low in high-glycemic carbohydrates (that is, blood sugar), here's what would happen: You would lose weight and measurably decrease your risk of heart disease.

Surprised? I'm not, and the Enabler Theory explains why. Simply put, high-glycemic carbohydrates—especially refined sugars, breads, potatoes, and white rice—instruct the body to begin the complex process of energy storage.

A thick, juicy steak dripping with saturated fat and protein will not cause a spike in blood sugar, and therefore on its own won't trigger the Storage Cascade. But add a heap of potatoes (a high-glycemic carbohydrate) to the meal and what happens? Up spikes the blood sugar, out flows insulin, and suddenly all that delicious fat in the steak is enabled to be stored as extra pounds and inches. Since the fat in the steak happens to be saturated, the seemingly innocent spud may also contribute to an increase in so-called bad LDL cholesterol. (More on the various types of fats and cholesterol later.) In this all-too-common example, the high-glycemic

potatoes act as a delivery system for shuttling the fat and protein calories to your thighs!

Substitute a low-glycemic carbohydrate, however, such as sautéed spinach, and your body hears a very different message: hold the insulin, stabilize blood sugar, don't bother storing energy in the form of fat but instead burn some of it for energy right now. Same steak, thinner thighs.

The Enabler Theory explains some of the complex interactions between different foods, and why so much of the dietary guidance we receive is just plain wrong. Those high-glycemic carbohydrates we once thought so benign in reality provoke glucose/insulin surges that enable the body to begin the complex process of energy storage, which, unless you happen to be running a marathon, may result not only in weight gain but also in undesirable increases in blood lipids (bad cholesterol) and artery-clogging plaques.

The Enabler Theory may also explain why, thirty years after the low-fat ethos took root in the American consciousness, Americans themselves are fatter than ever. Could it be that all those studies purporting to show the bad effects of fat intake were conducted using meals that also included high-glycemic carbohydrates?

These studies concluded—erroneously, it now appears—that fat alone was the culprit in weight gain, ignoring the enabling effect of high-glycemic carbohydrates in combination with fats. All those research subjects who lost weight on high-fat diets (while restricting carbohydrates) convince me that we've been fingering the wrong villain: It's not the fat that makes you gain or lose weight, but what you eat with it.

In the movie *Trading Places,* the Eddie Murphy character is basically a decent guy whose exposure to the wrong elements (poverty) forces him to behave badly. But put him in the right environment and he becomes a smashing success. Similarly, fat by itself is a perfectly decent energy source and nutrient, but put it in the company of high-glycemic carbohydrates and it behaves in ways we'd rather it didn't. The Wine and Food Lover's Diet is about creating the right environment for optimal health, where your body burns both sugar and fat for energy and thrives in what I call healthy equilibrium.

I can almost hear you saying, "Come on, Phillip, get real. Who wants to eat meat without carbohydrates?" To which I answer, "You're right. Not me." That's why the Wine and Food Lover's Diet recommends satisfying portions of low-glycemic carbohydrates—what I call "Savvy Carbs"—in combination with protein sources such as meat, poultry, fish, or tofu. By eating protein sources in combination with Savvy Carbs that have less of an enabling effect than high-glycemic carbohydrates, you can consume more of the carbohydrates without triggering a massive Storage Cascade. Eating very low-glycemic carbohydrates—my term for these is "Super-Savvy Carbs"—reduces the enabler effect even more. You'll find lists of Savvy Carbs and Super-Savvy Carbs on page 55, and lots of delicious recipes for preparing them later in the book.

The Echo Hunger Cycle

Get hungry. Eat a meal. Feel stuffed. Grow sleepy. Lose energy. Get hungry. Eat a meal...

Sound familiar? That is the pattern millions of Americans reenact day after day, and the consequences range from the mildly depressing to the downright disastrous. I call it the Echo Hunger Cycle, because the foods you eat don't satisfy, hunger bounces back way too soon, you

eat more than you need or want, and the cycle perpetuates. So you might as well add these to the list: Gain weight. Clog arteries. Become prediabetic. Buy diet books. Repeat cycle.

There's a simple reason why we feel Echo Hunger: The body reacts to the foods we eat in much the same way it reacts to the drugs we take when we are ill. After all, foods—like drugs—are composed of various chemicals, each of which produces an effect when ingested. And just as we physicians are careful when and how we combine drugs when prescribing for patients, so do all of us need to pay attention to the foods we eat and in what combinations we eat them.

When you eat a large helping of a high-glycemic carbohydrate—a baked potato, a bowl of white rice—you are creating the perfect conditions for Echo Hunger. (If there happens to be any fat in the meal, watch out: You've now set up a perfect Storage Cascade, and if the fat is saturated, you've enabled bad fat to be stored as well.) As we've seen, the carbohydrate causes a rapid spike in blood sugar, which in turn triggers a sudden release of insulin, which signals the body to start burning sugar and storing sugar and fat. What happens next? What goes up must come down, so following that sudden spike in glucose comes an almost equally precipitous fall.

Now here's where Echo Hunger comes in: as blood sugar drops, the body starts to worry about where it's going to find more energy. Because the body is very concerned about long-term survival, it would much rather find new sources of energy than burn its reserves. This is especially true when the body is in the throes of the Storage Cascade, because one of the features of the cascade is that, while the body is storing sugar and fat, it won't burn fat. Rather than burn some of the fat tucked handily around the waist or thighs, the body simply tells itself, "I'm hungry. Let's eat."

So just an hour or two after eating that baked potato or bowl of sweetened cereal, we're hungry again. (Hey, aren't there some cookies tucked behind the corn flakes?)

Happily, all of these processes—the Storage Cascade, the Enabler Theory, and the Echo Hunger Cycle—are 100 percent preventable. And the Wine and Food Lover's Diet shows you how.

The Savvy Solution

The Wine and Food Lover's Diet isn't a quick fix. It's a life-long approach to sensible eating that centers on a few basic concepts. Once you learn them, they will become second nature.

As you will see, every Wine and Food Lover's Diet meal revolves around a basic combination of foods that will help your body find its metabolic equilibrium—that precise point where it burns a healthy proportion of sugar and fat for maximum energy with minimal fat storage.

The combination is called the Meal Planning Trilogy because it involves three core foods in every dinner, many lunches, and even some breakfasts. (Some breakfasts and snacks use just one or two elements of the Trilogy). The formula goes like this:

1 protein + 2 low-glycemic carbs

Throughout *The Wine and Food Lover's Diet*, the term "Savvy Carb" refers to low-glycemic carbohydrates with a value of 55 or lower on the glycemic index; "Super-Savvy Carbs" are those with a glycemic value of 25 or lower. Most Super-Savvy Carbs are below 10. I'll explain the glycemic index and exactly how it ranks foods later on.

Here are examples of recipes from which you can create the Meal-Planning Trilogy.

PROTEIN

Petrale Sole Stuffed with Asparagus and Hazelnuts (page 112).
Dr. Phillip's Roast Chicken with Tarragon Sauce (page 136).
Roast Pork with a Walnut Crust (page 149).
Spicy Tofu with Tomato Sauce (page 157).

SAVVY CARBS

Cannellini Bean Salad with Feta Cheese and Mint (page 189).
Barley Risotto with Garlic and Almonds (page 194).
Lentils with Shallot and Herbs (page 196).
Quinoa Pilaf with Sunflower and Pumpkin Seeds (page 197).
South American Tabbouleh (page 200).

SUPER-SAVVY CARBS

Swiss Chard with Bacon (page 161).
Mushrooms Stuffed with Parmesan Cheese and Almonds (page 169).
Saffron-Braised Leeks (page 177).
Roasted Vegetables with Arugula Pesto (page 179).
Ratatouille with Chile (page 185).

This is only a partial list, but as you can see, there are plenty of ways to combine these foods into delicious, satisfying meals with virtually endless variety.

If you think the Wine and Food Lover's Diet requires you to give up the little indulgences that make life worth living, look at this list of foods that, in moderation and without enablers, you can enjoy guilt free:

Butter	Premium ice cream
Cheese	Steak
Coffee	Shrimp
Dark chocolate (preferably 60 percent cacao or more)	Heavy cream
	Wine

There are, however, a number of foods you'll want to avoid, or at least limit. These foods are generally high-glycemic carbohydrates and are low in fiber:

Processed baked products (cake, cookies, muffins, pancakes, bagels, pretzels, bread, scones)

Potatoes

White rice

Popcorn

Corn

Sweetened cereals

Raisins and other dried fruit

Candy

Sweetened canned fruits

Soft drinks sweetened with high-fructose corn syrup

The basic Wine and Food Lover's Diet approach recommends one protein and two low-glycemic carbohydrates (Savvy Carbs and/or Super-Savvy Carbs) for dinner. You can combine these elements differently to control the rate at which you lose weight. For example, in the Wine and Food Lover's Diet 28-Day Menu Plan (page 67), I recommend starting with a period of rapid weight loss by composing menus this way:

1 protein + 2 Super-Savvy Carbs

Once you've achieved your ideal weight and want to maintain it over the long term, or if you want to slow your rate of weight loss or simply plateau for a while, adjust the Trilogy to include one carbohydrate source with a slightly higher glycemic response:

1 protein + 1 Super-Savvy Carb + 1 Savvy Carb

To get you started on the right track, I've organized the 28-Day Menu Plan around the three basic daily meals. These delicious breakfast, lunch, and dinner menus range from simple to decadent. I've included recommendations for healthful snacking, tips for dining in restaurants

and ordering take-out food (among other eating occasions), and ways to adapt the diet to your individual eating preferences. You will also find wine-pairing recommendations, although I admit they reflect my own personal preferences. Feel free to substitute your preferred varietals, keeping in mind that discovery and experimentation are part of the fun of drinking wine.

No time for breakfast? Working through lunch? We're all busy, so I've created on-the-go breakfasts and lunches that will keep you fueled all day long. The Wine and Food Lover's Diet is flexible enough to accommodate everyone's personal tastes and preferences, but keep in mind that your body needs enough calories at either breakfast or lunch to avoid unhealthful afternoon snacks or overeating at dinner. Try to spread out your calorie intake throughout the day, rather than waiting until dinnertime to consume most of your calories.

About That Wine

As you've noticed by now, I appreciate a glass of wine with a well-made meal. For me, a good dinner isn't complete without one. More than my half-French ancestry led me to conceive a diet for wine lovers. A mountain of research points to the health benefits of moderate wine consumption.

To be fair, there is a range of opinion on this topic. Some studies find no health benefit from any type of alcohol; others are inconclusive. To me, the large body of scientific evidence in support of moderate wine consumption is persuasive. More important, a little wine with my Wine and Food Lover's Diet dinners increases my enjoyment and satisfaction, and lets me feel indulgent and rewarded, which is all the incentive I need to stick to the program.

Plenty of well-known diets denounce all alcoholic beverages as diet defeaters. Some point to the calories as the culprit; others rail against the carbohydrates. I happen to think they've all got it wrong—on the science, on the psychology, and on the self-deprivation.

Whether to classify alcohol as a carbohydrate is the subject of some difference of opinion among people who've studied the question. Having looked at it from all sides, I'm prepared to state a firm conviction: it doesn't matter. The simple fact is that alcohol on its own has zero carbohydrates, and while wine may technically qualify as a carbohydrate, it doesn't behave as one: it will not raise blood sugar, so there is no glycemic response. Nor does wine contribute to a Storage Cascade, so it's not an enabler, which means you can enjoy it with, say, the fat in a nicely marbled steak. (Some argue that wine actually helps digest fat—hence the French term *digestif* for an after-dinner snifter.) True, wine doesn't promote weight loss, but in the context of the Wine and Food Lover's Diet, it won't inhibit it, either.

A lot of the confusion about this topic arises from the fact that alcohol is made from sugar. In the fermentation process, however, the sugar in grape juice converts to alcohol, to the point that a dry wine is virtually sugar free. There are exceptions: certain wines contain residual sugar, and others have had sugar added back during fermentation. But the vast majority of premium wines, including all of the most popular varietals, are fermented to dryness and have only trace amounts of residual sugar in the finished product.

While a glass or two of wine will not cause an appreciable spike in blood sugar, it can slow down the rate at which we burn fat, since alcohol and fat appear to utilize some of the same burning pathways. This is the reason I recommending limiting, or possibly eliminating, wine consumption during the early, rapid weight-loss phase of the diet. I'm willing to accept slower weight loss for greater enjoyment of meals (along with the other health benefits that wine offers). Whether or not to consume wine is a decision we can make individually.

As for the health benefits, statistics show that moderate wine consumption is associated with lower risk of stroke, heart disease, and diabetes, among other ailments. One explanation is that wine appears to increase the ratio of "good" HDL cholesterol to artery-clogging "bad" LDL cholesterol. The antioxidants found in red wine, in particular, reduce the oxidative stress on cells, which in turn appears to reduce the risk of certain cancers. In my mind, all these benefits, as well as others I haven't mentioned, more than compensate for a small reduction in fat-burning efficiency.

As a food lover and diet expert, I'm on safe ground including wine as a component of the diet. As a physician, I want to be clear that a good deal of evidence confirms that heavy drinking can lead to all manner of ailments, both physical and social. For some individuals, there is no safe level of alcohol consumption, and nothing they read here should persuade them otherwise.

But for the vast majority of readers, the Wine and Food Lover's Diet not only allows but recommends a glass of wine with dinner, in part for the health benefits and more importantly for the emotional benefits. Any diet based on delicious meals, a glass of wine with dinner, and even an occasional dessert is a program that you will stay with over the long term. That is the critical difference between a short-term diet and successful, lifelong weight control.

What Works a Lot Works a Little

One of the virtues of the Wine and Food Lover's Diet is the control it gives you over the foods you eat and the rate at which you lose weight. If you want to achieve maximum weight loss in a short period of time, adapt the Meal-Planning Trilogy to one protein and two very low-glycemic Super-Savvy Carbs. If you're more comfortable with a measured pace, that's good, too. For the Super-Savvy Carbs, simply substitute Savvy Carbs, which are still low glycemic. Whether you prefer a sprint or a marathon, what's important is sticking to the plan long enough to feel truly better, at which point you won't want to go back.

No matter what your individual approach, the underlying principles of the Wine and Food Lover's Diet never change:

- Limit high-glycemic carbohydrates (potatoes, white rice, bread, and corn) but achieve satiety (a sense of fullness) by eating very low-glycemic carbs and low-glycemic carbs with protein and some fat.
- Stop counting. Not calories, not fat grams, not carbs. If you must think about numbers, try this for your main meal:

1 protein + 2 low-glycemic carbs = Meal-Planning Trilogy

1 protein + 2 Super-Savvy Carbs = rapid weight loss with some exercise

1 protein + 1 Super-Savvy Carb + 1 Savvy Carb = moderate weight loss or maintenance of healthy equilibrium and weight

- Eat until you are satisfied. High-glycemic foods like bread and cookies tell your body to keep eating and keep storing fat. But Trilogy combinations tell your body that it's full and satisfied—and keep it feeling that way for a longer time.

Following these formulas, you'll reverse the trend of insulin overload, which can lead to obesity, heart disease, and type 2 diabetes. You'll feel better, rediscover the youthful energy you thought was lost forever, and achieve a metabolic balance that makes it easy to change your relationship with food.

The Wine and Food Lover's Diet Recipes

The Wine and Food Lover's Diet will help you meet your weight control objectives, but only if you stick to the program. Fortunately, that's easy to do, because it doesn't involve the complicated recipes and exotic ingredients that would have you sneaking to a drive-through window before this book hits the floor.

Instead, you'll find a mix of simple work-week recipes—many ready in just thirty minutes—plus a selection of more involved recipes for weekend indulgence. If you enjoy cooking, there are recipes that would be right at home in a gourmet restaurant. If you find cooking a chore, there are lots of quick and easy recipes guaranteed to satisfy.

What they all have in common—and what makes menu planning such a breeze—is the Meal-Planning Trilogy. Just pick a protein, a Savvy Carb, and a Super-Savvy Carb (or two Super-Savvy Carbs for rapid weight loss) and you've got a delicious menu in seconds, and a satisfying meal in minutes. And don't forget dessert—yes, there are desserts, too.

If you don't like to cook, you can still lose weight on the Wine and Food Lover's Diet. The principles on which the Wine and Food Lover's Diet is based are applicable to a variety of eating situations, whether restaurants, take-out food, or supermarket prepared foods. Once you learn the basic metabolic messages sent by various foods, you'll naturally start to choose those that make you feel better.

Exercise

One last point I'd better make is sort of a good news, less good news thing. The less good news is that even a diet as brilliantly simple and easy to follow as this requires physical activity.

The good news is that it is only a little. Moderate exercise is optimal, but certainly a little is better than none, and you will find that the added vitality you feel on the Wine and Food Lover's Diet will give you the energy you need to exercise more than you have been used to doing.

What I mean by exercise is this: a brisk half-hour walk (or two fifteen-minute walks) every day, or a vigorous hour-long walk three times a week. Working in a garden counts, as does playing with kids or walking to the grocery store. No marathons, no weekend-warrior stuff. Just a little physical activity on a consistent basis.

The reason is simple. Like most cells in your body, those that form your muscle tissue can burn sugar or fat for energy. Muscles that are well toned (or even moderately toned) will actually burn fat preferentially. You don't have to be a body builder to reap this benefit: Moderate daily exercise, in concert with the food combinations recommended in the Wine and Food Lover's Diet, will turn your muscles into regular fat-burning machines.

Later on I'll explain exactly how this works and suggest a few easy ways to meet this objective. For now, why don't you set this book down, put on a pair of sneakers, and walk around the block while you congratulate yourself on this incredibly easy but rather momentous decision you've made: to embark on a lifestyle that will have you controlling your weight, feeling more alert, preventing disease, and enjoying healthy, satisfying meals from now on.

THE STORAGE CASCADE

When it comes to dieting, the conventional wisdom goes something like this: Burn more calories than you take in and you will lose weight.

The logic behind that is deceptively simple. Much of the extra weight you're carrying is actually stored energy. When your body demands more energy than is immediately available, it burns what's stored, and those extra pounds disappear.

The conventional wisdom is sound, as far as it goes. Trouble is, it doesn't go far enough, because it fails to take into account two essential truths. First, to create the necessary energy deficit, you need to exercise more or to consume fewer calories. For many, these two options—consistent, aggressive exercise or self-deprivation dieting— are just too difficult to sustain over the long term.

The second truth is that not all calories are created equal—at least not in the way they affect your metabolism. As the Storage Cascade and Enabler Theory demonstrate, certain foods send metabolic messages to your body, instructing it to burn or store energy. A 100-calorie portion of white rice (a high-glycemic carbohydrate) sends a very different metabolic message than the same number of calories of spinach (a low-glycemic carbohydrate).

The messenger, it turns out, is insulin, which instructs the body to begin the complex mechanism of excess calorie storage. The constellation of events that occurs in the body as it deals with the storage of sugar and fat and even the production of fat is what I call the Storage Cascade.

Insulin is a hormone produced by the pancreas, an organ in the abdomen that works like a little pump, releasing insulin into the bloodstream. Insulin is involved with several critical functions, but the one that most interests us here is its role in regulating blood sugar, called glucose. Insulin takes glucose into the body's cells, where it is converted to energy. Without glucose, our cells would be deprived of the fuel they need to function and survive. If not taken up by our cells, glucose builds up in the blood, ultimately damaging the eyes, kidneys, nerves, or heart.

So insulin is essential to our well-being. Too little insulin results in a disease called type 1 diabetes, also known as juvenile diabetes. With no insulin at all, you will die.

Because high-glycemic carbohydrates like bread, candy, potatoes, and white rice raise our blood sugar faster and higher than low-glycemic carbs, they stimulate the pancreas to produce more insulin. As the insulin flows to almost every cell in the body, it carries three important messages. First, it instructs the cells to burn sugar instead of fat for energy and to store sugar (in the form of glycogen) to burn later.

The second instruction insulin communicates directly to fat cells is to store and actually produce fat at the same time it instructs the liver to produce fat.

Fat production is a complex process that occurs when we introduce more sugar, in the form of high-glycemic carbohydrates, than our cells can immediately burn or store (in the form of glycogen). When our cells have burned or stored all the sugar they can, and there is still more unburned and unstored sugar in the blood, insulin helps instruct the liver to synthesize more fat from the excess. Fat begets fat, and insulin makes it happen.

For ancient hunter-gatherers, for whom food scarcity was a fact of life, the ability to manufacture fat—called lipogenesis—was an amazingly useful mechanism. But if you happen to be, say, an overweight radiologist from Marin County, what begins as a dollop of sour cream and a pat of butter on a high-glycemic Idaho spud will, in less time than it takes to let your belt out a notch, bump up the blood sugar, trigger a Storage Cascade with its insulin release, instruct your muscles to burn sugar and store what's left, and tell your fat cells to store fat and sometimes to make some more. That is the Storage Cascade, and over time this process will lead more and more of us to, well, more and more of us.

The third message insulin sends seems at first to be counterintuitive: It prevents cells from burning fat. When you think about it, though, it really is intuitive. The body's goal is long-term survival, which requires energy stores safely tucked away for use in extreme circumstances.

That's what fat is for, and insulin is the body's insurance that, when sugar is available, under no circumstances should fat be burned. It's a derivation of the law of conservation, and it comes into play whenever we have lots and lots of sugar in our blood, as is the case when we eat high-glycemic carbohydrates.

Pancreas to the Rescue

Having branded the pancreas as the Storage Cascade trigger, let's return to that tiny hormone pump. This time we'll cast it in the role of hero.

Not only does the pancreas manufacture insulin, but it's also responsible for a little-known hormone called glucagon. In many ways the mirror opposite of insulin, glucagon is secreted by the pancreas when too *little* blood sugar is available. It, too, carries an important message to our cells: If you need fuel, try burning some fat.

The Wine and Food Lover's Diet relies on glucagon to reverse the Storage Cascade with a process I call the Burning Cascade. When we substitute low-glycemic carbohydrates for high, we are taking control of our blood sugar levels, avoiding the glucose spikes that trigger insulin release and replacing them with nice little boosts of glucagon, which in turn instruct our cells to find some fat and burn that for energy. While glucagon has the starring role in that process, protein plays an important supporting role. Consuming even a little protein with most or, better yet, *every* meal gives the pancreas a little nudge in the direction of more glucagon and less insulin.

While we always want to limit a Storage Cascade, we don't necessarily always want to encourage the Burning Cascade. Were we to eliminate all carbohydrates from our diet, thereby depriving our cells of energy from sugar, we would eventually burn all of our stored fat and soon turn to protein for fuel. The word for that is *starvation*, and it's a condition we all best avoid. Besides, by eliminating carbohydrates altogether, we miss out on many essential vitamins and other nutrients. The Wine and Food Lover's Diet helps us find a healthy equilibrium where we burn sugar and fat for energy, with a well-modulated trickle of insulin and glucagon in proper proportion.

Cardiovascular Disease and Insulin

Having been designed by nature as a means of survival in times of food scarcity, the Storage Cascade is an incredibly efficient way to gain weight. Unfortunately, it's also an effective means of increasing our risk of all manner of diet-related disease, including obesity, diabetes, stroke, and heart disease.

We've already touched on the first two, but it's worth mentioning insulin's role in cardiovascular disease, and how the Wine and Food Lover's Diet can reduce your risk.

That insulin carries its instruction to store fat to all the obvious places—waist, thighs, rear—is bad enough. But it also finds its way to less visible, but potentially more dangerous, locations—like the arteries that carry blood to and from the heart. The process of clogging the arteries, called arteriosclerosis or atherosclerosis, occurs when the artery walls begin to accumulate fat. As they narrow, the heart has to work harder to pump the same quantity of blood.

The fat stored in the walls of the arteries contains low-density lipoproteins (LDL), more commonly called bad cholesterol. And since LDL cholesterol is a fatty substance, insulin has the same effect on it that it does on regular fat

cells: It directs the body to store and possibly create it, too. (We'll talk more about fat, cholesterol, and heart disease a little later on.) The Wine and Food Lover's Diet helps reduce this risk in two ways: First, by avoiding the sudden glucose spikes that trigger the Storage Cascade and the message to store and produce cholesterol, and, second, by recommending the kinds of foods and exercise that can increase high-density lipoproteins (HDL), known as good cholesterol, which helps rid our bodies of LDL.

The same conditions that create the Storage Cascade also foster an environment for the oxidation of bad LDL cholesterol. Oxidized LDL cholesterol is especially harmful to blood vessels, as it both clogs them and weakens them. Visualize the way rust eats through metal, a process also called oxidation, and you'll get an idea of the way oxidized LDL cholesterol acts on blood vessels.

The prolonged release of excessive amounts of insulin during the Storage Cascade—the inevitable result of a diet rich in high-glycemic carbohydrates—will also numb the body's cells to the effects of insulin, leading to a condition known as insulin resistance. When the cells stop responding to insulin, they no longer receive the instruction to take up blood sugar, leading to the buildup of glucose in our bloodstream, a condition called prediabetes. Eventually, blood sugar levels are so high for so long that the condition becomes type 2 diabetes.

Unlike type 1, or juvenile, diabetes, where the pancreas doesn't produce enough insulin, type 2 diabetes occurs when too much insulin is released for too long, and cells simply stop responding to it. Meanwhile the pancreas kicks into overdrive, producing more and more insulin in a futile effort to lower blood sugar, which only exacerbates the accumulation of bad cholesterol.

Happily, the storage of fat in the arteries is, in most cases, reversible. Patients who have dramatically reduced the amount of carbohydrates in their diet, especially high-glycemic carbs, have brought their blood fats, including cholesterol and triglycerides (more on this later), back into line.

There is a strong current of opinion that eating meat, with its saturated fat, is a prescription for cardiovascular disease. But the truth is that saturated fat is taken up by cells and stored only when consumed with high-glycemic carbohydrates, triggering an insulin release that tells your body to store the fat. It's the Enabler Theory! As has been shown over and over again, fat alone isn't the issue. The sugar or starch eaten with fat poses this potentially serious problem by sending the metabolic message to begin the Storage Cascade and store fat.

Insulin and the Echo Hunger Cycle

Ever wonder why you grow sleepy after a big lunch? You might recall that high-glycemic carbohydrates, such as a big baked potato or a thick crust pizza, were on the menu. Or perhaps your lunch was rice cakes with low-fat yogurt (often full of added sugar) and some fruit. Do you also recall feeling intense hunger soon after you felt sleepy? Even after eating a modest 100-calorie snack like a portion of a candy bar, a cookie, or potato chips—which are supposed to quell your appetite for a while—hunger returns too soon. The overall effect is that you eventually eat too many calories.

I call this the Echo Hunger Cycle, and it turns out that the Storage Cascade and insulin specifically have a lot to do with it. After a sudden rise in blood sugar spurred by a meal of high-glycemic carbohydrates or a large overall load of carbohydrates that creates a commensurate spike in blood sugar, the body releases a burst of insulin to trigger a Storage Cascade. This has the effect of lowering blood sugar. But a rapid drop in blood sugar sets off another type of alarm: The brain perceives falling blood sugar levels as fuel shortage and orders the body to conserve fuel by burning less energy. It is sort of like driving your car's engine at a slower rate when the low-fuel light comes on in an effort to conserve enough fuel to make it to the gas station. The human equivalent of reduced engine speed is sleepiness.

In some people, a rapid fall in blood sugar goes beyond sleepiness to a condition called hypoglycemia—literally, too little sugar. In extreme cases a hypoglycemic individual can grow dizzy or even pass out, requiring an immediate dose of sugar to bring glucose levels back into balance. The easiest remedy for hypoglycemia is to eat.

Most of us are not clinically hypoglycemic, but the Echo Hunger we feel is a mild form of the same condition. The Wine and Food Lover's Diet will help you minimize Echo Hunger by avoiding its root cause: the rapid rise in blood sugar, followed by an almost equally precipitous fall. Eating a balanced meal of low-glycemic carbohydrates, proteins, and fats will smooth out blood sugar spikes and troughs, prevent the Storage Cascade, and prolong the feeling of satiety.

CARBOHYDRATES AND THE ENABLER THEORY

Now that the no-carb diet craze has faded, it's time to restore some sanity to the diet and nutrition conversation. After all, in a world with only three basic food types—protein, fats, and carbohydrates—it makes no sense to vilify one or another.

Yet that is exactly what so many popular diets try to do. First, fat was the villain, and suddenly the food industry reinvented every product on the shelf as "low fat" or "fat free." You know what happened? Thirty years later, obesity rates tripled, and Americans are fatter than ever.

Much the same thing can be said of the low-carb/no-carb fad. Millions of Americans, egged on by a few blockbuster diet books and their cheerleaders in the media, made carbohydrates the enemy. Their point is well taken; it just doesn't go far enough. A diet heavy on carbohydrates often does lead to weight gain (among other potential evils), but only if they are high glycemic and eaten in sufficient quantity to initiate a Storage Cascade, especially when combined with fats. Unfortunately, that information was omitted from the media hoopla and the low-carb marketing campaigns. Besides, simply reducing all carbohydrates is a deprivation diet, and I don't believe self-denial is a sustainable, long-term solution to weight control.

The Wine and Food Lover's Diet takes a different approach. It recognizes that carbohydrates are the easiest energy source for the body and the preferred energy source for the brain. In other words, carbs are a critical component of a sensible diet.

Remember that only two ready sources of energy power the body: fats and carbohydrates. (The body can convert protein into blood sugar for energy, but not as readily as carbohydrates.) Some cells, like those in the brain, vastly prefer energy from carbohydrates, while well-toned muscles will burn fat preferentially over carbohydrates if body chemistry is in balance. (More on that later.)

Because the body reacts to different foods differently, the key is choosing Savvy or Super-Savvy carbs (see pages 13–14), in the right proportions, to provide the fuel we need to power our cells without triggering a Storage Cascade. Choosing wisely starts with understanding a few basics about carbohydrates.

Carbohydrate is really just another word for sugar. The ultimate fate of all carbohydrates, except fiber, is blood sugar. There are only two types of sugars we need to be concerned with here. Simple sugars, called monosaccharides or disaccharides, have just one or two molecules and tend to dissolve quickly in the blood, converting rapidly and easily into glucose (sugar in the blood, or blood sugar). Table sugar and the sugar found in milk and beers that aren't fermented dry are simple sugars. So is fructose, the sugar in fruit.

The second type of sugar that we need to know about is called complex carbohydrates, often referred to as polysaccharides, because they have three or more molecules and can, but do not always, dissolve more slowly. Green vegetables and most starchy foods contain polysaccharides, or complex sugars.

Because simple sugars typically dissolve quickly in the blood, they promote the release of insulin, which in turn signals the body to burn sugar instead of fat for energy, to store sugar and fat, and even to produce fat—in other words, the Storage Cascade. It stands to reason that eating a lot of simple sugars will prevent weight loss and long-term weight control. Since those same simple sugars lead directly to the Echo Hunger Cycle, they fail to provide long-lasting satiety. All in all, and for lack of a more colorful term, we'll call those simple-sugar foods "bad carbs."

Unfortunately, just because a particular carbohydrate is complex doesn't necessarily make it a "good" carb. While categorizing foods as simple or complex sugars is often a pretty good guideline to whether a carbohydrate is "bad" or "good," it's not always that clear, and the glycemic index, explained below, tells us why.

The body reacts to different foods in different ways, so even though a baked potato and a bowl of steamed white rice are complex carbohydrates, and even though they contain some fiber, they are both high-glycemic foods. This means that eating more than a small amount with a pat of butter, a dollop of sour cream, or a juicy steak may activate the Enabler Theory, trigger the Storage Cascade, and lead to Echo Hunger. Brown rice is only marginally better because, like white rice and potatoes, it is high in starch. Starch is technically a complex carbohydrate, but it can break down just as quickly—in some cases even quicker—than simple sugars, which is why starchy foods tend to have a higher glycemic index value. What's more, potatoes and white rice have relatively little nutritional value beyond the energy they provide—another reason to limit starchy carbohydrates. Green leafy vegetables offer much more nutritional value than starchy plant sources such as potatoes or white rice, and have a markedly lower glycemic index value. So not only are they less likely to trigger a Storage Cascade, but they also provide essential vitamins and minerals that those starchy, high-glycemic carbohydrates often do not.

Now to add to the confusion, just as some complex carbohydrates dissolve quickly and therefore are implicated in the Storage Cascade, simple sugars can break character and dissolve slowly depending on what the sugar is paired with. Ice cream has lots of simple sugar, but because it also contains lots of fat, which slows down digestion, the sugar tends to dissolve more slowly. Still, I only recommend full-fat ice cream in moderation, and not with enablers like a cone or mix-ins that contain flour products, such as cookie dough.

The sugars in fibrous vegetables are released

very slowly into the bloodstream. The sugars in celery dissolve slowly in the blood because celery is high in water and fiber. The water dilutes the total amount of carbohydrates in the celery, and the fiber tends to blunt the glycemic response by slowing down the digestion of the carbohydrate source. Fiber is a polysaccharide that, by itself, contributes no sugar molecules to the blood, so it has no effect on blood sugar. (This is the reason food labels subtract fiber grams from total carbohydrates to arrive at *net* carbohydrates.) There are many reasons to eat lots of fiber: promoting regularity is one, and lowering LDL cholesterol is another. But protecting against colon cancer is one thing fiber doesn't do. From the standpoint of the Wine and Food Lover's Diet, fiber is important because it blunts the glycemic response of carbohydrates, reducing the insulin release that signifies the Storage Cascade.

As a rule of thumb, if the carb is processed, refined, easily digestible, or white, it's probably a bad carb. If it's a whole food, minimally processed, high in fiber (and therefore digested more slowly), and green or otherwise colorful, it's most likely a good carb.

Fortunately, there are plenty of delicious good carbs to choose from, and those are the ones that fit into the Wine and Food Lover's Diet under the categories Savvy Carbs or Super-Savvy Carbs.

When Fat Was Good

Viewed in an evolutionary context, functions like the Enabler Theory, the Storage Cascade, and the Echo Hunger Cycle make perfect, even elegant sense. But while changes in culture and technology happen quickly, over just a few generations, changes to the genetic programming in which those basic survival techniques are rooted can take hundreds or thousands more generations.

Only during the last hundred years or so have we developed technologies like sugar refining, fat hydrogenation, and concentrated fructose syrups. It will likely take thousands of years, however, to genetically reprogram the human race.

Our genes originally were adapted for a hunter-gatherer lifestyle, which entailed hunting up to four times per week and gathering for two or three days a week. Both pursuits required frequent physical activity. Hunter-gatherers ate diets consisting entirely of whole and natural foods with low sugar content, and experienced periods of feast and famine. The principle of natural selection dictates that, during periods of abundant food, individuals whose genes favored efficient storage of food energy had a survival advantage when the next famine arrived. Survival of the fittest was based on the ability to store fat!

Although those miserly, calorie-hoarding, stone-age genes were a boon to the ancients, for the vast majority of us with access to plenty, they are anything but.

Alas, we can't undo a thousand generations of genetic programming. So the answer to weight control is a diet and a lifestyle more akin to those for which the body is actually designed. This is a diet based on whole foods that are naturally low-glycemic (unrefined and minimally processed) combined with moderate physical activity: the Wine and Food Lover's Diet.

Does this mean we have to drop our laptops and car keys, grab a spear and a basket, and head for the woods instead of the drive-through? Well, yes—but only for the exercise, not the food. There are plenty of delicious menu options that are both less strenuous and entirely consistent with your ancient genetic code. (A hundred of them are right in this book.)

We will, however, have to learn how different foods affect us: which metabolic messages they're sending and how we can amplify the beneficial messages and censor the others. Luckily, a tool called the glycemic index, or GI, makes this relatively easy.

The glycemic index measures the insulin-producing effect of carbohydrates and therefore the likelihood that the carbohydrate source will initiate the Storage Cascade. Every carbohydrate source is assigned a numerical value based on how high and how quickly it raises the blood sugar. The higher and longer the increase in blood sugar, the higher the GI value. Those carbohydrates with a GI ranking above 70 are considered high (pure glucose is assigned a value of 100), while a value below 55 is considered low-glycemic and in most people will not increase blood sugar sufficiently to initiate a significant Storage Cascade. Carbohydrates with a GI value of 55 or below qualify as Savvy Carbs on the Wine and Food Lover's Diet; a value of 25 or below is Super-Savvy. Such a low-glycemic value will cause something more like a Storage Trickle than a cascade, which means our muscles will get the message to burn fat for energy rather than sugar.

For a more comprehensive picture of how carbohydrates affect the release of insulin, you can look at a carbohydrate's glycemic load (GL). While the GI value describes how rapidly particular carbohydrates turn into sugar, the GL tells you the quantity of carbohydrates in a serving of a particular food. Put another way, the GI helps us choose which foods to eat, and the GL helps us determine how much. Take pasta, for instance. While al dente pasta is technically low glycemic (cooking increases the starchiness of pasta and therefore the glycemic value), the amount of net carbohydrates can still be considerable if you eat a large quantity, leading to a significant Storage Cascade.

To understand fully a food's effect on blood sugar, you need to know both values. For example, the carbohydrates in watermelon have a high GI, but since watermelon is mostly water and a little fiber, its glycemic load is relatively low. A GL of 20 or more is considered high; a GL of 10 or under is low. As noted above, a particular food's glycemic effect is influenced by how it is cooked, how much fiber and fat it contains, what it's paired with, and other factors.

Personally, I find it a bother to calculate the GI and GL values of foods I'm trying to eat and enjoy. The beauty of the Wine and Food Lover's Diet is that you don't have to calculate anything.

Earlier I promised that the Wine and Food Lover's Diet lets you stop counting overall calories, fat grams, and carbohydrate grams, and I stand by that promise. Certainly, you can learn the GI and GL values of everything you eat, or you can just mix and match foods from the lists in this book. Eventually, the selection process will become second nature: The lower the GI and GL of the foods you eat, the better you will feel, and soon you will naturally gravitate to those foods and away from those that rank higher on the glycemic index or carry a higher glycemic load.

All you really need to know is that high-glycemic carbs tend to increase blood sugar rapidly, thereby triggering a Storage Cascade with its insulin release, which in turns leads to the Echo Hunger Cycle, weight gain, and an increase in risk factors, such as LDL cholesterol and triglycerides, associated with heart disease. Low-glycemic carbohydrates, on the other hand, cause a slow, steady rise in blood sugar, minimizing the glycemic response, moderating the insulin release, avoiding the Storage Cascade by permitting cells to burn fat instead of sugar, and keeping you feeling fuller, longer, ultimately leading to weight loss and weight control.

Knowing the effect different foods have on the body and its metabolism is useful information, but it doesn't qualify as a diet and it sure isn't a lifestyle. That's where *The Wine and Food Lover's Diet* comes in. The recipes in this book incorporate all the principles discussed above, so if the actual science doesn't interest you, you can skip it and dig right in.

The Meal-Planning Trilogy

If you organized your diet around the U.S. Department of Agriculture's food guide pyramid, you'd get about 60 percent of your daily calories from carbohydrates—much of it high-glycemic bread, pasta, white rice, and cereal. The rest would come from protein and fat. But that's not how our early ancestors lived, and if you're serious about losing weight and preventing disease, you won't live that way either. Such a diet might make sense if we were preparing ourselves for a period of famine, but it makes no sense for humans who expect three square meals a day, and then some.

Because it's based on the way the body actually operates (and not, as some pyramid critics charge, on the way food industry lobbyists operate), the Wine and Food Lover's Diet turns that equation around to put your metabolism to work for you rather than against you. To do that we must minimize the role of high-glycemic carbohydrates in favor of a combination of low-glycemic carbs, proteins, and healthy fats.

While I take issue with the content of the food guide pyramid, I am not reticent about borrowing the three-sided figure to visualize the cornerstone of the Wine and Food Lover's Diet, a concept I call the Meal-Planning Trilogy. Consisting of one main-dish protein and two low-glycemic carbohydrates, the Trilogy is the fundamental principle guiding every Wine and Food Lover's Diet dinner,

as well as many lunches and some breakfast recipes.

We touched on the Trilogy on pages 13–14, perhaps without fully explicating how the concepts behind it help us lose weight, keep it lost, and prevent disease—sensibly, effortlessly, and sustainably over the long term. By now you may better understand how Trilogy combinations work with your metabolism to exert conscious control over the metabolic processes that cause weight gain.

The concept of control over the foods you choose to eat is important to the long-term success of the diet. With control comes the power to determine the rate at which you lose weight—rapid weight loss or a more measured pace (or no weight loss, just easy maintenance). Whereas deprivation diets seem to control the dieter, the Wine and Food Lover's Diet puts *you* in control.

If rapid weight loss is the goal, the Meal-Planning Trilogy consists of one protein (typically fish, poultry, or meat) and two Super-Savvy Carbs—those carbohydrates with a very low GI value of 25 or under. In due course, when you decide to moderate the rate at which you lose weight or maintain your present weight, the Trilogy will include one protein and incorporate one Super-Savvy Carb and one Savvy Carb. Savvy Carb sources are still low glycemic, with a GI value of 55 or lower. But now your menus can include some starch such as in the **Barley Risotto with Tomatoes and Lemon** (page 193) and **Quinoa-Chile Skillet Bread** (page 199) or, if you're not wheat sensitive, al dente pasta.

These formulas are useful, but at this point may seem a little abstract. To understand fully the Trilogy concept, let's look at an actual Wine and Food Lover's Diet menu, the one I call my surefire dinner, because it's the one I turn to whenever I need to reassert control.

- Protein: **Dr. Phillip's Roast Chicken with Tarragon Sauce** (page 136)

- Super-Savvy Carb: **Spinach with Toasted Garlic and Pine Nuts** (page 176)
- Super-Savvy Carb: **Button Mushrooms with Thyme, Rosemary, and Basil** (page 180)
- Wine pairing: Chardonnay or Pinot Noir

First, notice the Trilogy: my favorite roasted chicken recipe for the protein, and spinach and mushrooms as the two Super-Savvy Carb sources. With all due respect to the USDA, that's *my* idea of a pyramid. Now note the little indulgences that turn an ordinary dinner into a pleasurable experience: pine nuts that add texture and richness to the spinach, fresh herbs that flavor the mushrooms, and a glass of wine. This is anything but a deprivation diet. What's more, you don't need a diet scale to weigh the portions, because the portions are reasonable and satiating for most. If it turns out that one portion isn't enough and you want an extra bite or two of chicken, go right ahead. A second helping of mushrooms? Be my guest. You can even top up your wineglass, if you want. Now that you're in control and more attuned to the signals your body is sending, you are far more likely to stop eating when it is time to stop.

The important thing is to eat until you are satisfied—the word for that is *satiety*—so you won't feel deprived. Don't overdo it, of course, but neither should you deny yourself. On the Wine and Food Lover's Diet, it's all but impossible to OD on spinach or mushrooms or even chicken, because the satiety mechanisms kick in, signaling your brain to tell your hands to put down the fork. For a lot of complicated reasons I will touch on later, high-glycemic carbs may thwart the satiety mechanism, allowing us to continue eating long after we've had enough.

Keep in mind that the dishes in my surefire menu happen to be my favorites, but I won't be offended if they're not yours. I encourage experimentation: Mix and match to your heart's content, so long as you stay with the basic Meal-Planning Trilogy configuration. There are more than a hundred recipes in this book to choose from, but don't feel limited to those. Pick ingredients from the lists on pages 54–57, then construct your own menus to your own taste.

Aside from ranking very low or low on the glycemic index, all of the carbohydrates I encourage eating have at least one thing in common: They are nutritious. Each one provides many of the essential nutrients, antioxidants, vitamins, and fiber, ensuring that you get the nutrition you need without wasting calories on foods that offer no tangible benefit.

But these foods have something else in common—something they *don't* provide that many high-glycemic carbs do. None of these low-glycemic carbs contribute significantly to the bad environment that encourages the production or storage of triglycerides—a precursor to bad LDL cholesterol—or the oxidation of LDL, one of the primary causes of coronary artery disease. They won't increase your risk of cancer—not of the breast, the colon, the pancreas, or other vital organs—as a steady diet of high-glycemic carbs will, over time.

And as I've discussed, they won't elevate your blood sugar to the point where large quantities of insulin begin to pump into your cells, carrying the message to store and produce fat, and in-structing cells not to burn fat for energy.

I'll talk more a little later about the role of Savvy Carbs and Super-Savvy Carbs in disease prevention. For now, keep in mind how different foods, especially high-glycemic carbohydrates, send different metabolic messages to your body, and that you alone have the power to censor those messages by making the right food choices.

THE TRUTH ABOUT FATS AND CHOLESTEROL

Thirty years ago, for reasons that have a lot more to do with marketing than science, fats became the dietary villain. Even now, the low-fat/fat-free myth persists: just reduce the amount of fat you consume and the pounds will melt away magically. Unfortunately, as any of the millions of frustrated low-fat dieters will attest, it doesn't work for the long term.

What started as a fad in the 1980s is today a fiasco. Manufacturers of low-fat and fat-free foods have grown fat, figuratively speaking, perpetuating the myth that fat causes fat, even as millions of Americans have grown fatter, literally, year after year. I call it the fat-free fiasco, but in truth it's worse than that: When you consider the health implications of rampant obesity—including the near-epidemic incidence of diabetes and coronary artery disease—the fat-free myth takes on a sinister dimension.

The scientific fact is that, generally speaking, fat is good. Not all fats, certainly, and not in excess, but the healthy monounsaturated fats in, for example, olive oil are absolutely essential for good health. Even the saturated fats in animal products, though a bit more controversial, have a role to play in good nutrition. Remember, the body has, for eons, been burning fats as the primary fuel, so to brand them as villainous is just plain silly. Clearly there is a lot of bad information out there, which the Wine and Food Lover's Diet addresses head-on.

Let's start with a simple definition: Fats are one of the three main classes of foods (the others being carbohydrates and protein) and, with sugar, are one of our two major sources of energy. While carbohydrates (with the exception of fiber) eventually turn into blood sugar, fats stay fats for the most part until they are burned for energy. Fats also help the body absorb certain vitamins, they keep the skin and cell membranes healthy, and they are one of the ways the body stores energy for future use.

I should add that, typically in extreme circumstances, the body can use protein for energy by converting it to sugar. When we eat sugar as a primary source of energy day in and day out, the body will come to prefer sugar as an energy source over fat. When there is insulin floating around and the body is prevented from burning fat, some of the dietary protein will be converted to sugar. If this happens for too long, the body more easily converts protein to sugar. The result is a decrease in body mass—not a decrease in fat, mind you, but in muscle. With severe carbohydrate restriction, the body will start consuming itself in as little as a few days.

Fats are divided into two broad categories: unsaturated and saturated. From a chemical standpoint, unsaturated fats are composed of molecules in which not all positions are occupied by hydrogen atoms. These tend to be liquid at room temperature. Vegetable oils such as corn oil, safflower oil, and canola oil are examples. The molecules in saturated fats, as the name implies, are fully occupied by hydrogen atoms. These fats, like butter, tend to be solid at room temperature.

Unsaturated fats are further divided into two more varieties: monounsaturated, found in foods like olives, avocados, pumpkin seeds, many nuts, and canola (made from the rapeseed plant, whose seeds are pressed for the oil), and polyunsaturated, found in corn and most other types of vegetable oils. While the chemical differences between monounsaturated and polyunsaturated fats are interesting to those with a scientific bent, it's far more important to understand the health and nutrition aspects of each. For example, monounsaturated fats help reduce the level of LDL, or bad cholesterol, while polyunsaturated fats in some circumstances may actually reduce HDL, or good cholesterol.

Some polyunsaturated fats are important, specifically omega-3 fatty acids, derived from fish and grass-fed animals, and omega-6 fatty acids, found in plant sources such as corn oil, cottonseed oil, and soybean oil. These are often called essential fatty acids because they aren't made by the body and have to be ingested. These fatty acids are important for brain function, immune response, and other vital functions. Omega-3 fatty acids are widely touted to improve the lipid profile of your blood, or the ratio of good HDL cholesterol to bad LDL cholesterol. Omega-3s may raise both good and bad cholesterol, which would cast a little doubt on their overall benefit. Most studies have shown that omega-3s lead to an improvement in the ratio of good to bad cholesterol, and it's this ratio that seems to be important rather than specific quantities. Omega-3s have also been shown to reduce triglycerides in the blood, which is clearly beneficial.

Saturated fats, where the molecule is completely occupied, or saturated, by hydrogen atoms, are primarily found in animal fats and dairy products. The controversy around saturated fats gets quite intense, especially when vegetarians are involved, and centers not on whether saturated fat is necessary for good nutrition (it isn't) but whether it is harmful (which it typically is, but needn't be).

It's interesting that the highest concentration of saturated fats is produced in animals that consume large amounts of enablers (high-glycemic carbohydrates) such as grain-fed animals. The same thing happens in humans: eat high-glycemic carbs, accumulate saturated fat. Free-range or grass-fed animals, which typically have much less saturated fat, were the only types of animals consumed by humans for the eons preceding the advent of industrial feedlots. My feeling is that most of us can consume some saturated fat, in moderation and without enablers. There is plenty of evidence to support this. According to numerous studies, people on severely carbohydrate-restricted diets who eat large amounts of saturated fats have shown not only a decrease in total cholesterol, bad LDL cholesterol, and triglycerides, but also an increase in good HDL cholesterol. I should also point out that, because we digest fat more slowly than other food types, we tend to feel fuller longer after eating it. This feeling of fullness, called satiety, helps forestall the Echo Hunger Cycle and bolsters our resistance to between-meal snacking.

The Wine and Food Lover's Diet steers a middle course. On the one hand, you want to limit the amount of saturated fat, because it's too difficult and impractical to eliminate Storage Cascades completely. On the other hand, you want to lose weight by reducing the frequency and intensity of Storage Cascades. So the Wine and Food Lover's Diet includes some foods with saturated fat—for example, butter and beef and lamb, preferably grass-fed—but only in combination with Savvy Carbs and Super-Savvy Carbs.

Whatever your personal feelings about eating meat—and there are plenty of ethical, environmental, and economic reasons to avoid it—the body is undeniably equipped to digest the range of fat in meat. (Those canine teeth in our jaws aren't there for decoration.) I happen to be a meat eater, both because it's a good source of protein with moderate amounts of fat and because I happen to like the taste. For those reasons, I include meat in many Wine and Food Lover's Diet recipes. But there are many vegetarian choices among this book's recipes, so regardless of your personal bent, please read on.

Before we explore how fats affect our metabolism, it's important to mention a third category of fats that I believe is directly responsible for much of the diet-related disease plaguing our culture: trans fats. Trans fats are engineered fats created as far back as the 1920s and are used to extend the shelf life of processed foods. Also known as hydrogenated or partially hydrogenated oils, these fats are solid at room temperature and, were they not truly lethal, could be considered a miracle of modern science for their ability to keep crispy foods crisp, and chewy foods chewy, and to deter rancidity. Saturated fats are actually more stable with less of a propensity to go rancid than unsaturated fats and the development of trans fats was a way to take advantage of that property by turning an unsaturated vegetable oil into an artificially saturated fat. Even the typically reticent U.S. government says that "there is no safe level" of trans fats in the diet—a statement that will get no argument from me. Eat trans fats with enablers, and you set the stage for a particularly deadly Storage Cascade.

Fat on the Move

Most of us eat a combination of saturated and unsaturated fats (the elemental form is called triglycerides), much of which is absorbed in the intestines. Because fat can't mix with blood to travel around the body (think oil and vinegar), the fats you eat combine with protein carriers called chylomicrons, which carry them through the bloodstream and lymph system to fat and muscle tissue, where they will be stored until the body needs to burn fat for energy. If the body is getting all the energy it needs from carbohydrates, the stored fat will not be used for energy and instead will accumulate.

With the exception of brain cells, which prefer sugar under most circumstances, almost every other cell in the body can derive energy from fat or sugar. In most cases, when a cell calls for energy, it looks first for sugar; if none (or not enough) is immediately available, it looks to fat. It's a lot like a hybrid engine using gas, then electricity.

When you restrict the amount of sugar available for energy—by limiting the amount of carbohydrates you consume—your body will burn fat. That is the fundamental premise behind low-carb diets: cut off the sugar supply so your body burns up the available fat. But if you cut off the supply of carbs *and* fat, your body starts converting protein into energy. That is the fundamental premise behind starvation.

The goal of the Wine and Food Lover's Diet is to manage the amount and type of carbohydrates we consume to strike a healthy equilibrium between energy sources. Instead of burning the sugar and storing the fat, we manage our metabolism to burn sugar *and* fat.

Storing Fat

The body stores fat for exactly the same reason some people save money: the inevitable rainy day. In times of famine, the body will defend against starvation and death by drawing on the fat it stored when food was plentiful. As a survival mechanism, the design makes perfect sense.

Unfortunately, when we attempt to lose weight, we're actually fighting many millennia of human development when the body was focused on perfecting the system to *increase* fat storage. But don't let that discourage you. By understanding *how* the body stores fat, we can develop strategies to forestall it. The Wine and Food Lover's Diet is that strategy.

We have already seen how this fat-storage mechanism works. We consume more calories than we can immediately burn, leading to a spike in blood sugar, which in turn triggers the pancreas to release insulin and other hormones. In addition to signaling our cells to store fat, the Storage Cascade also instructs the liver, and the fat cells we've already stored, actually to

produce fat—which, it turns out, contains a lot of saturated fat. This is a complex chain of distinct events, evolved over thousands of years of natural selection.

Insulin is the linchpin of the Storage Cascade. It not only tells cells to absorb sugar and store fat, but also instructs cells *not* to use fat for energy unless and until they really need it. If we can manage the release of insulin and other components of the Storage Cascade into the bloodstream—in effect, censor the metabolic message sent to our cells—we can begin to strike a balance between energy sources, instructing our cells to burn sugar *and* fat for energy.

By the way, the cells in muscle tissue prefer to burn fat over sugar for energy, and the better toned the muscles, the more that fat-burning preference is expressed. I'll explore this further when we look at exercise, but it's important to understand that there are clear strategies available to us to prevent and reverse the accumulation of fat.

The accumulation of unsightly fat isn't the only downside to repeated Storage Cascades brought on by insulin in the bloodstream. Insulin has also been shown scientifically to increase the risk of certain cancers by triggering growth factors, and it is also known to increase the risk of, or even to cause, high blood pressure and osteoporosis.

If you're tempted to dismiss the risk posed by repeated Storage Cascades as merely the hallmarks of aging, you would be doing yourself a grave disservice. A growing body of scientific evidence suggests that too many Storage Cascades and not enough Burning Cascades are precisely what accelerate the aging process. Conclusion: The Wine and Food Lover's Diet not only helps you lose weight and prevent disease, but also keeps you looking and feeling younger.

By now the importance of managing insulin

should be crystal clear, not only to prevent fat storage but also to mitigate all of the other risks posed by too much insulin. It's useful to note that, while sugar and, to a much lesser extent, protein cause insulin release, fat doesn't. No matter how much fat you eat, it won't stimulate the release of a single drop of insulin. While that tidbit of knowledge may be interesting, it's impractical as a diet strategy because few of us ever consume fat by itself. (One diet I've come across does advocate primarily fat and a tiny bit of protein, but it causes such rapid weight loss that the dieter risks malnutrition.) Rather, we eat fat in combination with other foods—butter with bread, for example, or animal protein with animal fat—where the carbohydrates or protein acts as a delivery system for the fat.

As delivery systems go, it's hard to beat carbohydrates, and nothing delivers fat better than high-glycemic carbohydrates. Remember, fat alone will not cause insulin release or initiate a Storage Cascade. You need carbohydrates to do that. This is the truth that explodes the fat-free myth: The villain that causes you to store fat, gain weight, and increase your risk of diet-related disease is not fat, but what you eat it with. I call this the Enabler Theory.

Using food combinations to manage insulin release is one of the core principles that sets The Wine and Food Lover's Diet apart from other weight-loss approaches. By pairing fats with very low-glycemic carbohydrates, the recipes in *The Wine and Food Lover's Diet* let you indulge in modest amounts of saturated fats like cream and butter without initiating a diet-defeating Storage Cascade. While unsaturated fats like olive oil are healthier choices in the long run, I believe that completely denying yourself the foods you enjoy is not an effective strategy for lifelong weight control.

The Meal-Planning Trilogy is the key to incorporating fats in your diet without incorporating it into your hips, thighs, and tummy. The combination of one protein with two Super-Savvy Carbs (for rapid weight loss) or one Savvy Carb and one Super-Savvy Carb (for moderate weight loss and ongoing weight control) denies your metabolism the enabler foods that trigger an insulin release that initiates the Storage Cascade, which, in turn, instructs your cells to burn sugar instead of fat, to store fat, and even to produce fat.

The inclusion of fat in the Trilogy offers an important benefit as well: satiety. High-glycemic carbohydrates like cereal, white rice, bread, and potatoes quickly break down into blood sugar, causing an almost immediate spike in glucose. Initially, insulin sends a transient, short-lived satiety signal to your brain, letting it think you've eaten enough. Soon afterward, as your cells quickly burn or absorb all that blood sugar, your brain becomes aware that glucose levels are falling. Your brain interprets this information as a "low fuel" warning and immediately shifts into emergency response mode by (1) decreasing energy use (causing you to feel sleepy) and (2) asking you to replenish glucose (causing you to feel hungry). This is the Echo Hunger Cycle that leads to excessive calorie consumption.

By now you should be gaining a clear understanding of how all of these food-related processes interact and lead to weight gain.

HIGH-GLYCEMIC CARBS

1. Blood sugar rises rapidly.
2. Pancreas releases insulin.
3. Cells burn sugar, stop burning fat, store fat, produce fat.
4. Blood sugar falls rapidly.
5. Brain instructs body to decrease energy use (become sleepy).
6. Brain instructs body to replenish glucose (become hungry).
7. You eat more, gain weight.

The Wine and Food Lover's Diet, and the Meal-Planning Trilogy menus I recommend, provide a strategy to break that cycle.

Cholesterol and Triglycerides

To hear some people talk, cholesterol might as well be plutonium. In reality, cholesterol is a waxy, fatty substance found in the cells of all animals, humans included, and it is necessary for good health. When we eat animal cells, we necessarily ingest cholesterol. If we happen not to eat animals, the body manufactures the cholesterol it needs from other substances. That's a good thing, because cholesterol strengthens cell membranes; without it, we'd literally fall apart.

We also use cholesterol to help make hormones like estrogen, progesterone, and testosterone. A hormone made from cholesterol helps regulate water balance through the kidneys. Cholesterol helps with the absorption of fats through the action of bile in the digestive system. Cholesterol is secreted from glands in the skin to heal and protect against foreign organisms and to stave off dehydration.

Cholesterol also sticks to the walls of your arteries, constricting and, worse case, blocking blood flow to your heart.

No wonder, then, that cholesterol is so widely misunderstood—particularly when it comes to the differences between HDL and LDL, or good and bad cholesterol, respectively.

Our cells acquire cholesterol from food or, if none is available, can produce the cholesterol they need. But they can't break down the cholesterol once it has been used. Only the liver can process the unused cholesterol. Because cholesterol can't travel through the blood by itself, it needs to bond with a carrier molecule to transport it to the liver for proper disposal. These carriers are protein molecules called lipoproteins (*lipo* means "fat") and come in a few basic varieties. We'll talk about two of them here: high-density lipoproteins (HDL) and low-density lipoproteins (LDL). LDL is further divided into small, dense molecules that are bad and larger, not so dense molecules that are just carrying out the day's work of cholesterol in the body. The small, dense ones are also called the oxidized form of LDL.

High-density lipoproteins carry 15 to 40 percent of the cholesterol in your blood and are, generally speaking, good for you. The higher the percentage the better, and some people have up to 50 percent of their cholesterol as HDL cholesterol. Think of HDL molecules as tiny vacuum cleaners scooping up the bad cholesterol and bringing it to the liver for disposal. When there are plenty of little HDL cleaners to capture all the LDL cholesterol floating around, the risk of heart disease is reduced. (With this analogy you can see that it's not the absolute amount of cholesterol in your body, but the ratio of good to bad that counts.)

There is strong evidence that HDL actively protects blood vessel walls from the evils of small, dense LDL particles. One of our goals on the Wine and Food Lover's Diet is to decrease the ratio of LDL cholesterol to HDL. A low LDL to HDL ratio means that you are doing a good job of burning and getting rid of unneeded fat, whether from the waistline and thighs or, more importantly, from the walls of your arteries, which is why people with high levels of HDL run the *lowest* risk of heart attack. HDL levels reflect the amount of fat burned by the body. The more fat burned for fuel, the higher the HDL level.

A commonly performed test is the total cholesterol/HDL ratio. In this case the higher the HDL (what we want), the lower the ratio. A total cholesterol/HDL ratio below four is good. Most cholesterol in the blood is carried by LDL. Although we often refer to LDL as bad cholesterol, it actually performs an important function in transporting the cholesterol our cells need to the farthest reaches of our bodies.

Several factors render LDL cholesterol harmful, including genes, diet, and the nature of your blood chemistry. In the same way metal rusts (oxidizes) and weakens when exposed to oxidants, so do LDL molecules, creating oxidative stress on the molecules that can lead to heart disease. The small, dense LDL cholesterol is, for the most part, oxidized, and always seems to be present where arteries are clogged. Whether the LDL cholesterol causes fatty plaques to accumulate in the arteries or just shows up when arteries are already clogging isn't entirely clear. What we do know is that every time we trigger a Storage Cascade, LDL is present.

When we achieve a healthy equilibrium between sugar and fat burning for energy, LDL isn't necessarily bad for us. But when we are burning sugar and storing fat—in other words, during the Storage Cascade—the LDL oxidizes, increases in density and decreases in size, and begins its artery-clogging work that can lead, over time, to heart disease.

Triglycerides is the chemical term for the most common type of fat—in essence, the elemental form. We get triglycerides from the fat in our diet, and most of our body fat is composed of it. It should surprise no one that the accumulation of triglycerides increases the risk of heart disease and stroke. That accumulation is caused by—you guessed it—the ongoing stream of Storage Cascades that define the lifestyles of just about everyone who is overweight. It has been known for a long time that a high carbohydrate load (glycemic load) will lead to an increase in triglycerides and then the production of fat. This risk is independent from the artery-clogging buildup of LDL cholesterol, but the two are frequently found together.

Overeating carbohydrates (especially high-glycemic carbohydrates) above what is needed by the body for energy will trigger a Storage Cascade which will, in turn, result in insulin stimulated fat production. The fat will be, in large part, in the form of triglycerides from the liver and from fat cells. A measure of this phenomenon is fasting triglyceride levels. Measuring tri-glycerides after eating reflects the triglycerides that we've recently eaten. Fasting triglyceride levels reflect what we are making in the body. Elevated triglyceride levels are an independent risk factor for the development of heart disease.

The Wine and Food Lover's Diet helps control cholesterol and elevated triglyceride levels in several ways, most notably by moderating the cycle of Storage Cascades at the root of so many health problems, chiefly obesity, diabetes, heart disease, and stroke.

Managing Cholesterol

As I mentioned above, the issue with cholesterol is not so much the absolute amounts of LDL and HDL cholesterol in your blood, but the ratio between the two. Remember, one function of HDL is to scoop up and transport LDL cholesterol to the liver for disposal. If there is always enough HDL around to accomplish this, it hardly matters how much LDL is hanging around. Some LDL isn't necessarily harmful; what is harmful is the small, dense component, which, until recently, wasn't typically measured in lab tests.

IMPROVING THE RATIO OF HDL TO LDL

For at least one generation and probably longer, Americans have been admonished to "lower their cholesterol." Yet few of us understand what that means. In fact, there are two types of dietary cholesterol that concern us, only one of which we want to keep in check. By now most of us have heard the terms "good" and "bad" applied to cholesterol, so let's stay with those. Good cholesterol–called HDL for high-density lipoproteins–is an important marker for a healthy heart, and generally points to reduced risk of heart attack or coronary artery disease. But it's not the absolute level of HDL in the blood stream that's important; rather, it's the ratio of LDL cholesterol (low-density lipoprotein, or "bad" cholesterol) to HDL cholesterol that describes the risk of heart disease.

   While drug companies are hard at work looking for the magic bullet that will raise HDL or lower LDL cholesterol levels without any annoying side effects, there are steps you can take on your own to significantly improve your blood lipid profile–that is, the LDL/HDL ratio. The five steps, ranked by the effectiveness of the Wine and Food Lover's Diet as an HDL-raising tool, are:

1. **Lose weight:** If you're losing weight, then you're burning fat. The fat-burning process raises HDL cholesterol, so the more fat you burn for energy, the more you are raising HDL as a ratio to LDL so the ratio becomes a smaller number, which is a good thing. Of course, the converse is also true: When you're storing fat, in a storage cascade, insulin is telling your cells NOT to burn fat, and therefore not to improve their LDL:HDL ratio. No wonder, then, that people on a high-carbohydrate, low-fat diet typically have a low HDL, even though their LDL may be low, too.

2. **Drink some wine:** There is wide agreement among researchers that moderate amounts of alcohol actually help the liver transport key HDL components and increase the amount of HDL in the bloodstream. One glass of wine does this a little; two glasses does it even more. But excessive alcohol consumption poses serious health risks unrelated to cholesterol: your good LDL ratio will do you no good if you also have cirrhosis of the liver or a collision with a tree. Interestingly, the hormone estrogen does for women what an extra glass of wine does for men, which explains why women generally have higher HDL levels than men.

3. **Exercise:** Well-used muscles burn fat as well as sugar, and as we have seen, fat-burning raises HDL. Want to lose weight faster and improve your HDL profile without drugs? Stand up, open the door, go outside, walk in one direction for 15 minutes, turn around and walk back. Repeat.

4. **Eat some fat:** What? You heard me. Fat does not cause an insulin release, so there is no signal to your cells to stop burning fat and store it. Carbohydrate does that, but not fat. Fat reduces the glycemic effect of foods and is more satiating in the long term than carbohydrates, so eating fat helps you avoid over-eating. (But eating carbohydrates in combination with fat will instruct your cells not to burn fat but to store it—the Enabler Theory.

5. **Don't smoke:** This one's a no-brainer. Smoking decreases HDL concentrations in the blood and quitting smoking increases it. It's that simple.

When your metabolism is in healthy equilibrium—burning both sugar and fat for energy—you are automatically improving your LDL:HDL ratio and reducing your risk of heart disease. You're also losing or maintaining your weight and, chances are, feeling better about life in general.

Statin drugs are a class of pharmaceuticals that specifically decrease the amount of LDL cholesterol in the body. Many physicians feel that if dietary management of cholesterol isn't successful, statin drugs may be beneficial. These drugs have been shown to be effective in cutting the risk of heart disease. While statins offer tremendous benefits to some patients, I'm convinced that many of those individuals could successfully manage their cholesterol with dietary methods alone.

By now it should be clear that the root of all dietary evil isn't one particular class of foods, but the harmful patterns of dietary behavior we adopt, which tend to be self-perpetuating. Consuming fat with enablers causes a Storage Cascade, which in turn leads to the Echo Hunger Cycle, which drives us to consume more enablers... and on and on it goes, while we grow fatter, our cells weaker, our arteries narrower, and our lives ever shorter.

It's time to break that pattern, and *The Wine and Food Lover's Diet* shows you how.

PROTEIN IN PERSPECTIVE

Protein is the stuff that holds you together. It's a key component of muscle and gives structure to your body. Of all the materials of which you are formed, pound for pound protein is second only to water.

Not only are proteins structural, but they are very functional as well. Lipoproteins, for instance, transport fat through the bloodstream to all the places it needs to go (and several it probably shouldn't). Hemoglobin is a protein that distributes oxygen to body tissues—no hemoglobin, no life. Enzymes, too, are types of proteins—little work-horses that do all kinds of heavy lifting, from digesting food to removing toxins to bolstering the immune system.

And protein is a critical part of the Meal-Planning Trilogy menu, which incorporates it into every meal. The recipes in this book easily provide enough protein to sustain your body day to day without overloading it.

Proteins themselves are made up of building blocks called amino acids. Different combinations of amino acids produce different proteins. While the body is capable of manufacturing certain amino acids, some essential ones have to be imported, ideally via the diet. When we fail to eat enough of the foods that deliver these essential amino acids, we run the risk of developing deficiency syndromes, with consequences ranging from minor to catastrophic.

Vegetarians can be at particular risk of protein deficiency. While most animal sources provide complete proteins, vegetable sources need to be combined in ways that create complete proteins. For example, rice and beans together are a complete protein, while either one alone is not.

Of the three basic food types, protein has perhaps the most subtle effect on weight loss. The body will burn protein for energy, but not if a lot of sugar is present. The process of converting protein to a burnable form of blood sugar is complicated, and requires energy, so the resulting rise in blood sugar is delayed and muted, and is far less likely to stimulate a significant Storage Cascade compared to that seen after eating a carbohydrate laden meal. Nor is it likely to interfere with a Burning Cascade. (This phenomenon of a delayed rise in blood sugar is more of a concern for type 1 diabetics, who typically need to take long-term insulin after a protein-laden meal to counteract the delayed increase in blood sugar.)

Another effect of protein is to stimulate the release of glucagon. Like insulin, glucagon is a messenger hormone produced in the pancreas that instructs the body to convert glycogen into glucose in the liver, thereby raising the blood sugar (as opposed to insulin's effect of lowering it by forcing it into cells). But here is the important difference: Where insulin instructs the body to burn sugar and store fat, glucagon facilitates fat burning as the counterweight to insulin.

From a weight-loss standpoint, mixing in protein with carbohydrates moderates the glycemic effect of the carbohydrates, both because it "dilutes" the carbohydrate source and because it stimulates fat burning that counteracts the insulin-carb message to store fat.

I wouldn't be the least bit surprised if all of this has you a bit confused. The effect of protein on body chemistry is quite involved, and anything but the most cursory explanation will quickly grow tedious. At the risk of over simplifying, let's agree that protein in combination with high-glycemic carbohydrates will do little to avoid the Storage Cascade, but protein in combination with low-glycemic carbohydrates, as the Wine and Food Lover's Diet recommends, will not only help avoid the Storage Cascade but also promote fat burning. And protein combined with fat (the typical pork chop, say) has almost zero ability to initiate a diet-defeating Storage Cascade. The fat in that pork chop, however, can be enabled when eaten with a high-glycemic carbohydrate such as potato or corn. As we have seen, this combination creates ideal conditions for a Storage Cascade, and all the bad things that go with it.

Yet, as important as those effects are, perhaps the most important role protein plays in the success of your weight-loss program is its ability to keep you feeling fuller longer. This property, known as satiety, is what keeps you from returning to the fridge or the pantry too soon after a meal.

Because protein takes longer to break down and digest, it is one of the best tools we have to avoid the Echo Hunger Cycle that so often leads us to consume far more calories than we need to fuel our energy output. If blood sugar rises and falls at a more moderate pace, there is no insulin-triggered alarm sent to the brain, and no instruction to feel sleepy (reduce energy expenditure) and become hungry (refuel).

I can't overstate the importance of food combinations, for that is the key to minimizing Storage Cascades and promoting Burning Cascades, and the underlying premise of the Meal-Planning Trilogy menu I've described. In essence, every meal should have protein to modulate the glycemic effect of what is eaten, to promote satiety, to replenish the protein lost in normal body function, and to increase the enjoyment and satisfaction of your meals.

In a typical day, the Wine and Food Lover's Diet recommends the following intake of protein:

- A high-protein, low-glycemic breakfast to provide sustained energy throughout the day and avoid the Echo Hunger Cycle— a breakfast scramble, for example, with eggs for protein (go ahead, add some bacon or sausage, maybe a little cheese) and a bit of onions or peppers for flavor.
- A lunch that combines a small portion of protein with Savvy Carbs (or Super-Savvy Carbs), for the same reasons—a small salad with chicken or seafood.
- A dinner built around a center-of-the-plate protein, combined with a larger portion of Savvy and/or Super-Savvy Carbs, since they will be digested quicker than protein alone, allowing you to avoid a delayed blood sugar elevation while you sleep.

A day's worth of meals built around these basic guidelines will help you lose weight, maintain energy and alertness throughout the day, avoid between-meal or late-night snacking, and prevent you from feeling deprived, which is the bane of every diet I've encountered.

Which protein to eat is entirely your choice. I've included a complete list of protein recommendations in the section beginning on page 54. Here are a few points when it comes to selecting protein:

Fish, even fatty fish, is good for you, even the skin, even the fat. I would avoid shark, swordfish, tilefish, and king mackerel because of their potential to contain unsafe levels of mercury, but from a diet standpoint there are no bad alternatives.

Chicken meat with the skin on has more saturated fat. The skin is a relatively rich source but can be eaten if it is part of a meal that doesn't include enablers. Since I'm not eating **Mediterranean Spiced Chicken with Olives and Almonds** (page 130) with enablers in the first part of the diet, I'm not concerned with the saturated fat in the chicken. Skinless white meat has much less saturated fat and cholesterol than dark meat or white meat with skin, but it still contains some. If you insist on eating enablers in a meal with chicken, skinless white meat is the better choice.

WINE AND WEIGHT LOSS: A PERFECT PAIRING

Wine and food are so often mentioned in the same breath for a good reason. When paired correctly, each is the perfect complement of the other: Good wine makes good food taste better, and vice versa. Wine can also have positive effects on the attitude, which may help us appreciate more fully the sensual aspects of food.

Of course, there are plenty of reasons to avoid alcohol altogether—even the glass or two with dinner—but fear of gaining weight shouldn't be one of them. Unless you have a specific reason to stay away from alcohol, the Wine and Food Lover's Diet not only allows the moderate consumption of wine, but encourages it.

For purposes of the Wine and Food Lover's Diet, I'm going to limit the discussion to wine. Although some (but by no means all) of wine's benefits are available from distilled spirits, those beverages aren't as well suited to pairing with food, so I don't include them in the diet. As for beer, the jury is still out as to its glycemic impact. Remember, the Wine and Food Lover's Diet is all about enjoying food, and for me that not only suggests a glass or two of wine with dinner; it darn near requires it.

The benefits of drinking wine with food are many and, by now, well established. They tend to fall into two main categories: sensory and health. Let's deal first with the former, then the latter.

That some wine simply tastes good is obvious to most who've experienced its charms. No less an authority than Benjamin Franklin said, "Wine makes daily living easier, less hurried, with fewer tensions and more tolerance." While Franklin was commenting on the attitudinal benefits of wine, as a diet creator and food lover I'm more interested in its ability to enhance the flavor of food.

Specialists in food science will tell you that the two natural substances known to convey the flavor of food most effectively are fat and alcohol. That is why a nicely marbled steak, for example, tastes better than an overly lean cut of meat, and why cream makes coffee taste better than skim milk. A glass of wine with food has a similar effect—it enhances the flavor.

Another reason that I recommend wine with Wine and Food Lover's Diet recipes is the sense of indulgence it provides. With so many diets demanding sacrifice and self-deprivation, the Wine and Food Lover's Diet takes a different approach: The enjoyment of good food is a source of satisfaction in our lives, and anything that deepens that satisfaction—as wine surely does—is important to the success of the diet. Eat good food, drink a little wine, lose weight: Who could have a problem with that?

As for the health benefits, this topic is receiving a lot of attention. A rash of research studies and news reports links wine, in particular, to a decreased risk of heart disease and certain cancers, among other diseases. Wine leads to an increase in your good (HDL) cholesterol. Some studies have shown that regular consumption of alcohol can increase HDL considerably, thus improving the ratio of good to bad (LDL) cholesterol and decreasing your risk for heart disease. Increasing HDL cholesterol is one of the goals of the Wine and Food Lover's Diet, and this is one way to accomplish it. Increased levels of HDL cholesterol mean that the body is burning fat for energy—a main goal of the diet. Wine also helps improve insulin sensitivity, decreasing the risk of developing type 2 diabetes. Red wine, much more so than white, has also been shown to reduce LDL cholesterol, and its antioxidant properties can ameliorate the bad blood-chemistry environment that enables oxidized LDL cholesterol to do its damage.

Research also suggests that a little wine with meals can reduce inflammation in tissue cells, which not only strengthens our bodies on the inside, but also combats the visible effects of aging, helping you appear younger, longer.

All of these benefits accrue to anyone who drinks wine (especially red wine) in moderation, not just those on the Wine and Food Lover's Diet.

Although wine is made from grapes that are very high in sugar, the process of fermentation converts the sugar to alcohol, rendering the finished product virtually sugar free. As a result, wine ranks relatively low on the glycemic index, and by itself will not initiate a Storage Cascade. (However, it will do nothing to prevent a Storage Cascade should you choose to drink it with high-glycemic carbohydrates.)

As a doctor, I would be remiss not to point out the downside to alcohol consumption. While you're no doubt aware of it, excessive consumption of alcohol can—and often does—lead to serious illness. Too much alcohol consumed over a period of years can cause accumulation of fat in the liver, which will steadily erode its ability to clean your blood. Although fat accumulation is, for the most part, reversible, another alcohol-related liver disease, cirrhosis, is not. Cirrhosis is a chronic disease that, as it progresses, replaces healthy cells with scar tissue, decreasing liver function.

I don't mean to sound like a scold, but the behavioral aspects of excessive alcohol can pose risks, as well. Alcohol impairs our reflexes and judgment, affecting our ability to do serious things, like drive a car. That same loss of control and social inhibitions could lead us to make stupid dietary choices. I'm not equating the seriousness of driving drunk with, say, devouring fast-food french fries, but you get my point:

There are benefits to drinking alcohol, but not for everyone and only in moderation.

Wine and Food Lover's Diet Recommendations

For the first few weeks or so that you follow the Wine and Food Lover's Diet, during rapid weight loss, I recommend limiting consumption of wine to just one glass—or a glass and a half, if you must. While wine that has been fermented to dryness is low glycemic, it still has lots of calories that, in the early phase of the diet, will slow your pace. Also, the pathways used by the body to extract energy from alcohol are shared with those that extract energy from fat, so enough alcohol will slow the rate of fat burning and, ultimately, weight loss.

As you reach your weight-loss goal, it's okay to increase wine consumption: up to two glasses with a Wine and Food Lover's Diet dinner.

One last thought on wine pairings: Don't feel bound by the old myth that red wine is for red meat, and white wine for fish and poultry. I often enjoy a red wine with chicken or fish, especially when the protein is served with a bold-tasting sauce, such as my **Grilled Shrimp with Romesco Sauce** (page 124) or **Stuffed Chicken Breasts with Cascade Falls Sauce** (page 137). I mention this because red wine appears to offer more of the antioxidant properties that are so useful in preventing oxidation and inflammation and reducing the risk of heart disease. And because, generally speaking, I prefer red wine.

But if you happen to like white wine, and you want to drink it with a nice New York steak, go right ahead. The same applies to those who drink no wine at all. Remember, the only hard-and-fast rule in the Wine and Food Lover's Diet is that you eat what you like and like what you eat (and drink), so if that's your preference, I say, "Cheers."

A LITTLE EXERCISE GOES A LONG WAY

You already know that exercise is good for you. It burns calories, prevents disease, and, for almost everyone who does it, enhances longevity. Exercise also provides all manner of ancillary benefits, from focusing your thoughts to improving your appearance and self-esteem, to simply getting you out of the house.

So if exercise is so great, why don't more of us do more of it?

I suspect it has to do with a very widely held misconception that, for exercise to work as a weight-loss strategy, it has to be frequent, prolonged, vigorous, and painful. It's time to explode that myth.

That misconception is rooted in the simple arithmetic that to lose weight you have to burn more calories than you take in. True enough. Yet, because not all calories are created equal, it's also true that the *kind* of calorie you consume is as important as the quantity. By now you understand that some foods (high-glycemic carbohydrates, for example) promote fat storage and production, and others do not. So a 250-calorie portion of high-glycemic carbohydrates may lead to weight gain, while a 500-calorie portion of protein and low-glycemic greens may not.

Notice that I said "may" lead to weight gain. You'll recall that most cells in our bodies can burn sugar or fat for energy, and that they usually look for any available sugar (carbohydrates) first. But muscle cells *prefer* fat to sugar, and the more toned up and in shape those muscles, the more that fat burning preference is expressed.

By "toned" I do not mean six-pack abs. All it takes is a little activity, on a consistent basis, to get the cells in those muscle tissues burning away.

Note the key word in the preceding sentence. It's *consistent*, and herein is the key, because muscle tone is the product of regular exercise over time, regardless of the intensity, rather than short bursts of intense exertion.

I certainly don't want to discourage you from intense exercise. Short of driving yourself to injury or exhaustion, there's no upper limit on the amount of exercise you can safely perform. But for those who, for whatever reason, may lack the commitment of a marathoner or the discipline of a drill sergeant, let me reassure you: It doesn't take all that much to encourage muscles to burn fat.

Can you lose weight on the Wine and Food Lover's Diet without any exercise? Sure, you can lose some. But if you insist on the sedentary existence of the proverbial couch potato (even a low-glycemic one), you will have difficulty achieving the significant and lasting results you want. To turn your muscle cells into tiny high-performance fat burners, you're going to have to use them.

The Wine and Food Lover's Diet Strategy for Weight-Loss Success

Find a way to walk for fifteen minutes twice a day and you will dramatically improve the way your muscles burn fat. The important thing is to do it regularly, and in a way that is a pleasure, not a chore. Making exercise a part of your daily routine is the best way, because it tends to eliminate the "should I or shouldn't I?" conundrum. Every time you open the door to a new decision, you make it easy for yourself to say no. If exercise is part of your daily routine, you are much less likely to question it each time and, to turn a phrase, just do it.

Can you walk around the block every evening after dinner? Can you carve out fifteen minutes from your lunch hour? Once you get over that first hurdle—actually getting started—the rewards are so great and so immediate that it isn't difficult to keep it going. When you think about it, thirty minutes a day is equal to about one full week over the course of a year. If that one week per year enabled you to extend your life by, say, five years, would that be a reasonable return on your investment? Do the math: Over thirty years, you will have invested 30 weeks of exercise to extend your life by 260 weeks. Now consider the vastly improved quality of all those years, when you're feeling better, healthier, more confident. The technical term for this is no-brainer.

I admit that it's a bit silly to quantify the health benefit of exercise that way. But you get the point: The reasons to take that after-dinner walk or early-morning bike ride are pretty compelling, and the excuses we make not to are, well, just plain lame. So here's the plan: Put this book down and go outside and walk for fifteen minutes. When you return, I'll explain just how the aerobic exercise you just enjoyed shortens the distance between where you are and where you want to be.

Part of the Wine and Food Lover's Diet strategy is to create the conditions in your body that encourage your muscles to burn fat as well as sugar. In essence, those conditions are a metabolism in equilibrium, or balanced between burning sugar and burning fat for energy. Diet and exercise are the two main mechanisms for achieving metabolic equilibrium and teaching your muscles to burn fat instead of sugar, and it just so happens that both are directly and totally under your control.

Of the two primary types of energy-burning exercise, aerobic and anaerobic, the former encourages fat burning, while the latter promotes muscle development. Both types of exercise are important, because the more developed the muscles (achieved via anaerobic exercise), the more fat they burn during aerobic exercise. More muscle, more fat burning. (*Aerobic* simply refers to the presence of oxygen; if an activity entails a lot of movement, it's probably aerobic.

Walking is aerobic. Weight lifting is usually, but not always, anaerobic.)

Light to moderate aerobic exercise like walking, hiking, or raking leaves increases your heart and breathing rate to ensure that enough oxygen reaches your muscles to stoke the fat-burning furnace for energy production. (The body burns primarily sugar during the first few minutes of exercise, and will continue to burn some sugar as exercise continues, but will prefer to burn fat as energy demand increases, so long as sufficient oxygen is present.)

When you begin aerobic exercise, the muscles draw energy from only two sources: fat oxidation (oxidation in this case refers to the addition of oxygen while extracting the energy from fat) and carbohydrate oxidation (sugar burning). In a process known as up-regulation, the body meets the increasing demand for power by instantaneously improving its ability to oxidize both sugar and fat in order to create energy at the onset of exercise.

Whether muscles burn predominantly sugar or fat depends on many factors, some of which we can affect, through diet and more exercise. Other factors are beyond our conscious control. We want to concentrate on those factors over which we have some influence to increase fat burning.

Most of us have heard of carbo-loading, a technique that some endurance athletes (marathon runners, for example) use to stretch their fuel supply by filling their tank with more of the quickest burning fuel (carbohydrates) and thereby preserve the fat for use later in the race. These athletes typically have very well-toned muscles that burn fat very efficiently; the idea behind loading up on carbohydrates is to forestall fat burning as long as possible.

If your goal is to lose fat rather than preserve it, and there's no marathon in your immediate future, you'll be relieved to know that when lots of fast-burning carbohydrates aren't available, fat burning becomes the primary source of energy during aerobic exercise. While this dynamic is well known, the exact mechanisms that regulate the shift from one energy source to the other during exercise are not completely understood.

While it may make some sense for a marathoner to load up on carbohydrates the night before a race, I want to emphasize that it makes no sense for the typical "weekend warrior" athlete. Remember, the body's sugar (glycogen) storage capacity is relatively limited and easily "topped off." A meal heavy in carbohydrates will very quickly replenish your glycogen stores, leaving lots of excess carbohydrates to dispose of. As we have seen, disposal can happen only two ways: burn or store. If you don't immediately burn the excess sugar, the Storage Cascade will kick in, excess sugar will be converted to fat, and insulin will instruct your cells not to burn fat for energy—the exact opposite of what we want to happen.

We do know that short and strenuous exercise (anaerobic) generally increases sugar burning, and long and moderate-intensity exercise increases fat burning. This makes sense, since most of us have enough fat stored to provide energy for days, while our supplies of muscle glycogen, the storage depot for sugar, typically last for a period of minutes to a few hours. Our muscles will conserve its stores of glycogen during prolonged exercise by judiciously burning fat. If we carbo load, we can temporarily top off our sugar storage depots. If, as I recommend, we reduce carbohydrate storage, we are instructing the body to burn more fat during light to moderate exercise.

Regular exercise has also been shown to

decrease insulin resistance, meaning that your body can tolerate more glucose without going out of a healthy equilibrium and initiating a significant Storage Cascade. A brisk walk of fifteen minutes will decrease insulin resistance by up to 20 to 30 percent, so those who "just do it" can also, occasionally, just eat it without broadcasting as loud a metabolic message to burn sugar, store fat, and even produce fat.

If you need more reasons to start regular light to moderate exercise consider this: It also improves your blood lipid profile, increasing HDL cholesterol and improving the LDL to HDL ratio. One study of almost 50,000 people in eight different populations found that walking just two miles a day, give or take, significantly reduced triglyceride levels and increased HDL levels compared to those walking only a half mile a day. So you're not only losing weight or maintaining weight loss, but also markedly reducing your risk of heart disease.

When they stepped up to jogging instead of walking, subjects in the study further decreased triglycerides and elevated HDL levels. The biggest improvement of all was in people who exercised for thirty minutes three times per week. For all the success many people have with cholesterol-lowering statin drugs, some surely could achieve similar results with regular exercise. (If you do take a statin prescription, definitely consult your doctor before substituting exercise for medication.)

A GUIDE TO THE WINE AND FOOD LOVER'S DIET

Enjoy good food *and* lose weight? Stop denying yourself *and* feel full and satisfied? Never worry about counting calories, carbs, or fat grams?

If it sounds too good to be true, perhaps you need to listen harder. Not to me, but to your own body, and how different foods affect it. Learning to decode the messages different foods send your body is neither complicated nor challenging, but easy and natural. With that simple knowledge you will be empowered to take control of your diet, your weight, and even your health over the long haul.

The Wine and Food Lover's Diet is less of a diet regimen than a proven, lifelong *strategy* to help you change your relationship to food. It is not a deprivation diet that temporarily sheds some pounds, but a sustainable lifestyle that addresses your need to enjoy food and the companionship associated with it.

The Wine and Food Lover's Diet makes lifestyle change easy because in practically no time at all you'll feel better, both emotionally and physically. You'll be more alert and have more energy and stamina. You'll think about food less and enjoy it more. You can even slow down the aging process, so you'll look and feel younger. And before long, you'll naturally—unthinkingly—choose the foods that make you feel this way. For most of us, feeling is believing…which is all the motivation we need.

The Wine and Food Lover's Diet works because it uses your body's fundamental design and natural processes, which have evolved over thousands of years. Back then, the fat storage mechanism was critical to survival. The body adapted to an inconsistent food supply by carefully regulating how it burned and stored energy. Today, with food so readily available, your body works at cross-purposes: It will store and produce fat even when fat storage and production pose a direct threat to your health and well-being.

Happily, we can take those basic principles and put them to work for us—not to maintain and increase our weight through energy (fat) storage, as primitive humans needed to do, but to achieve a healthy weight and maintain it over the years. In other words, we can optimize our health by choosing and combining the foods that contribute to efficient energy utilization and disease prevention.

Many of you no doubt have tried other diets and found that most of them focus on a single idea: restricting one type of food (such as fat or carbs) or restricting all foods to reduce overall caloric intake. The problem with almost every regimen is that it is not sustainable over time. Soon you will tire of the self-denial of calorie restriction or grow weary of counting calories or grams.

Instead of that restrictive approach, we want to pursue a lifestyle that includes delicious, satisfying meals made with a wide variety of foods. Our goals on the Wine and Food Lover's Diet are to achieve a healthy equilibrium between burning sugar and fat for energy and to stimulate the release of glucagon and other hormones helpful in initiating a Burning Cascade, while mitigating the release of insulin, decreasing insulin resistance, and avoiding a Storage Cascade.

Too many of us follow a diet that lurches from one Storage Cascade to the next. This not only encourages our bodies to store fat, but also helps create the conditions for a host of diseases, among them diabetes, heart disease,

and cancer. The science of Storage Cascades is clear: too many will result in a reduced ability to burn fat, leading to increased triglycerides, increased bad (LDL) cholesterol, and decreased good (HDL) cholesterol.

Over time, the continuous chain of Storage Cascades will lead to a condition known as insulin resistance, when your body gradually loses its ability to respond to the metabolic message that insulin sends. In this event you become, in effect, prediabetic, a precursor to type 2 diabetes, where no fat burning will occur, and your fat cells will become efficient storage machines, causing you to grow fatter and fatter. Remember, food is like a drug, and people in constant storage mode are like addicts—in this case, sugar addicts. Once we kick the high-glycemic carb habit, we can break the chain of Storage Cascades and begin to restore metabolic equilibrium.

Wine and Food Lover's Diet Fundamentals

The Wine and Food Lover's Diet includes a 28-Day Menu Plan in which the first two weeks are designed for a more rapid weight loss and the second for gradual weight loss and for long-term weight control. The basic principles are the same for each phase, and you're free to design your own program—and control the rate at which you lose weight—as long as you follow the general guidelines.

The heart of the Wine and Food Lover's Diet is the basic three-part meal structure called the Meal-Planning Trilogy. Just as the U.S. government designed a pyramid-shaped nutrition guide, the Wine and Food Lover's Diet uses a three-sided figure as a guide to the balanced meal. In our case, the three components are:

1 protein + 1 Super-Savvy Carb + 1 Super-Savvy Carb, for rapid weight loss

1 protein + 1 Savvy Carb + 1 Super-Savvy Carb, for moderate weight loss or weight maintenance.

You may find it helpful to visualize the Trilogy not as a pyramid, but as a dinner plate divided into three parts—picture the Mercedes Benz logo as a dinner plate—with the compartments filled by a protein and two very low-glycemic carbohydrates (rapid weight loss), or a low-glycemic carbohydrate and a very low-glycemic carbohydrate (moderate weight loss). This formula will provide enough protein and carbohydrates to let you eat your fill and still lose weight. It also supplies a nice balance of all three food types, with the fat derived from animal protein (saturated fat) or from oil (unsaturated fat) used in cooking or as a salad dressing or from accents like nuts (monounsaturated and polyunsaturated fats) and cheese (unsaturated and saturated fat).

Keep in mind that, far from being your enemy, dietary fat is essential to good nutrition, and some fat in the diet is required to get your muscles to burn fat for energy. The type of fat you choose, however, is important, so try to use "good" monounsaturated fats like olive oil, canola oil, and nut oils such as hazelnut or almond in your cooking. The other type of fats you want to be sure to include in your diet are omega-3 fatty acids, found in fish or fish oil pills and dark green vegetables, as well as other sources. Most other vegetable oils such as corn oil are rich in omega-6 but not omega-3 fatty acids, *and* they are easily oxidized, which can exacerbate oxidative and inflammation stress.

One way to combat oxidative stress is to drink a glass of red wine with dinner. Not only will you benefit from its antioxidant effect, but it will make your food taste better and let you feel like you've indulged in a fine, satisfying meal. What's more, it just might improve your overall disposition as well. (Although wine offers real benefits for some, obviously it is not appropriate for everyone, so use your own judgment.)

The Meal-Planning Trilogy can take a variety of forms, depending on the meal. A Trilogy breakfast, for example, could have all three elements in one dish—a **Tomato, Basil, and Mozzarella Frittata** (page 89) or a **Baja Omelet with Avocado-Tomato Salsa Fresca** (page 90).

If you prefer a lighter breakfast, try **Creamy Hot Barley with Toasted Almonds** (page 79) or yogurt with nuts. The point is to include some protein, a little fat, and low-glycemic or very low-glycemic carbohydrates. I need to emphasize the importance of eating at least a small breakfast with basic Trilogy components. This will ensure that you have the energy to last until lunchtime and to avoid the urge to snack before lunchtime arrives.

Breakfast cereals with lots of sugar or high-glycemic carbohydrates like corn, wheat and white rice are a poor choice, because they start the day off with a big Storage Cascade and, soon after bring on the Echo Hunger Cycle. Cereals have been a breakfast staple only for the past hundred years or so. Before that, most people ate a portion of protein in the morning— usually the previous night's leftovers—which provided many hours of energy and satiety.

Lunch can be a similar combination of Trilogy foods: **Greek Salad** (page 96) or **Chicken Paillards and Caesar Salad** (page 140) with protein supplied by the feta cheese. Dinner provides an opportunity to focus on the Meal-Planning Trilogy with a nice variety of foods. The recipes in this book will give you a broad selection of dishes to choose from, but after a while you can find lots of ways to create your menus using the recommended ingredients. One advantage of these recipes is that, in addition to providing a balanced meal, they have portion sizes that will ensure you consume enough to feel satisfied without overdoing total calories.

Whether you choose to follow the menus and recipes in the Wine and Food Lover's Diet or feel confident to create your own recipes and menus, I've put together this comprehensive guide to the Meal-Planning Trilogy components and other foods used in the recipes so you know exactly what foods will lead you to success.

PROTEIN The recipes in *The Wine and Food Lover's Diet* are categorized by protein type: Seafood (including fish and shellfish), Poultry (including chicken and turkey; egg dishes are included in the Breakfast section), Meat (including pork, beef, and lamb), and Vegetarian (tofu). You'll find more detailed information about other recommended protein foods that aren't "complete" proteins, like nuts and cheese, in the Savvy Carb and Dairy sections.

Here are a few additional points to keep in mind when purchasing these protein sources:

- Avoid fish varieties that may contain high levels of mercury. This is especially important for pregnant and nursing women. These varieties are swordfish, tilefish (also known as golden bass or golden snapper), Atlantic king mackerel, and shark.

- I look for free-range poultry. It is the healthiest choice because the birds consume what they evolved into being able to eat, and they produce a healthier spectrum of fats.

- I prefer eggs from chickens that have been fed in a free-range environment with flax seed containing omega-3 precursors. These eggs, available in most supermarkets, have higher levels of omega-3 fatty acids and are much better for you. I normally eat whole eggs (even with cheese) in recipes like **Tomato, Basil, and Mozzarella Frittata** (page 89). On occasion, I opt for egg whites only, for variety, but eating the whole egg makes me feel fuller and more satisfied, and since I'm not eating them with high-glycemic carbohydrates like toast or hash browns that act as enablers, I don't have to worry about the saturated fat being enabled.

- Grass-fed or free-range animals are much healthier for you and have a wider range of good fats including omega-3 fatty acids normally associated with fish. Grass-fed-beef is a decent source of omega-3 fatty acids, and the amount of unhealthy long-chain fatty acids is markedly lower than in beef raised on corn or grain. When grass-fed beef or pork isn't available, I buy center-cut pork and lean beef filets because they contain the least amount of saturated fat. If I choose a meal that includes a protein higher in saturated fat, like **Spicy Grilled Baby Back Ribs** (page 151), I am conscious of the

RECOMMENDED PROTEINS

Bacon (nitrite-free)

Beef: filet mignon, tenderloin, ground beef, veal

Eggs

Fish: catfish, flounder, grouper, halibut, mahi-mahi, orange roughy, red snapper, salmon, sardines, sole, trout, tuna

Lamb chops

Pork: shoulder (trimmed of fat), center-cut boneless loin pork chops, bone-in rib pork chops, boneless pork loin, baby back ribs

Poultry: chicken, turkey

Prosciutto

Sausage: Italian, andouille, and turkey (free of nitrite and fillers)

Shellfish: calamari, clams, crab, lobster, oysters, scallops, shrimp

Tofu

saturated fat and try to avoid a Storage Cascade by pairing it with Super-Savvy Carbs only like **Napa Cabbage Slaw with Pumpkin Seeds** (page 183).

- It's important to read the ingredient labels on processed and cured beef products like sausage. In some cases, they may contain nitrites, filler carbohydrates, and sugar, which should be avoided. Look for words like dextrose, which is a sugar additive.

RECOMMENDED SUPER-SAVVY CARBOHYDRATES

Artichokes

Arugula

Asparagus

Avocados

Bell peppers

Bok choy

Broccoli

Broccolini

Brussels sprouts

Cabbage, all varieties

Cauliflower

Celery

Chiles, all varieties, both fresh and canned

Citrus: grapefruit, lemon, lime

Cucumber

Dandelion greens

Dark, leafy greens: chard, collard greens, kale, mustard greens, spinach, turnip greens

Eggplant

Endive

Fennel

Frisée

Garlic

Green beans

Herbs, fresh, all varieties

Jicama

Kohlrabi

Leeks

Lettuce, all varieties

Mushrooms, all varieties

Nuts, all varieties except cashews

Okra

Olives, all varieties, with or without brine

Onions, all varieties

Peanuts

Pea shoots

Radicchio

Seeds: pumpkin, sesame, sunflower

Shallots

Snowpeas

Spaghetti squash

Sprouted vegetables such as sunflower sprouts

Sugar snap peas

Summer squash, all varieties

Tomatillos

Tomatoes

NOTE: When it comes to choosing Super-Savvy Carbs, nearly all green vegetables meet the criteria.

SAVVY CARBOHYDRATES

Barley

Beans: cannellini, cranberry, lima, pinto, soy/ edamame

Berries: blueberries, raspberries,

strawberries (technically very low-glycemic, but placed here because the sugar can slow weight loss)

Black-eyed peas

Butter beans and other shelling beans

Chickpeas

Dark chocolate,

preferably 60 percent cacao or more

Green peas

Lentils, all varieties

Quinoa

OILS AND OTHER COOKING FATS You may be wondering why so many of my Wine and Food Lover's Diet recipes use certain oils and cooking fats. The simple answer is that, like most fats, they add flavor and richness to the recipes and help make you full and satisfied.

A NOTE ABOUT BUTTER Butter has been used for thousands of years because it's quite flavorful, is more solid and therefore spreadable at room temperature, less likely to go rancid when exposed to light and air, and, in my opinion, sort of decadent. It's butter that unleashes the rich mushroom flavor in **Button Mushrooms with Thyme, Rosemary, and Basil** (page 180). Eaten without enablers, butter is filling, satisfying, and delicious and won't be implicated in a Storage Cascade and related cardiovascular risks. I recommend unsalted butter in my recipes. If you choose to use salted butter, sample each recipe to check for saltiness.

DAIRY PRODUCTS Dairy products offer numerous benefits. They can help increase fat-burning proficiency by up to 60 percent when eaten as part of a calorie-restricted diet, but remember that a little goes a long way. A teaspoon of crème fraîche adds a tremendous amount of flavor to **Leeks and Pattypan Squash with Tarragon and Crème Fraîche** (page 163). Using a small amount of dairy adds only a small amount of saturated fat. When eaten without enablers, the small amount of saturated fat will not contribute to the cardiovascular risk to nearly the same degree as when dairy is combined with enablers like bread, potatoes, and white rice. In fact, in Europe, dairy products, especially cheese, are consumed in much greater proportions than in America, and the Europeans, in general, have a lower incidence of heart disease.

I choose not to drink milk because it contains lactose, or dairy sugar, which encourages the Storage Cascade. For those of you who like to start your morning with coffee, I suggest opting for a small or dry (made mostly with foam) cappuccino. A big portion of milk can initiate a Storage Cascade, which will set you up for a diet-defeating Echo Hunger Cycle.

Cheese is great for snacking, as an ingredient in salads and other dishes, and for dessert because it contains protein and fat for satiety and it doesn't initiate a Storage Cascade or result in Echo Hunger. I recommend purchasing the highest quality cheese and avoiding anything labeled "cheese food" or fat-free. These tend to have unhealthful additives such as starches.

SEASONINGS AND CONDIMENTS Seasonings are a terrific way to add flavor and variety to foods, and you'll notice that I use them liberally in my recipes. Dried or fresh herbs and other aromatics such as garlic, basil, tarragon, chives, and thyme will not lead to a Storage Cascade. The same is true of ground spices like cinnamon and cayenne pepper.

Salt is an essential ingredient in bringing out the flavor of food, and I use kosher salt when I cook Wine and Food Lover's Diet recipes. The size and shape of kosher salt crystals help meat retain moisture while adding an appealing crispiness to surface. Kosher salt and sea salt, an alternative to kosher, tend to dissolve less readily than table salt, so despite their increased size they will result in a less salty finished dish.

In the recipes, I add both freshly ground black and white pepper (I confess to being a bit of a food geek, so if you prefer monochromatic pepper, go right ahead).

I also like to use condiments like Dijon mustard, capers, green curry sauce, red wine vinegar, pimientos, Worcestershire sauce, and fish sauce. All of these add wonderful flavors to dishes and pose little, if any, risk to our diet strategy.

Having been raised in the South, I find it perfectly natural to add a little extra kick to my meals, as you'll see in **Scrambled Eggs with Green Onions, Chicken, and Hot Sauce** (page 81). I usually reach for the Tabasco or Crystal hot sauce brands, but there are hundreds of varieties to explore.

FLOUR Because of its high-glycemic value, flour is one of those ingredients you won't find in my recipes. Personally, I stay away from most flour-based foods, although I will admit an occasional weakness for a piece of crusty French bread (my family was French before it was Southern). I recommend avoiding flour completely during the 28-Day Menu Plan, and only moderate consumption, at most, as you progress on the Wine and Food Lover's Diet.

Some recipes call for chickpea or soy flour, or nut flours made from almonds and hazelnuts, to thicken sauces or produce a nice crust in savory dishes like **Spice-Crusted Fish Fillets with Arugula-Mint Pesto** (page 118). These flours also provide structure in sweet dishes like **Flourless Chocolate Cakes** (page 217).

BEVERAGES Drinks sweetened with sugar or high-fructose corn syrup, such as soda or juice drinks, initiate the Storage Cascade, and I don't recommend them. These highly refined sugars have been blamed for a portion of the obesity epidemic in the United States and are particularly hard for the body to process.

As for 100 percent fruit juice, although they may be natural sugars (fructose), they are nonetheless quickly digested and associated with weight gain.

RECOMMENDED BEVERAGES

Cappuccino, made with mostly foam	Iced tea, nonsweetened
Coffee	Water, still or sparkling
Espresso	Wine, red or white (1 to 2 glasses at dinner)
Hot tea	

SWEETENERS If you must use a processed sweetener on some foods or beverages, Splenda is your best option. Keep in mind, however, that artificial sweeteners tend to increase rather than satisfy your craving for sweets.

GETTING STARTED

There has to be a better word than *diet* to describe this simple approach to losing weight. After all, most of us have unpleasant associations with that word: discipline, self-denial, deprivation and—let's be honest—hunger. Most diets that I've encountered seem to require eating too much of the foods I don't particularly care for, or too little of those foods I really enjoy.

I never set out to create a new diet. To the contrary, I'd had about as much serial dieting as I could stomach. But there I was, eating nearly the entire bread basket while consuming fruity cocktails before dinner, wondering why I was gaining weight. There had to be a better way.

Then one day I found it. Amazingly, that's all it really took: one day. I skipped the bread and potatoes, and paid close attention to how it made me feel. When I woke the next morning, I felt better. I was more alert and energetic, readier than ever to start a new day. The next evening I decided to test the new theory and went back to the high-glycemic bread and white rice. Sure enough, when the alarm went off the next morning, I felt sluggish and groggy. I tested this reaction over the next several days and nights, and each time had the same result.

Eventually this test became known as the Feel-Good Challenge.

The Feel-Good Challenge

Here's how the challenge works. Eat whatever you enjoy for dinner tonight, but skip the high-glycemic foods: potatoes, bread, white rice, corn, fruit, sweet sauces like barbecue or plum, and sweetened drinks. A glass of wine is fine. Eat until you're full, but don't overdo it.

Ideally, in this experiment you'll avoid consuming additional foods for the rest of the evening. If you can't resist a nighttime snack, pick one from the Wine and Food Lover's Diet list, like some **Rosemary Roasted Nuts** (page 202). Same goes for beverages. Skip dessert this time.

When you wake up tomorrow morning, pay close attention to how you feel. Do you feel alert, energized, and leaner? Or do you feel bloated, tired, and crabby? Write down some key words to describe it if you want to keep track.

Tomorrow night, eat everything you typically have for dinner, including potatoes, bread, white rice, pasta, fruit, or any high-glycemic carbohydrates you wish to eat. When you wake up the next morning, note how you feel and write it down. Do you feel any different than you did the morning before?

The Feel-Good Challenge is a simple experiment illustrating how everything on your plate affects how you feel. At first you'll need to pay attention to the foods you eat and the metabolic messages they're sending. Before long, selecting the right foods will become second nature. Soon you won't miss the potatoes, pasta, bread, and white rice. And here's the good news: If you do miss them now and then, there's nothing wrong with indulging yourself. Even if you overdo it, you're only four to five hours away from resetting your metabolism.

But before we discover just how easy all this is, let's pause for a brief reality check: The Wine and Food Lover's Diet isn't a quick fix. No short-term diet will lead to lifelong weight control. Common sense says that we can't simply shed some extra pounds and then return to the same old ways that got us in trouble in the first place.

Over the long haul, the Wine and Food Lover's Diet will help you change your relationship to the foods you eat. It will give you the knowledge you need to decode the messages different foods send your body. And it will make it easy to change your lifestyle because, before long, you'll prefer the way it makes you feel.

In fact, it might be easier to think of the Wine and Food Lover's Diet as a lifestyle rather than a diet. The difference is important. Maybe you've experimented with diets that promise dramatic results with a quick-start phase characterized by extreme self-deprivation. If you've got the self-discipline, and don't mind the emotional toll such diets exact, you will probably lose weight in a hurry. Unfortunately, once the quick-start phase is over, or your tolerance for self-deprivation is exhausted, the weight you lost will come right back. I know this, because it happened to me. More than once.

We've all heard the old saw that a particular diet "was so good I've tried it dozens of times." This describes the experience of too many dieters who have achieved early success in losing weight, only to regain quickly the pounds they've lost. The sad truth is that few dieters maintain their new, lower weight over time.

If you reduce your caloric intake, you will definitely shed pounds. But when you resume your previous level of caloric consumption, you will rapidly add back weight. This makes sense, because it's exactly what your body was designed to do. Remember, your metabolism works very hard to avoid starvation, and the antidote to starvation is the Storage Cascade. In other words, from a biological standpoint, weight gain is a good thing.

That's why the Wine and Food Lover's Diet is honest about this fundamental truth. I will not promise you a short period of intense self-deprivation, followed by a lifetime of having your cake (or bread, corn, white rice, or potatoes) and eating it, too.

What the Wine and Food Lover's Diet does promise is this: You can achieve and maintain an ideal weight and better overall health not by temporarily adjusting your diet, but by adjusting your lifestyle based on a thorough understanding of the effects different types of foods have on your body and well-being. That's why this book explains the Enabler Theory, the Storage Cascade, the Echo Hunger Cycle, the Trilogy menu, and other key Wine and Food Lover's Diet principles.

Whether you choose to read this as a diet book with recipes or a cookbook with diet information is entirely up to you. The recipes are simple, varied, and delicious, but once you understand the basics of the Wine and Food Lover's Diet, you can apply them to the foods you like to eat and still lose weight.

Armed with the scientifically demonstrated Wine and Food Lover's Diet principles, you can make informed choices about when and why to reintroduce high-glycemic carbohydrates.

If potatoes are important to you, eat them occasionally, in sensible portions, with foods low in fat, especially saturated fats because of the Enabler Theory. Take the Feel Good Challenge often, and listen carefully to what your body is telling you. Once you make the connection between what you eat and how you feel, high-glycemic foods rapidly lose their appeal. While you may think that life without french fries or crusty sourdough bread isn't worth living, you may well change your mind when you discover how much better you feel without them. At the very least, you will find that the interval between high-glycemic carb consumption will lengthen as your desire for such foods decreases. Feeling physically better—more energetic, vibrant, alert, and satisfied—is the key to changing your lifestyle, and it can happen naturally, effortlessly.

The Wine and Food Lover's Diet is presented here as a 28-Day Menu Plan. But you can just as easily think of it as a 28-year plan, because once you feel the difference it makes—not just in your weight, but in how you feel—it won't feel like a diet anymore. It will be the way you eat. One of the most important aspects of the diet is the way it puts you in control. Where other diets severely narrow your choice of foods and prescribe very precise portion sizes, the Wine and Food Lover's Diet invites you to take control. You can adjust the food choices and combinations to suit your own tastes and goals. Do you want to lose a lot of weight rapidly, or take a more measured pace? The choice is yours.

The instrument of control is the Meal-Planning Trilogy: one protein, plus two low-glycemic carbs. Want to lose weight faster? Adjust your Trilogy to one protein plus two Super-Savvy Carbs.

The 28-Day Menu Plan in the next chapter is my recommendation for moderate weight loss. You may decide to follow the plan essentially to the letter and find that you will lose a significant amount of weight in the first month. At that point, you can choose to adjust your Trilogy combinations, or repeat the plan as written. (The first two weeks are biased toward more rapid weight loss.) Again, it's entirely up to you. Eventually, when your metabolism is in equilibrium—burning both sugar and fat for energy—you will naturally move from weight loss to lifelong weight maintenance.

Remember, there are two ways we can regulate the rate of weight loss: exercise and the Meal-Planning Trilogy. Choosing two Super-Savvy Carbs to enjoy with your dinnertime center-of-the-plate protein will accelerate weight loss; combining one Super-Savvy Carb and one Savvy Carb with your protein will moderate the pace of weight loss. Aggressive, consistent exercise will accelerate weight loss, and like a falling object, the rate of acceleration will itself accelerate as your newly toned muscles become more efficient fat burners. Even moderate physical activity is sufficient to induce your muscles to burn some fat, so it's up to you to choose how much exercise is right for you.

No two metabolisms are exactly alike, and yours may respond differently to the Trilogy variations. Experiment a little. Go back and forth from rapid weight loss (two Super-Savvy Carbs plus a protein) to maintenance (one Savvy Carb plus one Super-Savvy Carb plus a protein) to see what works for you. The point is to stick with the Trilogy formula, adjust it as necessary or desired, and pay attention to the results. You might be able to eat a Savvy Carb like **Barley Risotto with Garlic and Almonds** (page 194) every night and still lose weight rapidly. You'll just have to try it and see.

Your choice of protein also plays a role in the rate of weight loss you'll experience. A rib-eye steak, with its higher saturated fat content, paired with a Super-Savvy Carb and a Savvy Carb, may slow your weight loss, while **Dr. Phillip's Roast Chicken with Tarragon Sauce** (page 136) with the same carbs may not. Again, a little experimentation will make clear which combinations work best for you. The same goes for how often you snack and eat dessert. You can do both, but be prepared to wait a little longer for the results you want.

My goal is both simple and transforming: To give you the tools to live a healthy, energetic, vibrant, and long life. No more feeling fat, hungry, or guilty about what you eat. From now on, food is a source of enjoyment, of fellowship, of affirmation. The Wine and Food Lover's Diet will help you change your relationship to food; when that happens, it isn't a diet, but a way of life.

Strategies and Tips for Success

Even though the Wine and Food Lover's Diet is a proven path to weight loss, it's not a miracle cure. It will require some thought and consistency. A little advance preparation sure won't hurt. Here are a few simple tips to make it easier:

BREAKFAST   Breakfast doesn't work for everyone, but it's critical that you fuel your body with enough of the right calories early in the day, either at breakfast or at lunch. Try not to wait until late afternoon or dinnertime to consume most of your calories.

I recommend a moderate breakfast that includes protein—whether eggs, yogurt, nuts, or sausage, for example. If you fill yourself up at breakfast, with the right foods in the right combinations, a small lunch is all you'll need to keep going until dinner. Last night's leftovers are a delicious and easy way to start the day. In most cultures around the world—and in the United

States up until the early twentieth century—the first meal of the day was made from the previous day's dinner, like steak with eggs.

SNACKS   The Wine and Food Lover's Diet menus provide the right combinations of foods and the right portion sizes for most appetites, so chances are you won't be thinking about eating between meals. If you do want a snack, here are some ideas best enjoyed on an occasional basis (perhaps one time per day/every other day):

- One ounce of real cheese, any variety, such as Gruyère, Brie, string cheese, or Monterey Jack
- Handful of olives, any variety, such as green or Kalamata, with or without brine
- One to two ounces of dark chocolate, preferably 60 percent cacao or more, with or without nuts
- Four to six ounces of plain yogurt sprinkled with toasted almonds or hazelnuts
- One-half cup raspberries, blueberries, or strawberries with a dollop of whipped cream
- Handful of nuts, any kind except cashews

On days when I eat a more substantial breakfast, like **Tomato, Basil, and Mozzarella Frittata** (page 89), sometimes all I need is a snack like **Jalapeño Jack Cheese Melt with Toasted Pumpkin Seeds** (page 205) or yogurt sprinkled with almonds to keep me going until my Meal-Planning Trilogy dinner. Refer to the lists of Savvy Carbs and Super-Savvy Carbs (page 55) for other ideas that suit your personal taste buds. You'll also want to try the snack recipes later in the book, such as **Spiced Chickpeas** (page 203) and **Deviled Eggs** (page 207).

RESTAURANT DINING   For me, a restaurant meal is a congenial way to connect socially with others, and provides an opportunity to reward myself.

Here are some simple suggestions for applying Wine and Food Lover's Diet principles to restaurant meals:

- For breakfast, opt for eggs any style—scrambled, cooked over easy, or made into an omelet. Ask the server to hold the toast and hash browns/home fries, as they are enablers.
- For lunch and dinner, it's easier to ask the server to hold the bread rather than trying to ignore it when it's sitting right there on the table.
- As a starter, order a small salad with a sugarless dressing like Caesar, ranch, or Italian, or ask for olive oil and vinegar and dress the salad yourself with a splash of each. Some restaurants serve sweetened balsamic vinaigrettes; consider dressing your own salad instead.
- A seafood appetizer that includes scallops, calamari, or grilled shrimp, as long as the seafood is not breaded and deep-fried, is also a great option. If you like crab cakes, enjoy them at home—try **Seafood Cakes with Lemon Crème Fraîche** (page 127)—rather than the restaurant versions, which often include a generous dose of bread crumbs.
- For your main course, ask the waiter to substitute an extra vegetable like sautéed spinach or broccoli for the high-glycemic potatoes or white rice that often accompany the entrée. As with your appetizer choice, stay away from breaded and deep-fried foods like chicken Parmesan.
- I don't hesitate to ask the server if a dish contains flour. It's surprising how many dishes do. Ask if the chef can leave out the flour, or choose another item.
- If you have a hankering for pasta, follow an Italian custom and order a small plate as an appetizer (ask that the pasta be cooked al dente, which is less glycemic).

- When choosing dessert, consider a piece of flourless chocolate cake, a scoop of premium ice cream (without the cone), a wedge of cheesecake (don't eat the crust), a custard dessert like panna cotta, a soufflé, or some fresh berries with whipped cream.

TAKE-OUT FOOD When I don't have the time or inclination to cook, I may find myself buying take-out food, often pre-packaged from a grocery store. Here are some of my favorites:

- Rotisserie chicken (check for sugar in the ingredients) with vegetables
- Fajitas without the tortillas
- Salsa and guacamole, great condiments for spicing up a protein such as grilled chicken fajitas or a pork chop
- Stir-fry dishes like chicken or shrimp with vegetables, without sauces that contain flour, cornstarch, or sugar
- Indian tandoori-style chicken, lamb, or fish (making sure sauces do not contain flour, cornstarch, or sugar), or lentils and spinach with cheese, garnished with yogurt sauce
- Barbecued poultry or meat with a dry rub only, avoiding the sugar-laden sauce

RESETTING YOUR METABOLISM If you go a few days when your attention to what you eat wavers—when you're traveling, say—or you find yourself adding a pound or two back or reaching a plateau, choose a few of your favorite days from the first fourteen days of the 28-Day Menu Plan that consist of a Trilogy of protein plus Super-Savvy Carb plus Super-Savvy Carb, and get back in the game. Remember, no matter what happens, you're only a few hours away from resetting your metabolism and regaining your healthy equilibrium of burning sugar and fat.

If you eat a large bowl of pasta (a high-glycemic load) or snack on some popcorn (a high-glycemic food) and find yourself caught up in the Echo Hunger Cycle, your best bet to break the cycle is to eat a healthful snack of the correct combinations of protein, low-glycemic carbohydrates, and fat, such as a handful of almonds or a very low-glycemic snack such as a piece of cheese. Your body will probably crave more sugar, but snacking on high-glycemic carbs will only trigger the Storage Cascade and the metabolic message to consume even more high-glycemic carbohydrates. That's why you're more likely to crave that second chocolate chip cookie rather than a second chicken breast.

EXERCISE A moderate level of activity on a consistent basis is all you need to give your muscles the tone they need to burn fat and sugar efficiently for energy. Ideally you should spend thirty minutes a day (all at once or in two fifteen-minute periods) enjoying a brisk walk or jog, perhaps a little longer on the weekends. Aerobic exercise is what gets the muscles burning fat, but anaerobic exercise will strengthen your muscles to make them more efficient fat burners. I recommend a daily dose of aerobic activity with less frequent (but no less consistent) anaerobic exercise for conditioning.

Starting the Wine and Food Lover's Diet

I've organized the first two weeks of the diet for rapid weight loss, with dinners focused on the center-of-the-plate protein and plenty of Super-Savvy Carbs, complemented with occasional Savvy Carbs and desserts. Breakfasts and lunches follow the same general outline: protein and Super-Savvy Carbs. Happily, you will notice the results immediately: You'll wake up each morning feeling vibrant and energetic.

Each week, as the pounds drop off, feel free to add more Savvy Carbs to your Trilogy combinations. It's important to eat the foods you enjoy. I am not opposed to rapid weight loss, but it will do you no good to deprive yourself for two weeks, lose ten pounds, then quickly regain them when you resume your old habits. I'd rather you ease into the program, discover for yourself how much better you feel, then gradually adopt these principles for the long haul.

Now that you understand the science behind the Wine and Food Lover's Diet and have helpful tools like the Meal-Planning Trilogy, it's easy to apply the principles and customize the Wine and Food Lover's Diet to meet your lifestyle and achieve your personal goals for weight loss and optimal health. If you want to lose more weight more quickly, on day five substitute a Super-Savvy Carb like **Roasted Asparagus with Pecorino Romano and Hazelnuts** (page 170) for the **Barley Risotto with Tomatoes and Lemon** (page 193), a Savvy Carb, and eat desserts like **Hazelnut Swirl Chocolate Brownies** (page 214) less frequently. If you're satisfied with your weight and want only to maintain it, and if you're exercising regularly, mix in more Savvy Carbs. Remember, eating the right foods in the right combination will help you lose weight, but it is imperative that you exercise regularly, even if it's light to moderate physical activity.

The recipes in the 28-Day Menu Plan are organized into the appropriate portion sizes for most people and are designed to keep you feeling satisfied until it's time for the next meal. When you end a meal feeling satisfied—and stay satisfied longer—you're much less likely to crave more foods and eat more.

In some of the menus, I've recommended starters like the **Classic Savvy Salad** (page 93) and **Sesame-Seed Popcorn Shrimp** (page 104), which you can enjoy as a first course or with the main course. Either way, these dishes are considered one of the two Savvy or Super-Savvy Carbs listed on the Trilogy menu.

I've included measurements to help you get started, but I don't expect you to live your life by a scale—either in the kitchen or in the bathroom. As your eating habits change and you use the Feel-Good Challenge to get in touch with your body's signals, you won't need to measure quantities or count anything. Your body will tell you what you need to know.

Feel free to repeat meals. If something works, and you enjoy it, why argue? I ate **Dr. Phillip's Roast Chicken with Tarragon Sauce** (page 136), **Spinach with Toasted Garlic and Pine Nuts** (page 176), and **Button Mushrooms with Thyme, Rosemary, and Basil** (page 180) for days in a row, all while losing lots of weight. As you'll see, I suggest it several times in the 28-Day Menu Plan because I think it exemplifies the science behind the diet as a surefire way to feel good the next day.

You can also mix and match among menus. If you don't eat red meat, for instance, substitute another main dish. For dinner on day four, replace the **Roast Pork with a Walnut Crust** (page 149) with **Pecan-Crusted Chicken Breasts** (page 133). If you're a vegetarian, tofu is a great alternative to animal protein; try the **Spicy Tofu with Tomato Sauce** (page 157). You could also add sautéed tofu to any of the vegetable dishes to make a one-dish Trilogy. Or, if you

prefer **Roasted Asparagus with Pecorino Romano and Hazelnuts** (page 170) to **Brussels Sprouts with Pancetta** (page 175), it's fine to substitute one Super-Savvy Carb for another.

If your schedule leaves no time for breakfast or demands that you work through lunch, you'll also find ideas for on-the-go breakfasts and lunches, including recipes that you can prepare in advance and bring to work, such as **Thai Chicken Omelet Cups** (page 82) for breakfast, **Cannellini Bean Salad with Feta Cheese and Mint** (page 189) for lunch, and **Turkey Rolls with Roasted Bell Pepper and Hummus** (page 206) for lunch or a snack.

Because successful weight control depends on your ability to stick to the program, the recipes in the book are designed to be prepared and cooked in thirty minutes to one hour. Many dishes are perfect for freezing and microwave reheating, ready to enjoy at your convenience.

Whether you follow these recipes and suggestions explicitly is less important than learning the basic Wine and Food Lover's Diet concepts: the importance of avoiding enablers and the resulting Echo Hunger Cycle; how to combine foods in the Meal-Planning Trilogy format; and understanding the metabolic messages certain foods send. You don't need these precise recipes to lose weight, but they will make losing weight a lot more enjoyable.

Bon appétit!

THE WINE AND FOOD LOVER'S DIET

28-DAY MENU PLAN

WEEK 1

Day 1

BREAKFAST
Odette's Omelet Cups
(PAGE 83)

LUNCH
Classic Savvy Salad
(PAGE 93) with 3 ounces of
sliced turkey breast

DINNER
MAIN DISH
Dr. Phillip's Roast
Chicken with Tarragon
Sauce (PAGE 136)

SUPER-SAVVY CARB
Spinach with Toasted
Garlic and Pine Nuts
(PAGE 176)

SUPER-SAVVY CARB
Button Mushrooms with
Thyme, Rosemary, and
Basil (PAGE 180)

WINE
Pinot Noir, my favorite
varietal, goes well with
the tarragon sauce,
toasted nuts, and herb-
flavored mushrooms. If
you prefer a white wine,
a Chardonnay would be
a good choice.

Day 2

BREAKFAST
1 turkey or chicken
sausage (nitrite free and
without fillers) with
1 hard-boiled egg

LUNCH
Chopped Romaine Salad
with Bacon and
Almonds (PAGE 97)

DINNER
MAIN DISH
Fillets of Sole with
Classic Butter Sauce
(PAGE 116)

SUPER-SAVVY CARB
Kale Two Ways
(PAGE 181)

SUPER-SAVVY CARB
Saffron-Braised Leeks
(PAGE 177)

WINE
A Chardonnay with
crisp fruit flavors would
balance the richness of
the classic butter sauce.

Day 3

BREAKFAST
Plain yogurt, 6 to
8 ounces, with nuts of
choice and cinnamon

LUNCH
Sliced roast beef,
4 ounces, with ½ cup
shredded iceberg or
romaine lettuce, drizzled
with olive oil and
garnished with 2 dill
pickle halves

DINNER
MAIN DISH
Stuffed Chicken Breasts
with Cascade Falls
Sauce (PAGE 137)

SUPER-SAVVY CARB
Fennel with Shallots and
White Wine (PAGE 166)

SUPER-SAVVY CARB
Spaghetti Squash with
Summer-Ripe Tomato
Sauce (PAGE 171)

WINE
Serve a rich Chardonnay
or a rustic red such as a
Cabernet Franc.

Day 4

BREAKFAST
Creamy Hot Barley with Toasted Almonds **(PAGE 79)**

LUNCH
Fresh Mozzarella, Tomato, and Basil Salad **(PAGE 105)**

DINNER
SALAD AND STARTERS (COUNTS AS A SUPER-SAVVY CARB)
Savvy Salad with Toasted Pumpkin Seeds and Melted Gruyère **(PAGE 107)**

MAIN DISH
Roast Pork with a Walnut Crust **(PAGE 149)**

SUPER-SAVVY CARB
Roasted Asparagus with Pecorino Romano and Hazelnuts **(PAGE 170)**

WINE
To match the toasted nut flavors, choose an Italian Barbera or other fruity, medium-bodied red wine.

Day 5

BREAKFAST
1 turkey or chicken sausage (nitrite free and without fillers) with 1 hard-boiled egg

LUNCH
Caesar Salad **(PAGE 140)**

DINNER
MAIN DISH
Roast Halibut with Spinach Salsa **(PAGE 111)**

SUPER-SAVVY CARB
Sweet Pea Shoots with Garlic **(PAGE 172)**

SUPER-SAVVY CARB
Barley Risotto with Tomatoes and Lemon **(PAGE 193)**

WINE
Sauvignon Blanc would play off the spinach and pea shoots and also balance the acidity of the tomatoes and lemon in the risotto.

Day 6

BREAKFAST
Tomato, Basil, and Mozzarella Frittata **(PAGE 89)**

LUNCH
Classic Savvy Salad **(PAGE 93)**

DINNER
MAIN DISH
Double-Cut Pork Chops with Green Peppercorns **(PAGE 145)**

SUPER-SAVVY CARB
Cauliflower with Smoked Mozzarella **(PAGE 164)**

SUPER-SAVVY CARB
Collard Greens with Garlic **(PAGE 182)**

WINE
The smoked cheese, garlicky greens, and green peppercorns call for a medium-bodied Rhône-style wine like a blend of Mourvèdre, Grenache, and Syrah, or a Mourvèdre alone.

Day 7

BREAKFAST
Thai Chicken Omelet Cups **(PAGE 82)**

LUNCH
Greek Salad **(PAGE 96)**

DINNER
MAIN DISH
Chicken Breasts Stuffed with Cheese and Spinach **(PAGE 128)**

SUPER-SAVVY CARB
Leeks and Pattypan Squash with Tarragon and Crème Fraîche **(PAGE 163)**

SUPER-SAVVY CARB
Broccolini with Pesto **(PAGE 165)**

DESSERT
Hazelnut Swirl Chocolate Brownies **(PAGE 214)**

WINE
The emphasis on herbal flavors leads me to choose a light, crisp white such as Pinot Gris or Pinot Grigio, or a light-bodied red such as Chianti.

Day 8

BREAKFAST
Plain yogurt, 6 to
8 ounces, with nuts of
choice and cinnamon

LUNCH
Turkey Rolls with
Roasted Bell Pepper and
Hummus **(PAGE 206)**

DINNER
**SALADS AND STARTERS (COUNTS
AS A SUPER-SAVVY CARB)**
Arugula and Cherry
Tomatoes with
Warm Hazelnut Dressing
(PAGE 94)

MAIN DISH
Seared Halibut with
Lemon-Butter Sauce
(PAGE 115)

SUPER-SAVVY CARB
Roasted Vegetables with
Arugula Pesto **(PAGE 179)**

WINE
A Sauvignon Blanc
would stand up to the
rich lemon-butter sauce
and pesto.

Day 9

BREAKFAST
Three-Pepper and
Cheddar Omelet **(PAGE 86)**

LUNCH
Greek Salad **(PAGE 96)**

DINNER
MAIN DISH
Spicy Tofu with Tomato
Sauce **(PAGE 157)**

SUPER-SAVVY CARB
Button Mushrooms with
Thyme, Rosemary, and
Basil **(PAGE 180)**

SAVVY-CARB
Swiss Chard Stuffed
with Barley **(PAGE 186)**

WINE
To match the robust
tomato sauce and herb-
flavored mushrooms,
serve a medium-bodied
Sangiovese.

Day 10

BREAKFAST
1 turkey or chicken
sausage (nitrite free and
without fillers) with
1 hard-boiled egg

LUNCH
Caesar Salad **(PAGE 140)**

DINNER
MAIN DISH
Pork Cutlets with Lemon
Sauce and Hazelnuts
(PAGE 147)

SUPER-SAVVY CARB
Brussels Sprouts with
Pancetta **(PAGE 175)**

SUPER-SAVVY CARB
Spinach with Toasted
Garlic and Pine Nuts
(PAGE 176)

DESSERT
Berries with Toasted
Nuts and Spiced
Whipped Cream
(PAGE 208)

WINE
To bring out the
sweetness of pork, look
for a medium-bodied
Zinfandel.

Day 11

BREAKFAST
Creamy Hot Barley with Toasted Almonds
(PAGE 79)

LUNCH
Sliced turkey breast, 4 ounces, with ½ cup shredded iceberg or romaine lettuce and 1 sliced tomato, drizzled with olive oil

DINNER
SALAD AND STARTERS (COUNTS AS A SUPER-SAVVY CARB)
Warm Zucchini Salad
(PAGE 95)

MAIN DISH
Pecan-Crusted Chicken Breasts (PAGE 133)

SUPER-SAVVY CARB
Roasted Vegetables with Arugula Pesto (PAGE 179)

WINE
The nuts in both the chicken and the pesto would be well matched with a Zinfandel or Grenache.

Day 12

BREAKFAST
Scrambled Eggs with Green Onions, Chicken, and Hot Sauce (PAGE 81)

LUNCH
Shaved Zucchini with Arugula and Pecorino Romano (PAGE 108)

DINNER
MAIN DISH
Flounder with Lemon Zest and Capers (PAGE 117)

SUPER-SAVVY CARB
Roasted Broccoli with Pecorino and Pecans
(PAGE 167)

SAVVY CARB
Quinoa Pilaf with Sunflower and Pumpkin Seeds (PAGE 197)

DESSERT
Chocolate Soufflés
(PAGE 218)

WINE
Chardonnay goes particularly well with the roasted vegetables and the nuts, as well as with the fish.

Day 13

BREAKFAST
Teleme Cheese Frittata with Thyme and Chives
(PAGE 87)

LUNCH
Classic Savvy Salad
(PAGE 93)

DINNER
SALADS AND STARTERS (COUNTS AS A SUPER-SAVVY CARB)
Sesame-Seed Popcorn Shrimp (PAGE 104)

MAIN DISH
Dr. Phillip's Roast Chicken with Tarragon Sauce (PAGE 136)

SUPER-SAVVY CARB
Sweet Pea Shoots with Garlic (PAGE 172)

WINE
The variety in this menu calls for a Sauvignon Blanc with herbal and fruity flavors.

Day 14

BREAKFAST
Plain yogurt, 6 to 8 ounces, with nuts of choice and cinnamon

LUNCH
Fresh Mozzarella, Tomato, and Basil Salad
(PAGE 105)

DINNER
MAIN DISH
Beef Tenderloin with Red Wine and Shallot Sauce (PAGE 153)

SUPER-SAVVY CARB
Swiss Chard with Bacon
(PAGE 161)

SUPER-SAVVY CARB
Saffron-Braised Leeks
(PAGE 177)

WINE
Mark the halfway point of the menu plan with this celebratory dinner and break out your best bottle of Cabernet Sauvignon or Bordeaux-style wine.

WEEK 3

Day 15

BREAKFAST
Three-Pepper and
Cheddar Omelet (PAGE 86)

LUNCH
Turkey Rolls with
Roasted Bell Pepper and
Hummus (PAGE 206)

DINNER
MAIN DISH
Grilled Grouper with
Warm Tomato Salsa and
Arugula Salad (PAGE 114;
ARUGULA SALAD COUNTS AS A
SUPER-SAVVY CARB)

SUPER-SAVVY CARB
Roasted Asparagus with
Pecorino Romano and
Hazelnuts (PAGE 170)

DESSERT
Trail Bark (PAGE 212)

WINE
To highlight the herbal
and vegetable flavors
of this menu, serve
a crisp white such as a
Sauvignon Blanc or
Pinot Grigio.

Day 16

BREAKFAST
1 turkey or chicken
sausage (nitrite free and
without fillers) with
1 hard-boiled egg

LUNCH
Greek Salad (PAGE 96)

DINNER
MAIN DISH
Pan-Roasted Salmon
with Cucumber Salsa
(PAGE 121)

SUPER-SAVVY CARB
Green Beans with
Chile-Lime Mayonnaise
(PAGE 178)

SAVVY CARB
Cannellini Bean Salad
with Feta Cheese and
Mint (PAGE 189)

WINE
A Chardonnay or a
light- or medium-bodied
red wine, such as a
Beaujolais, served cold,
would complement the
fresh, summery flavors
in this menu.

Day 17

BREAKFAST
Creamy Hot Barley with
Toasted Almonds (PAGE 79)

LUNCH
Portobello Mushrooms
Stuffed with Turkey
(PAGE 109)

DINNER
SALAD AND STARTERS (COUNTS
AS A SAVVY CARB)
Goat Cheese Spread
with Roasted Peppers
and Endive (PAGE 99)

MAIN DISH
Seared Tofu Pockets with
Tahini-Lemon Sauce
(PAGE 156)

SUPER-SAVVY CARB
Spinach with Toasted
Garlic and Pine Nuts
(PAGE 176)

WINE
Goat cheese and
Sauvignon Blanc make a
classic combination.
The fruit flavors in the
wine will balance the
tahini-lemon sauce.

Day 18

BREAKFAST
Odette's Omelet Cups
(PAGE 83)

LUNCH
Chopped Romaine Salad with Bacon and Almonds (PAGE 97)

DINNER
MAIN DISH
Grilled Pork Chops with Merlot-Shallot Sauce (PAGE 146)

SUPER-SAVVY CARB
Brussels Sprouts with Pancetta (PAGE 175)

SUPER-SAVVY CARB
Mushrooms Stuffed with Parmesan Cheese and Almonds (PAGE 169)

WINE
Following the rule that one should drink the same wine, or a closely related one, used to make a dish, the choice for this menu is easy: Merlot.

Day 19

BREAKFAST
Tex-Mex Scrambled Eggs (PAGE 92)

LUNCH
Sliced turkey breast, 4 ounces, with ½ cup shredded lettuce and 1 sliced tomato, drizzled with olive oil

DINNER
MAIN DISH
Spiced Chicken Burgers (PAGE 138)

SUPER-SAVVY CARB
Napa Cabbage Slaw with Pumpkin Seeds (PAGE 183)

SAVVY CARB
Tomato, Cucumber, and Barley Salad with Lime and Mint (PAGE 191)

WINE
The sprightly flavors of the slaw and barley salad and the spicy burgers call for a dry rosé or dry Chenin Blanc.

Day 20

BREAKFAST
Plain yogurt, 6 to 8 ounces, with nuts of choice and cinnamon

LUNCH
Chicken Paillards and Caesar Salad (PAGE 140)

DINNER
MAIN DISH
Herbed Lamb Chops with Cucumber, Tomato, and Mint Salsa (PAGE 154)

SUPER-SAVVY CARB
Saffron-Braised Leeks (PAGE 177)

SUPER-SAVVY CARB
Classic Savvy Salad (PAGE 93)

WINE
To match the richness of the herbed meat and its accompaniments, serve a spicy red such as a Zinfandel, or offer Rioja, which is more sedate, but just as flavorful.

Day 21

BREAKFAST
Scrambled Eggs with Green Onions, Chicken, and Hot Sauce (PAGE 81)

LUNCH
Classic Savvy Salad (PAGE 93)

DINNER
SALADS AND STARTERS (COUNTS AS A SUPER-SAVVY CARB)
Calamari with Arugula and Shaved Pecorino Romano (PAGE 101)

MAIN DISH
Grilled Chicken Thighs with Roasted Red Pepper and Tomato Sauce (PAGE 139)

SUPER-SAVVY CARB
Roasted Broccoli with Pecorino and Pecans (PAGE 167)

WINE
Since this dinner moves from seafood to a robust chicken dish, consider serving two wines: Sauvignon Blanc first, followed by a light-bodied red such as Dolcetto.

WEEK 4

Day 22

BREAKFAST
Plain yogurt, 6 to 8 ounces, with nuts of choice and cinnamon

LUNCH
Greek Salad (PAGE 96)

DINNER
MAIN DISH
Dr. Phillip's Roast Chicken with Tarragon Sauce (PAGE 136)

SUPER-SAVVY CARB
Spinach with Toasted Garlic and Pine Nuts (PAGE 176)

SUPER-SAVVY CARB
Ratatouille with Chile (PAGE 185)

DESSERT
Trail Bark (PAGE 212)

WINE
For this chicken preparation and its spinach and ratatouille accompaniments, I recommend a slightly spicy red, such as Malbec or Grenache.

Day 23

BREAKFAST
Creamy Hot Barley with Toasted Almonds (PAGE 79)

LUNCH
Roasted Eggplant, Bell Pepper, and Tomato Salad (PAGE 98)

DINNER
SALADS AND STARTERS (COUNTS AS A SUPER-SAVVY CARB)
Prosciutto-Wrapped Shrimp (PAGE 102)

MAIN DISH
Mediterranean Spiced Chicken with Olives and Almonds (PAGE 130)

SUPER-SAVVY CARB
Green Beans with Chile-Lime Mayonnaise (PAGE 178)

WINE
To mirror the shrimp with prosciutto and the Mediterranean flavors of the chicken, offer a spicy red such as Zinfandel or Sangiovese. I'd serve it cold.

Day 24

BREAKFAST
1 turkey or chicken sausage (nitrite free and without fillers) with 1 hard-boiled egg

LUNCH
Caesar Salad (PAGE 140)

DINNER
MAIN DISH
Pork Chops with Greek Herbs and Cabbage (PAGE 150; CABBAGE COUNTS AS A SUPER-SAVVY CARB)

SAVVY CARB
Barley Risotto with Garlic and Almonds (PAGE 194)

WINE
The combination of pork and cabbage would be complemented by a dry, crisp Riesling or Pinot Blanc, or a light, fruity red such as Beaujolais or Gamay Beaujolais.

Day 25

BREAKFAST
Plain yogurt, 6 to
8 ounces, with almonds
and cinnamon

LUNCH
Sliced turkey breast,
4 ounces, with ½ cup
shredded lettuce and
1 sliced tomato, drizzled
with olive oil

DINNER
MAIN DISH
Chicken with Crab,
Asparagus, and Lemon–
Crème Fraîche Sauce
(PAGE 131)

SUPER-SAVVY CARB
Kale Two Ways (PAGE 181)

SAVVY CARB
Lentils with Shallot and
Herbs (PAGE 196)

WINE
To underscore the
sweetness of the crab
and balance the creamy
citrus sauce, serve a
Chardonnay.

Day 26

BREAKFAST
Teleme Cheese Frittata
with Thyme and Chives
(PAGE 87)

LUNCH
Turkey Rolls with
Roasted Bell Pepper and
Hummus (PAGE 206)

DINNER
APPETIZERS AND SALADS (COUNTS
AS A SUPER-SAVVY CARB)
Classic Savvy Salad
(PAGE 93)

MAIN DISH
Seafood Cakes with Lemon
Crème Fraîche (PAGE 127)

SUPER-SAVVY CARB
Roasted Vegetables with
Arugula Pesto (PAGE 179)

DESSERT
Flourless Chocolate
Cakes (PAGE 217)

WINE
The floral flavors of a
rich white wine such as
Semillon or Viognier
would pair well with the
rich, buttery flavors of
this menu.

Day 27

BREAKFAST
Tex-Mex Scrambled
Eggs (PAGE 92)

LUNCH
Chopped Romaine
Salad with Bacon and
Almonds (PAGE 97)

DINNER
MAIN DISH
Snapper Baked in
Parchment (PAGE 120)

SUPER-SAVVY CARB
Broccolini with Pesto
(PAGE 165)

SAVVY CARB
South American
Tabbouleh (PAGE 200)

WINE
Although the main
dish is fish, I'd serve
a Pinot Noir with an
alcohol level well under
14 percent.

Day 28

BREAKFAST
Baja Omelet with
Avocado-Tomato Salsa
Fresca (PAGE 90)

LUNCH
Classic Savvy Salad
(PAGE 93)

DINNER
MAIN DISH
Grilled Shrimp with
Romesco Sauce (PAGE 124)

SUPER-SAVVY CARB
Fennel with Shallots and
White Wine (PAGE 166)

SAVVY CARB
Italian Butter Beans
(PAGE 201)

WINE
You made it, and you
deserve a treat. Choose
a high-quality brut
(meaning very dry) rosé
sparkling wine or
Champagne. It will
match the robustness of
grilled shrimp and its
zesty sauce and the
delicate licorice flavor
of the fennel.

THE WINE AND FOOD LOVER'S DIET RECIPES

Now that you've absorbed all the thinking that goes into the Wine and Food Lover's Diet, it's time to start getting something out of it. Happily, what you'll get is delicious. And why not? For so many of us, food is not just for sustenance. More importantly (for me, at least), it is for enjoyment, as well. I guarantee you'll find dozens of ways to enjoy good food on the pages that follow.

In creating these recipes, I've drawn on my experience as both a medical doctor and a lifelong devotee of gourmet food. What's interesting is that both of these paths, though quite distinct, lead to the exact same destination.

From a scientific standpoint, you might say that I arrived at the Wine and Food Lover's Diet through a process of reverse engineering—that is, studying the basic design and function of the human body and how it has evolved over the millennia. That understanding led to a fundamental approach to diet and nutrition based on the Storage Cascade: The body is designed to maximize energy storage from the widely available foods (easily digested carbohydrates) to sustain it in lean times. Once you understand how and why the body stores (and even creates) fat, you can design a meal plan to avoid it. The Wine and Food Lover's Diet is intended to promote accelerated weight loss in the early weeks and moderate

weight loss, or sustainable weight control, over the longer term.

From the standpoint of a food lover, the Wine and Food Lover's Diet recipes are not engineered at all. They are intended to maximize the sensual experience of eating. My fondest memories— whether of family, friends, romance, whatever— revolve around food. That my genetic background is, in large part, French, certainly doesn't hurt; without a doubt, I've inherited the French love of good food. I'm on firm ground when I say that there is not a recipe in this book that wouldn't withstand the scrutiny of my Continental forebears.

Having established my credentials in both scientific knowledge and culinary passion, I should also mention that I don't have a lot of patience for the act of cooking. Not that I don't enjoy it, because I do, immensely. But like most of you, between work and kids (and exercise!) and everything else, I don't have time to prepare complicated recipes. This is why most of the recipes in *The Wine and Food Lover's Diet* are designed to go from page to plate in thirty to forty-five minutes, sometimes less, with simple ingredients, few pots and pans, and minimal steps.

So now I invite you to don your apron, fire up the stove, and turn the page. It's time to start enjoying food again.

CREAMY HOT BARLEY WITH TOASTED ALMONDS

SERVES 4

A bowl of warm whole-grain cereal is a great way to start the day. Barley, a Savvy Carb, is high in fiber and therefore is digested slowly, causing a low, even release of blood sugar. This kind of breakfast keeps you well fueled and feeling satisfied until lunch and often longer. I cook a large pot of barley once a week or so, keeping it tightly covered in the refrigerator. With my barley already prepared, I can scoop what I need for breakfast into a bowl, add some crème fraîche, and microwave the barley on high until hot. This allows me to have a quick, healthy breakfast and make it to work on time. The recipe may be doubled. Just be sure to use a very large pot. I use pearl barley because it is readily available and cooks faster than hulled barley, found at health-food stores. Hulled barley has only the very outer coating removed, so is higher in fiber than pearl barley. It is equally delicious but takes another fifteen to twenty minutes of simmering. You could also make this recipe with low-glycemic quinoa, an excellent alternative for anyone with gluten sensitivity.

1 tablespoon unsalted butter

1 cup pearl barley

2¾ cups water

¾ teaspoon kosher salt

½ cup almonds, walnuts, or pecans, or a mixture

½ cup crème fraîche

Ground cinnamon

1   In a large saucepan over medium heat, melt the butter. Add the barley and cook, stirring frequently, until thoroughly coated with butter and lightly toasted, about 5 minutes. Reduce the heat, if needed, to prevent scorching. Add the water and salt and bring to a boil. Reduce the heat to low, cover, and simmer until the barley is tender but still slightly chewy, about 45 minutes. Add more water, ¼ cup at a time, if the barley becomes too dry. Do not drown the barley; all the water should be absorbed just as the barley is done. Drain the barley, if necessary. You should have about 3 cups.

2   Meanwhile, in a small, dry skillet over medium heat, toast the almonds, stirring constantly, until they just begin to turn light brown, about 3 minutes. Immediately pour them into a small bowl to cool. Roughly chop the almonds.

3   Place the barley in a bowl. Stir in the almonds and crème fraîche until well mixed. Divide among 4 bowls, dust each portion with a pinch of cinnamon, and serve warm.

SCRAMBLED EGGS WITH GREEN ONIONS, CHICKEN, AND HOT SAUCE

SERVES 2

It's important to eat a good breakfast with plenty of protein. Eggs provide complete protein, do not raise your blood sugar, and—this may be hard to believe—can help increase your HDL cholesterol (the good kind) when eaten without starchy or sugary foods. In this recipe, you get a tasty double dose of protein. The chicken not only makes the dish more interesting but serves to increase your feeling of satiety so you can work throughout the morning without getting hungry.

2 cups water

Kosher salt

1 skinless, boneless chicken breast half (about 5 ounces), cut into 1-inch cubes

1 tablespoon unsalted butter

2 green onions, white and light green parts, thinly sliced

5 eggs, lightly beaten

Freshly ground pepper

1½ teaspoons finely chopped fresh chives

Hot sauce such as Tabasco or Crystal

1   In a saucepan over high heat, bring the water to a boil. Add a pinch of salt and the chicken. Reduce the heat to low and simmer gently, uncovered, until the chicken is opaque throughout, about 5 minutes. Drain well and set aside.

2   In a skillet over medium heat, melt the butter. Add the green onions and cook, stirring frequently, until softened, about 1 minute. Reduce the heat to medium-low and add the eggs, chicken, and salt and pepper to taste. Using a spatula and long, slow strokes, gently stir the eggs all over the sides and bottom of the pan until they are firm but not dry, about 1 minute. Divide among 2 warmed plates and sprinkle with the chives. Add a dash or two of hot sauce and serve.

THAI CHICKEN OMELET CUPS

SERVES 6

THAI CHICKEN FILLING

One 14-ounce can unsweetened coconut milk

1 tablespoon Thai green curry paste

1 tablespoon freshly squeezed lime juice

1 tablespoon fish sauce

3 cloves garlic, minced

¼ cup coarsely chopped fresh cilantro

2 skinless, boneless chicken breast halves (about 5 ounces each)

OMELET BASE

12 eggs

½ cup shredded Gruyère or Jarlsberg cheese

1 teaspoon freshly ground pepper

½ teaspoon kosher salt

½ teaspoon Thai green curry paste (optional)

1 large red bell pepper, seeds and ribs removed, cut into about ⅓-inch dice

½ cup torn fresh mint leaves

⅓ cup unsalted peanuts, chopped

On the Wine and Food Lover's Diet, we set our metabolic clocks at breakfast by eating a good portion of protein plus some fat. I particularly like this recipe because it has plenty of protein and tastes slightly spicy and exotic but not too much so. Coconut milk, notorious for its saturated fat content, should not deter you from trying this recipe. It is used as a marinade only, and very little, if any, remains in the finished dish. For more flavor punch, a little green curry paste may be added to the omelet base. Omelet cups freeze well for up to 2 months, individually wrapped in plastic wrap and then placed in a freezer bag. When you are ready to eat one, take it out of the plastic wrap before reheating it, still frozen, in a microwave on high for 2 to 3 minutes. To make this recipe, you will need a jumbo muffin pan with six cups, each of which has a 1-cup capacity.

1   To make the filling: In a bowl, whisk together the coconut milk and curry paste. Whisk in the lime juice, fish sauce, garlic, and cilantro. Add the chicken and turn to coat well in the marinade. Cover the bowl and refrigerate for at least 2 hours or for as long as overnight.

2   Preheat the oven to 375°F. Drain the chicken and place in a small baking dish. Bake until the chicken is opaque throughout, about 30 minutes. Leave the oven on. Let the chicken cool slightly while you make the omelet base.

3   To make the omelet base: Place the eggs, cheese, pepper, salt, and curry paste (if using) in a blender and process until smooth. Divide among six 1-cup nonstick jumbo muffin cups.

4   Cut the chicken into thin strips and divide among the cups. Add the bell pepper and mint, dividing evenly. Sprinkle with the peanuts. Bake until lightly browned and puffed, 15 to 25 minutes. The omelets will puff up like a soufflé and then deflate a bit when removed from the oven. Serve hot.

ODETTE'S OMELET CUPS

SERVES 6

My mother, Odette, is from France and introduced me to many foods unknown to most kids in Arkansas, where I grew up. Egg dishes, especially on holidays, were a specialty. One of these was a delicious quiche made with spinach, tomatoes, and mushrooms—a trio of Super-Savvy Carbs. Here is a crustless version that is wonderful for breakfast or lunch. I often make a batch of omelet cups on Sunday so they are ready for me to grab for breakfast or lunch as I head to the car. To freeze the cups, wrap them individually in plastic wrap. They can be frozen for up to 2 months. To reheat, place the frozen cups in a microwave on high for 2 to 3 minutes. For this recipe, you will need a jumbo muffin pan with six cups, each of which has a 1-cup capacity.

1   Preheat the oven to 375°F.

2   To make the filling: In a large skillet over medium heat, warm the oil until it shimmers. Add the garlic and cook, stirring frequently, until softened, about 1 minute. Add the tomatoes, mushrooms, spinach, and salt and pepper to taste. Stir and toss the vegetables until they release their liquid. Continue to cook, stirring occasionally, until the pan is nearly dry, 5 to 7 minutes. Stir in the basil. Let cool for 5 minutes.

3   To make the omelet base: Place the eggs, the ½ cup cheese, the pepper, and the salt in a blender and process until smooth. Divide among six 1-cup nonstick jumbo muffin cups. Add the filling, dividing it evenly among the cups.

4   Bake for 15 minutes. Meanwhile, in a small, dry skillet over medium heat, toast the pine nuts, stirring constantly, until they just begin to turn light brown, about 1 minute. Immediately pour them into a small bowl to cool. Set aside.

5   Sprinkle the omelet cups with the additional ½ cup cheese and the pine nuts. Bake until golden brown and firm, 5 to 10 minutes longer. The omelets will puff up like a soufflé and then deflate a bit when removed from the oven. Serve hot.

VEGETABLE FILLING

1 tablespoon olive oil

1 clove garlic, finely chopped

½ pint basket cherry tomatoes, quartered

12 button mushrooms (about 8 ounces), stems removed and caps quartered

4 cups well-rinsed baby spinach leaves

Kosher salt

Freshly ground pepper

1 tablespoon finely chopped fresh basil

OMELET BASE

12 eggs

½ cup shredded Gruyère or Jarlsberg cheese

1 teaspoon freshly ground pepper

½ teaspoon kosher salt

1 tablespoon pine nuts

½ cup shredded Gruyère or Jarlsberg cheese

SHRIMP AND PEA OMELET CUPS WITH SUMMER HERBS

SERVES 6

SHRIMP AND PEA FILLING

1 tablespoon unsalted butter

1 clove garlic, very finely chopped

12 large shrimp (about 12 ounces), peeled and deveined

½ cup baby green peas

3 tablespoons finely chopped fresh basil

2 tablespoons finely chopped fresh mint

OMELET BASE

12 eggs

½ cup shredded Gruyère or Jarlsberg cheese

1 teaspoon freshly ground pepper

½ teaspoon kosher salt

The delicate pink of the shrimp and the bright green of the peas give this recipe special eye appeal. Since it partners two proteins, shrimp and eggs, it has great appetite-satisfying power as well. If you, like me, feel particularly rushed in the morning, you may think that the Wine and Food Lover's Diet would never work for you. Who has time to make breakfast? Omelet cups can be prepared quickly and can even be made ahead. You can bake them without a filling for weekday breakfasts or with a colorful, flavorful filling like the one here for weekends. They are delicious, endlessly variable, and even portable. To freeze the cups, wrap them individually in plastic wrap. They can be frozen for up to 2 months. To reheat, place the frozen cups in a microwave on high for 2 to 3 minutes. For this recipe, you will need a jumbo muffin pan with six cups, each of which has a 1-cup capacity.

1   Preheat the oven to 375°F.

2   To make the filling: In a skillet over medium heat, melt the butter. Add the garlic and cook, stirring frequently, until softened, about 1 minute. Add the shrimp and cook, turning occasionally, until bright pink and opaque, about 1 minute. Stir in the peas, basil, and mint. Let cool.

3   To make the omelet base: Place the eggs, cheese, pepper, and salt in a blender and process until smooth. Divide among six 1-cup nonstick jumbo muffin cups Add the shrimp mixture, making sure that each cup has 2 shrimp.

4   Bake until lightly browned and puffed, 15 to 25 minutes. The omelets will puff up like a soufflé and then deflate a bit when removed from the oven. Serve hot.

THREE-PEPPER AND CHEDDAR OMELET

SERVES 4

PEPPER FILLING

1 tablespoon olive oil

½ green bell pepper, seeds and ribs removed, chopped

½ yellow bell pepper, seeds and ribs removed, chopped

½ red bell pepper, seeds and ribs removed, chopped

1 small yellow onion, finely chopped

OMELET

8 eggs

¼ cup water

Kosher salt

Freshly ground pepper

2 teaspoons olive oil

1 cup shredded Cheddar cheese

On the Wine and Food Lover's Diet, you can eat whole eggs and full-fat cheese. Eggs contain omega-3 fatty acids. Research suggests that these essential protein building blocks enhance brain function. The bell peppers, Super-Savvy Carbs, provide a burst of color and texture, while the cheese adds protein, dairy calcium, and a wonderful savory flavor.

1   To make the filling: In a large skillet over medium heat, warm the oil until it shimmers. Add the peppers and onion and cook, stirring, until softened, about 5 minutes. Let cool for a few minutes.

2   To make the omelet: Arrange the broiler rack about 5 inches from the heat source and preheat the broiler. In a bowl, whisk together the eggs, water, and salt and pepper to taste until frothy. In an ovenproof skillet over medium heat, warm 1 teaspoon of the oil. Add half of the egg mixture, stir briefly, and then let the eggs begin to set around the edges. Using a spatula, lift the edges and tilt the pan to allow the uncooked egg to run underneath. Cook until the eggs are almost set but still moist.

3   Spread half of the filling and ¼ cup of the Cheddar cheese over half of the eggs. Fold the uncovered half of the eggs over the filling. Sprinkle ¼ cup of the cheese evenly over the top. Place the pan in the broiler and cook until the cheese melts, about 30 seconds. Slide the omelet onto a warmed serving plate and keep warm. Make a second omelet with the remaining ingredients.

4   To serve, cut each omelet in half and arrange on 4 warmed plates.

TELEME CHEESE FRITTATA WITH THYME AND CHIVES

SERVES 2

Frittatas make a wonderful, relaxed late breakfast on the weekend, especially when paired with a simple and delicious salad such as the Savvy Salad with Toasted Pumpkin Seeds and Melted Gruyère (page 107). Frittatas, a sort of crustless quiche, are great fun to cook because of the way they puff up in the oven. They are also smart because the toppings can be infinitely varied. To turn this frittata into a supper dish, add Super-Savvy Carbs such as sautéed spinach or sautéed mushrooms to your menu. The cooked vegetables could also be stirred into the egg mixture. Teleme is a luscious, soft cheese that originated in Northern California. Taleggio, which has a similar texture but a stronger flavor, or mild Brie may be substituted if Teleme is unavailable.

1 tablespoon unsalted butter

5 eggs, lightly beaten

Kosher salt

Freshly ground pepper

3 to 4 ounces Teleme cheese, cubed

3 tablespoons finely chopped fresh chives

1 tablespoon finely chopped fresh thyme

1   Arrange the broiler rack about 6 inches from the heat source and preheat the broiler, or preheat the oven to 450°F. In a large, ovenproof skillet over medium heat, melt the butter. Pour in the eggs and season to taste with salt and pepper. Stir briefly and then let the eggs begin to set around the edges. Using a spatula, lift the edges and tilt the pan to allow the uncooked eggs to run underneath. Cook until the eggs are set on the bottom and still liquid on top.

2   Turn off the heat and scatter the cheese, chives, and thyme evenly over the top of the eggs. Place the pan in the broiler or oven and cook until the eggs are set, the edges are puffed, and the cheese is melted, 1 to 2 minutes. Do not overcook; the eggs should remain moist. Slide the frittata onto a plate, cut in half, and serve.

TOMATO, BASIL, AND MOZZARELLA FRITTATA

SERVES 2

A breakfast high in protein, with some healthy fat and Savvy or Super-Savvy Carbs, is ideal. The carbohydrates offer short-term satiety, protein supplies medium-term satiety, and fats give long-term satiety, sustaining your energy all morning. The tomatoes are a Super-Savvy Carb, and the cheese and eggs provide some fat and lots of protein. The high protein content of this summery-tasting frittata helps you burn fat for energy.

10 fresh basil leaves

1 tablespoon olive oil

1 clove garlic, very finely chopped

5 eggs, lightly beaten

Kosher salt

Freshly ground pepper

About 1 large handful cherry tomatoes, halved, or quartered if large

¼ cup shredded mozzarella cheese

1   Arrange the broiler rack about 6 inches from the heat source and preheat the broiler, or preheat the oven to 450°F. Stack half of the basil leaves on top of one another and roll into a tight cylinder. Cut the rolled leaves crosswise to make thin strips. Repeat with the remaining leaves and set aside.

2   In a large, ovenproof skillet over medium heat, warm the oil. Add the garlic and cook, stirring frequently, until softened, about 1 minute. Pour in the eggs and season to taste with salt and pepper. Stir briefly and then let the eggs begin to set around the edges. Using a spatula, lift the edges and tilt the pan to allow the uncooked eggs to run underneath. Cook until the eggs are set on the bottom and still liquid on top.

3   Turn off the heat and scatter the basil, tomatoes, and cheese evenly over the top of the eggs. Place the pan in the broiler or oven and cook until the eggs are set, the edges are puffed, and the cheese is melted, 1 to 2 minutes. Do not overcook; the eggs should remain moist. Slide the frittata onto a plate, cut in half, and serve.

BAJA OMELET WITH AVOCADO-TOMATO SALSA FRESCA

SERVES 4

AVOCADO-TOMATO SALSA FRESCA

3 tomatoes, diced

1 avocado, pitted, peeled, and cut into ¼-inch dice

3 green onions, white and light green parts, thinly sliced

1 small jalapeño chile, seeds removed and finely chopped

2 tablespoons finely chopped fresh cilantro

2 tablespoons freshly squeezed lime juice

½ teaspoon kosher salt

CRABMEAT OMELET

8 ounces cooked crabmeat, picked over and shells removed

½ small red bell pepper, seeds and ribs removed, finely chopped

2 teaspoons finely chopped fresh chives

Juice of 1 lemon

8 eggs

¼ cup water

2 teaspoons olive oil

Kosher salt

Freshly ground pepper

4 ounces Monterey Jack cheese

1 ripe avocado, pitted, peeled, and sliced

4 sprigs fresh cilantro

Voted chef of the year by *Chef* magazine in 2004, Bernard Guillas, executive chef at La Jolla Beach & Tennis Club in La Jolla, California, draws inspiration from cuisines around the world. This is the Wine and Food Lover's Diet adaptation of one of his popular weekend brunch dishes.

The crabmeat adds a richness to the omelet, while the chunky, lightly spicy fresh salsa offers a south-of-the-border flair. You can indulge in all this without guilt, as the recipe uses Super-Savvy Carbs, protein, and healthful fats. These add up to a feeling of satiety without initiating a rise in blood sugar.

1   To make the salsa fresca: In a glass or ceramic bowl, gently stir together the tomatoes, avocado, green onions, jalapeño, cilantro, lime juice, and salt. Cover and refrigerate for at least 1 hour to blend the flavors.

2   To make the omelet: Arrange the broiler rack about 5 inches from the heat source and preheat the broiler. In a small bowl, toss together the crabmeat, bell pepper, chives, and lemon juice. Set aside.

3   In another bowl, whisk together the eggs and water until frothy. In an ovenproof skillet over medium heat, warm 1 teaspoon of the oil. Add half of the egg mixture, stir briefly, and then let the eggs begin to set around the edges. Using a spatula, lift the edges and tilt the pan to allow the uncooked eggs to run underneath. Cook until the eggs are almost set but still moist.

4   Spread half of the crabmeat mixture over half of the eggs. Season to taste with salt and pepper. Fold the uncovered half of the eggs over the filling. Cut the cheese into 8 equal slices and arrange 4 slices on top. Place the pan in the broiler and cook until the cheese melts, about 30 seconds. Slide the omelet onto a warmed serving plate and keep warm. Make a second omelet with the remaining ingredients.

5   Cut each omelet in half and arrange on warmed plates. Garnish each omelet with a few slices of avocado and a cilantro sprig. Divide the salsa among 4 ramekins and serve with the omelets.

TEX-MEX SCRAMBLED EGGS

SERVES 2

¼ cup pumpkin seeds

2 avocados, pitted and peeled

2 large shallots, finely chopped

1 tablespoon very finely chopped fresh chives

Juice of 1 lime

Kosher salt

Freshly ground pepper

2 teaspoons olive oil

3 cups well-rinsed baby spinach leaves

One 4-ounce can diced green chiles, preferably Ortega, drained

⅛ teaspoon ground cumin

5 eggs, lightly beaten

½ cup shredded Monterey Jack cheese

2 tablespoons purchased salsa verde, preferably Herdez, or tomato salsa

After a long night shift on call as a radiology resident in Texas, I would head to a Tex-Mex restaurant called El Napolito, in Galveston, arriving just in time for the famous breakfasts. I particularly enjoyed all the colorful and creative ways that the restaurant served eggs. This recipe brings back memories of those satisfying flavors. I've used two Super-Savvy Carbs here: avocados and spinach. Avocados are rich in monounsaturated oil, the kind that helps raise good cholesterol.

1   In a small, dry skillet over medium heat, toast the pumpkin seeds, stirring constantly, until they just begin to turn light brown, about 2 minutes. Immediately pour them into a small bowl to cool.

2   In a bowl, mash the avocados with a fork to the desired consistency. Stir in half of the chopped shallots, the chives, and the lime juice. Season to taste with salt and pepper. Set the guacamole aside.

3   In a large skillet over medium heat, warm the oil until it shimmers. Add the remaining shallots and cook, stirring frequently, until softened, about 2 minutes. Add the spinach and stir and toss until wilted. Stir in the chiles, pumpkin seeds, and cumin. Season to taste with salt and pepper.

4   Reduce the heat to medium-low and add the eggs. Using a spatula and long, slow strokes, gently stir the eggs all over the sides and bottom of the pan until they are firm but not dry, about 1 minute. Sprinkle with the cheese. Divide among 2 warmed plates and top each serving with 1 tablespoon salsa verde. Pass the guacamole at the table.

CLASSIC SAVVY SALAD

SERVES 4

A friend in Austria, Dr. Peter Kullnig, taught me his secret: "First you must salt the leaves. Then you add just enough oil to coat the leaves and no more." Since then, I apply his principle to all my salads. Classic Savvy Salad, my favorite, includes only a few ingredients. That makes it a terrific showcase for a high-quality extra-virgin olive oil, which adds an important flavor component. Olive oil is significant for another reason, too. It contains a very high level of monounsaturated fats, the type shown to help raise good (HDL) cholesterol levels. The salad has essentially no glycemic effect, meaning it does not cause a rapid spike in blood sugar. You can easily vary the salad by using different oils such as flavored olive oils or pumpkin seed or hazelnut oil, and substituting walnuts or pecans for the almonds—all of which count as Super-Savvy Carbs.

2 tablespoons sliced almonds

8 cups butter lettuce or baby romaine leaves, rinsed and thoroughly dried

½ teaspoon kosher salt

2 to 3 tablespoons extra-virgin olive oil

1½ teaspoons red wine vinegar

Freshly ground pepper

¼ cup freshly grated Parmesan cheese (optional)

1   In a small, dry skillet over medium heat, toast the almonds, stirring constantly, until they just begin to turn light brown, about 1 minute. Immediately pour them into a small bowl to cool. Set aside.

2   Place the lettuce leaves in a large bowl and sprinkle lightly with the salt. Toss well with tongs. Add the oil, 1 tablespoon at a time, tossing the leaves thoroughly after each addition and adding just enough oil to coat the leaves lightly. Sprinkle with the vinegar and toss. Season to taste with pepper and toss again. Taste for seasoning and adjust with salt and pepper.

3   Divide the salad among 4 salad plates. Sprinkle with the almonds, dividing evenly, and top with the Parmesan (if using).

ARUGULA AND CHERRY TOMATOES WITH WARM HAZELNUT DRESSING

SERVES 4

About 10 hazelnuts

8 cups arugula leaves, rinsed and thoroughly dried

8 cherry tomatoes, quartered

½ teaspoon kosher salt

3 tablespoons hazelnut oil or extra-virgin olive oil

1½ teaspoons Dijon mustard

1 teaspoon red wine vinegar (optional)

Freshly ground pepper

2 tablespoons freshly grated Parmesan or pecorino romano cheese

What a relief to know that salad dressing will not make you fat—but will help make you healthier. Recipes in *The Wine and Food Lover's Diet* use oils that are high in healthful monounsaturated fat and are full of flavor, such as nut oils and extra-virgin olive oil. Arugula is a Super-Savvy Carb. It has dark green, deeply lobed leaves and a lightly peppery flavor that makes a good foil for strongly flavored dressings like this one with toasted hazelnuts, another Super-Savvy Carb.

1   In a small, dry skillet over medium heat, toast the hazelnuts, stirring constantly, until they just begin to turn light brown, about 5 minutes. Immediately enclose them in a clean kitchen towel and rub vigorously to remove the dark brown skins. Do not worry if tiny pieces of skin remain on the nuts. Pour the nuts into a colander and shake to separate the nuts from the flakes of skin. Coarsely chop the nuts and set aside.

2   In a large bowl, combine the arugula and tomatoes. Sprinkle with the salt. Toss well with tongs. In a small skillet over medium heat, warm the oil. Add the nuts and cook, stirring, just until they sizzle in the oil. Remove from the heat and place on an unused burner for 1 minute. Standing back to avoid being spattered, carefully whisk in the mustard and the vinegar (if using). Pour the dressing over the arugula and tomatoes and toss thoroughly. Season to taste with pepper and more salt, if needed, and toss again.

3   Divide the salad among 4 salad plates. Sprinkle with the cheese and serve.

WARM ZUCCHINI SALAD

SERVES 4

Not only is this salad great looking, but it is great fun to eat. Zucchini, a Super-Savvy Carb, is cut into wide strips resembling pasta ribbons, which are then very gently and quickly cooked. The bell pepper and tomatoes, both Super-Savvy Carbs, add contrasting colors and textures. The warm vegetables and dressing are arranged on top of a tangle of mixed lettuces, adding even more crunch and color. The pine nuts, butter, and Parmesan add rich flavor notes, too, but they have a more serious purpose. Their fat content adds to your feeling of satiety. And when the salad is eaten without enablers, such as bread or crackers, foods that cause a rapid increase in blood sugar, the fats are burned as energy.

1   In a small, dry skillet over medium heat, toast the pine nuts, stirring constantly, until they just begin to turn light brown, about 1 minute. Immediately pour them into a small bowl to cool. Set aside.

2   Stack half of the basil leaves on top of one other and roll into a tight cylinder. Cut the rolled leaves crosswise to make thin strips. Repeat with the remaining leaves and set aside. Using a vegetable peeler, mandoline, or sharp knife, cut each zucchini lengthwise into thin strips resembling wide noodles. Discard the pieces that are mostly skin.

3   In a large skillet over medium heat, warm the oil. Add the shallot and cook, stirring frequently, until softened, about 2 minutes. Add the bell pepper and cook, stirring frequently, for 2 minutes. Add the zucchini strips and gently stir and toss, being careful not to break the strips, until just cooked through, about 2 minutes. Add the butter and mustard and stir until the butter melts and the vegetables are evenly coated. Add the tomatoes and stir just until heated through. Season to taste with salt and pepper.

4   Divide the greens among 4 salad plates. Arrange the vegetables on top of the greens, dividing evenly. Top with the toasted nuts, basil strips, Parmesan, and oregano, dividing evenly, and serve.

---

2 tablespoons pine nuts

10 large basil leaves

2 zucchini (about 6 ounces each)

1 tablespoon olive oil

1 shallot, very finely chopped

1 small red bell pepper, seeds and ribs removed, cut into ¼-inch dice

1 tablespoon unsalted butter

1½ teaspoons Dijon mustard

2 handfuls cherry tomatoes, quartered

Kosher salt

Freshly ground pepper

4 generous cups mixed baby salad greens, rinsed and thoroughly dried

¼ cup freshly grated Parmesan or Gruyère cheese

2 teaspoons finely chopped fresh oregano

GREEK SALAD

SERVES 4

8 cups mixed baby salad greens, rinsed and thoroughly dried

1 small cucumber, peeled, halved lengthwise, seeded, and thinly sliced crosswise

½ small red onion, thinly sliced

1½ teaspoons finely chopped fresh oregano

½ teaspoon kosher salt

4 to 5 tablespoons extra-virgin olive oil

1 tablespoon red wine vinegar (optional)

Freshly ground pepper

3 tablespoons crumbled feta cheese

3 tablespoons finely chopped kalamata olives

I eat salads nearly every day because they can be so satisfying, especially when they include ingredients like olives, a Super-Savvy Carb, and cheese. Traditionally, a Greek salad combines cucumbers, tomatoes, olives, and feta cheese and is dressed in olive oil. I like to add salad greens for more color and crunch and a little vinegar to punch up the flavor. Kalamata olives, large, purple-black Greek olives with a tapering oval shape, are cured in wine vinegar and have a mild taste and a meaty texture. They, like olive oil, are full of heart-healthy monounsaturated oils.

1   In a large bowl, combine the greens, cucumber, onion, and oregano. Sprinkle lightly with the salt and toss well with tongs. Add the oil, 1 tablespoon at a time, tossing the vegetables thoroughly after each addition and adding just enough oil to coat the leaves lightly. Sprinkle with the vinegar (if using) and toss again. Season to taste with pepper and more salt, if needed (remember that the feta tends to be salty), and toss again.

2   Divide the salad among 4 plates. Sprinkle with the feta and olives, dividing them evenly.

CHOPPED ROMAINE SALAD WITH BACON AND ALMONDS

SERVES 2

Here's a quick and easy salad that is full of flavor. I've teamed romaine with fresh herbs, toasted almonds, and feta cheese. There is plenty of crunch, color, taste, and protein to keep you feeling satisfied and happy for hours. Romaine does not wilt rapidly after being dressed, but don't wait too long before serving, as its cut edges may brown.

1 In a skillet over medium heat, cook the bacon, stirring occasionally, until browned and crisp, about 7 minutes. Remove to paper towels to drain.

2 In a small, dry skillet over medium heat, toast the almonds, stirring constantly, until they just begin to turn light brown, about 2 minutes. Immediately pour them into a small bowl to cool.

3 In a large bowl, whisk together the lemon juice, salt, pepper, and mustard. Gradually whisk in the oil until well mixed.

4 Cut the lettuce leaves crosswise into ½-inch pieces (you should have about 4 cups). Add to the bowl with the tomato, thyme, oregano, feta, and reserved bacon and almonds. Toss to coat well with the dressing. Taste the salad, adjust the seasoning with more salt and pepper if needed, and serve.

2 slices nitrite-free bacon, cut crosswise into ¼-inch pieces

⅓ cup blanched, slivered almonds

1 tablespoon freshly squeezed lemon juice

¼ teaspoon kosher salt

⅛ teaspoon freshly ground pepper

½ teaspoon Dijon mustard

2 tablespoons plus 1 teaspoon extra-virgin olive oil

1 head romaine lettuce

1 tomato (about 6 ounces), finely chopped

1 tablespoon finely chopped fresh thyme

1 teaspoon finely chopped fresh oregano

⅓ cup crumbled feta cheese

ROASTED EGGPLANT, BELL PEPPER, AND TOMATO SALAD

SERVES 4

2 tablespoons pine nuts

1 large globe eggplant, cut into ½-inch cubes

Kosher salt

2 red bell peppers

2 large tomatoes, halved

3 tablespoons olive oil, plus more for brushing

Freshly ground pepper

1 tablespoon Dijon mustard

2 teaspoons freshly squeezed lemon juice

3 cups baby arugula or baby romaine leaves, rinsed and thoroughly dried, coarsely chopped

1 cup fresh mint leaves, coarsely chopped

½ cup crumbled feta cheese

If you worry that without potatoes, rice, or bread at dinner, you will be hungry, make yourself some roasted eggplant. It has a tender, yet substantial texture and takes on robust flavors that are sure to satisfy. The bright and pungent dressing marries the rich, caramelized roasted vegetables with the crisp flavor of arugula and mint. When topped with the crumbed feta and toasted pine nuts, the salad makes a colorful and satisfying lunch as well as a side dish for roasted chicken or grilled tofu.

1   In a small, dry skillet over medium heat, toast the pine nuts, stirring constantly, until they just begin to turn light brown, about 1 minute. Immediately pour them into a small bowl to cool. Set aside.

2   Put the eggplant in a colander, sprinkle with salt, toss, and let stand for about 20 minutes to remove any bitterness. Rinse well under cold running water and drain. Dry by pressing the cubes firmly between paper towels or in a kitchen towel.

3   Arrange the broiler pan about 5 inches from the heat source and preheat the broiler. Place the bell peppers on the broiler pan and broil, turning as needed, until charred all over, about 10 minutes. Place the roasted peppers in a bowl, cover, and set aside until cool enough to handle. Working over a bowl to catch the juices, pull the blackened skins from each pepper and discard. Pull out the stems and remove the seeds and ribs. Tear the peppers into strips about ¾ inch wide. Set aside. Strain any juices into a jar and reserve for use in salad dressings.

4   Preheat the oven to 400°F. Liberally brush the eggplant cubes and tomato halves all over with oil. Dust the eggplant with pepper. Season the tomatoes to taste with salt and pepper. Arrange the eggplant on one side of a baking sheet and put the tomatoes on the other side, cut side up. Roast until the eggplant is tender and lightly browned and the tomatoes are softened, about 15 minutes. Stir occasionally so the eggplant cooks evenly, and remove any cubes that are done. Let the vegetables cool just until you can handle them. You want them to be warm when you serve them. Coarsely chop the tomatoes.

5   While the vegetables are roasting, in a small bowl, whisk the 3 tablespoons oil, mustard, and lemon juice together. In a large bowl, combine the arugula and mint and sprinkle lightly with salt and pepper. Add about half of the dressing and toss until the arugula and mint are evenly coated. Divide the salad among 4 plates.

6   Top the greens with the roasted eggplant and tomato, dividing evenly. Set roasted pepper strips in a crisscross pattern on top of the salad. Drizzle with the remaining dressing and sprinkle with the pine nuts and feta.

GOAT CHEESE SPREAD WITH ROASTED PEPPERS AND ENDIVE

SERVES 4

This recipe combines the sweetness of roasted bell peppers, the tangy taste of fresh goat cheese, the nutty character of toasted Parmesan cheese, and the satisfying crunch of endive. It makes great finger food and is also easy to make ahead—all in all, a terrific party dish or cocktail party appetizer. On the Wine and Food Lover's Diet, cheese serves an important role as a provider of protein and calcium. Its fat content will also help you feel full longer.

1 Arrange the broiler rack about 5 inches from the heat source and preheat the broiler. Place the bell peppers on the broiler pan and broil, turning as needed, until charred all over, about 10 minutes. Place the roasted peppers in a bowl, cover, and set aside until cool enough to handle. Turn off the broiler and preheat the oven to 375°F.

2 Working over a bowl to catch the juices, pull the blackened skins from each pepper and discard. Pull out the stems and remove the seeds and ribs. Tear the peppers into strips about ¾ inch wide. You will need 8 strips; set them aside. Strain any juices into a clean jar and reserve with the remaining roasted pepper strips for another use, such as a salad.

3 Line a baking sheet with parchment paper. Arrange tablespoonfuls of the Parmesan several inches apart on the parchment paper. Flatten the cheese into even circles, being careful not to leave any holes. Bake until the cheese melts and turns a very light brown, 3 to 4 minutes. Watch carefully, as the cheese browns quickly. Let the Parmesan crisps cool. Remove from the paper and reserve.

4 In a bowl, mash together the goat cheese, crème fraîche, lemon juice and zest, and herbs. Season to taste with salt and pepper. Choose 8 of the largest endive leaves and place 2 on each of 4 plates, or arrange on a platter. Lay a pepper strip lengthwise in each leaf. Reserve any remaining endive for another use. Spoon some of the cheese spread onto each leaf, dividing evenly. Place a Parmesan crisp, standing on edge, in the spread. Garnish each leaf with a chive and serve.

---

2 large red bell peppers

½ cup freshly grated Parmesan cheese

4 ounces fresh goat cheese, at room temperature

¼ cup crème fraîche

1 tablespoon freshly squeezed lemon juice

1 tablespoon freshly grated lemon zest

1 tablespoon finely chopped mixed fresh herbs such as flat-leaf parsley, thyme, and basil

Kosher salt

Freshly ground pepper

1 head endive, end trimmed and separated into individual leaves

8 fresh chives

CALAMARI WITH ARUGULA AND SHAVED PECORINO ROMANO

SERVES 4

My neighbor, Christina Van de Camp, makes a simple pasta dish by topping just-cooked pasta with fresh arugula and shaved pecorino, then tossing them together. The heat of the pasta wilts the leaves and melts the cheese. Since the Wine and Food Lover's Diet avoids wheat products, I substitute calamari, or squid, for the pasta. Calamari is easily and quickly cooked, and its texture is similar to al dente pasta— tender and still slightly chewy. You can find the tubes, or bodies, already cleaned and ready to use at a local fish market.

1   Put the arugula in a bowl and set aside. Using a vegetable peeler or cheese plane, cut the cheese into thin shavings until you have about ¼ cup. Set aside.

2   In a skillet over medium heat, warm the oil until it shimmers. Add the garlic and cook, stirring frequently, until softened, about 1 minute. Add the calamari and cook, stirring frequently, until opaque throughout, about 3 minutes.

3   Place the hot calamari in the bowl with the arugula. Season to taste with salt (keeping in mind that the cheese added later is salty) and pepper. Toss well with tongs. The arugula will wilt. Divide evenly among 4 warmed salad plates. Top with the cheese shavings and serve.

---

2 cups baby arugula leaves, rinsed and thoroughly dried

1 to 2 ounces pecorino romano cheese

2 tablespoons extra-virgin olive oil

2 cloves garlic, very finely chopped

1 pound calamari tubes, cut crosswise into rings about ¼ inch wide

Kosher salt

Freshly ground pepper

PROSCIUTTO-WRAPPED SHRIMP

SERVES 4

8 jumbo shrimp (about 12 ounces), peeled and deveined

8 large basil leaves

3 strips prosciutto (about 2 ounces), cut lengthwise into 8 thin strips

Freshly ground white pepper

1 tablespoon olive oil

Classic Savvy Salad (optional; page 93)

People on a diet often feel that their social lives are restricted due to the many foods they are not allowed to eat. On the Wine and Food Lover's Diet, however, you won't feel isolated and unable to entertain friends with your own cooking. This starter is not only sophisticated and elegant, but also quick and easy to prepare for company. You can serve the shrimp on their own as finger food or on top of a Classic Savvy Salad as a first course. For special occasions, I embellish the cooked shrimp with a light drizzle of truffle oil.

1   Wrap each shrimp with a basil leaf and then with a strip of the prosciutto. If the strips do not hold together on their own, secure with toothpicks. Dust with white pepper.

2   In a skillet over medium heat, warm the oil until it shimmers. Add the shrimp and cook, turning once, until bright pink, 1 to 2 minutes per side.

3   Divide the salad (if using) among 4 salad plates. Top each serving with 2 shrimp and serve.

SESAME-SEED POPCORN SHRIMP

SERVES 4

1 egg

Kosher salt

Freshly ground white pepper

½ cup sesame seeds

12 large shrimp (about 12 ounces), peeled, with tails intact, and deveined

2 tablespoons grapeseed oil

Popcorn shrimp, an addictive specialty of the New Orleans area, are made by dipping shrimp in batter and frying them until succulent. A spicy sauce is the customary accompaniment. Since wheat flour is not part of the Wine and Food Lover's Diet, I had to look for an alternative way to duplicate the crunchy texture I like so much. Sesame seeds, with their healthy dose of mono- and polyunsaturated oil and minerals such as calcium, make a terrific coating. Serve these shrimp on their own or on top of a green salad.

1   In a bowl, lightly beat together the egg and salt and pepper to taste. Spread the sesame seeds on a plate. Add the shrimp to the beaten egg mixture and toss until well coated. Remove the shrimp, letting any excess egg drip back into the bowl. Turn the shrimp in the sesame seeds until evenly coated.

2   In a skillet over medium heat, warm the oil until it shimmers. Add the coated shrimp and cook, turning once, until bright pink, 1 to 2 minutes per side. Serve hot.

FRESH MOZZARELLA, TOMATO, AND BASIL SALAD

SERVES 2

This salad is a classic Italian combination. Make it in the height of summer when tomatoes are at their ripest and basil its most fragrant. Heirloom tomatoes, grown from seeds of older varieties, have a wonderful variety of shapes, colors, textures, and tastes. I like to serve several types together, mixing green zebra-striped tomatoes with large orange slicers and perhaps some cherry tomatoes for added contrast of size and shape. Really fresh mozzarella is, thankfully, becoming more widely available. It has a mild flavor and a succulent texture. When very fresh, the cheese nearly bursts with moisture. It comes packed in whey and can be found in the refrigerator section of specialty markets. Tomatoes qualify as Super-Savvy Carbs.

10 fresh basil leaves

4 ripe tomatoes, preferably heirloom, cut into ½-inch-thick slices

5 ounces fresh mozzarella cheese, drained and cut into ½-inch-thick slices

Kosher salt

2 to 3 tablespoons toasted pumpkin seed oil or extra-virgin olive oil

Freshly ground pepper

1   Stack half of the basil leaves on top of one other and roll into a tight cylinder. Cut the rolled leaves crosswise to make thin strips. Repeat with the remaining leaves and set aside.

2   Arrange alternating slices of tomatoes and mozzarella cheese on 2 plates. Sprinkle lightly with salt. Top with the basil, dividing evenly. Drizzle with the oil, 1 tablespoon at a time, being careful not to add too much. Season to taste with pepper and serve.

SAVVY SALAD WITH TOASTED PUMPKIN SEEDS AND MELTED GRUYÈRE

SERVES 4

This is my version of a salad served at Häuserl Im Wald (Little House in the Woods), a restaurant in Graz, Austria. The chef's use of pumpkin seeds and pumpkin seed oil fits right in with the Wine and Food Lover's Diet's focus on heart-healthy mono-unsaturated oils. The original salad included a sheep's milk cheese that is hard to find outside of Austria. Gruyère, which melts well, is an excellent substitute. A little cheese is melted on each salad plate and sprinkled with pumpkin seeds, then the salad is arranged beside the cheese. You take a small bite of melted cheese and toasted pumpkin seeds along with a few leaves of lettuce. A special variety of pumpkin seeds grown in Styria, a region of Austria, does not have the usual seed coat that makes the oil easy to extract. Therefore, the seeds are toasted first and then pressed. The resulting deep green-brown oil is redolent of toasted pumpkin seeds. The oil breaks down if heated, so it is used only to dress salads or as a finishing touch for other dishes such as eggs or sautéed chicken breast. You can find authentic Styrian pumpkin seed oil online. Roasted pumpkin seed oil made in the United States can be purchased at specialty-food stores. Store the oil, after opening, in a cool, dark place and use within two months. Alternatively, you can substitute extra-virgin olive oil.

½ cup pumpkin seeds

8 cups mixed salad greens

½ teaspoon kosher salt

2½ tablespoons toasted pumpkin seed oil or extra-virgin olive oil

1 scant teaspoon apple cider vinegar

Freshly ground pepper

4 ounces Gruyère, Jarlsberg, or Port Salut cheese, cut into 4 equal slices

1   Preheat the oven to 300°F. In a small, dry skillet over medium heat, toast the pumpkin seeds, stirring constantly, until they just begin to turn lightly brown, about 2 minutes. Immediately pour them into a small bowl to cool. Set aside.

2   Place the salad greens in a large bowl and sprinkle with the salt. Toss well with tongs. Add the oil, 1 tablespoon at a time, tossing the leaves thoroughly after each addition. Sprinkle with the vinegar and toss again. Season to taste with pepper and more salt, if needed, and toss again.

3   Place a slice of cheese just off center on each of 4 salad plates. Set the plates in the oven and cook the cheese until it is melted and bubbling, about 3 minutes. (You can also melt the cheese in a microwave on high for 20 seconds.) Remove the plates from the oven and scatter some of the pumpkin seeds over the cheese, dividing evenly. Divide the salad greens among the plates. Scatter the remaining pumpkin seeds over the top. Serve while the cheese is still warm.

SHAVED ZUCCHINI WITH ARUGULA AND PECORINO ROMANO

SERVES 4

2 tablespoons sliced almonds

1 zucchini (about 8 ounces)

1 ounce pecorino romano cheese

8 cups baby arugula leaves, rinsed and thoroughly dried

¼ cup extra-virgin olive oil

2 tablespoons freshly squeezed lemon juice

Kosher salt

Freshly ground pepper

Dan Baker, the chef of Marché aux Fleurs restaurant in Ross, California, shared this recipe with me. The shaved zucchini looks similar to pappardelle pasta but does not have the same glycemic effect, meaning that the squash, a Super-Savvy Carb, does not cause a rapid rise in blood sugar. The slightly spicy character of the arugula makes a nice contrast with the sweetness of the zucchini. When choosing the zucchini, look for one that is fat and even in shape from one end to the other. This will make it easier to slice lengthwise.

1   In a small, dry skillet over medium heat, toast the almonds, stirring constantly, until they just begin to turn light brown, about 1 minute. Immediately pour them into a small bowl to cool. Set aside.

2   Using a vegetable peeler, mandoline, or sharp knife, cut the zucchini lengthwise into thin strips resembling wide noodles. Discard the pieces that are mostly skin. Place the zucchini in a large bowl. Using a vegetable peeler or cheese plane, cut the cheese into thin shavings. Add the cheese and arugula to the zucchini.

3   In a small bowl, whisk together the oil and lemon juice. Season to taste with salt and pepper and whisk again. Pour about half the dressing over the salad and gently toss, being careful not to break the zucchini strips. Add more dressing, as needed, until the salad is lightly and evenly coated. Divide among 4 salad plates and sprinkle with the almonds.

PORTOBELLO MUSHROOMS STUFFED WITH TURKEY

SERVES 6

When I was first on the Wine and Food Lover's Diet, I ate mushrooms, a Super-Savvy Carb, nearly every night because they are so meaty and satisfying. Portobello mushrooms are particularly meaty, and marinating them enhances their already rich flavor. This recipe, adapted from a dish made by Bernard Guillas, executive chef at La Jolla Beach & Tennis Club in La Jolla, California, uses turkey sausage to fill the mushrooms. Be sure to choose a brand without carbohydrate fillers and sugar.

1   Preheat the oven to 375°F. Using a spoon, scrape the gills from the underside of each mushroom cap. In a bowl, whisk together the vinegar, oil, rosemary, and salt and pepper to taste. Hold each mushroom over a large baking dish and spoon the oil mixture on both sides. Let marinate in the dish for 15 minutes. Drain the mushrooms and arrange, gill side up, on a baking sheet. Bake until tender and juicy, about 10 minutes. Let cool.

2   Turn off the oven. Arrange the broiler rack about 5 inches from the heat source and preheat the broiler. In a large bowl, stir together the sausage, egg, Parmesan, parsley, sun-dried tomatoes, oregano, thyme, and salt and pepper to taste until well mixed. Divide into 6 equal portions. Spoon a portion into each mushroom cap, smoothing the filling to form an even layer. Place mushrooms on a baking sheet and broil until the stuffing is golden brown, about 5 minutes, or until the sausage is cooked through.

3   To serve, divide the salad (if using) among 6 salad plates and place a warm stuffed mushroom alongside.

---

6 portobello mushrooms, each about 5 inches in diameter, stems removed

¼ cup red wine vinegar

¼ cup extra-virgin olive oil

1 tablespoon finely chopped fresh rosemary

Kosher salt

Freshly ground pepper

3 fresh turkey sausages (about 6 ounces each), casings removed and meat crumbled

1 egg

¼ cup freshly grated Parmesan cheese

2 tablespoons finely chopped fresh flat-leaf parsley

2 tablespoons chopped oil-packed sun-dried tomatoes, drained

1 tablespoon finely chopped fresh oregano

1 teaspoon finely chopped fresh thyme

Classic Savvy Salad (page 93) omitting the nuts and cheese (optional)

ROAST HALIBUT WITH SPINACH SALSA

SERVES 2

This pretty, green variation of a tomato salsa tastes great with any roasted, seared, or sautéed fish. In one recipe, you get two parts of your Meal-Planning Trilogy dinner: a protein and a Super-Savvy Carb. Halibut is a source of essential omega-3 fatty acids.

1   To make the salsa: Bring a large pot of salted water to a boil and prepare a bowl of ice water. Stir the spinach into the boiling water and cook just until the color brightens and the leaves wilt, about 1 minute. Drain the spinach and plunge into the ice water. Drain again and squeeze the spinach with your hands to remove the excess water. Roughly chop the spinach.

2   Place the spinach, olive oil, and garlic in a food processor and process until smooth. Using a rubber spatula, scrape the mixture into a bowl. Fold in the shallots, cucumber, and cilantro (if using). Season to taste with salt and black pepper. Pour into a bowl and refrigerate until ready to serve. You should have about 1 cup. The salsa can be prepared up to 1 day ahead, but is best if made within several hours of serving.

3   Preheat the oven to 450°F. Pat the fillets dry with paper towels and lay them on a plate. Season both sides with the salt and white pepper.

4   In a large, ovenproof skillet over medium-high heat, warm the grapeseed oil until it is very hot. Add the fillets and cook until browned on the first side, about 2 minutes. Turn and cook on the second side until browned, about 2 minutes. Immediately place the pan in the oven and cook until the fish is opaque throughout and flakes when tested with a knife but is still moist, about 7 minutes. The timing will depend on the thickness of the fillets.

5   Transfer the fillets to 2 warmed plates. Spoon a generous amount of salsa over and beside the fillets and serve.

SPINACH SALSA

2 cups well-rinsed baby spinach leaves

¼ cup extra-virgin olive oil

1 clove garlic

2 shallots, finely chopped

½ cup peeled, seeded, and diced cucumber (¼-inch dice)

1 tablespoon roughly chopped fresh cilantro (optional)

Kosher salt

Freshly ground black pepper

2 halibut fillets (about 5 ounces each)

½ teaspoon kosher salt

½ teaspoon freshly ground white pepper

2 tablespoons grapeseed oil or canola oil

PETRALE SOLE STUFFED WITH ASPARAGUS AND HAZELNUTS

SERVES 2

10 pencil-thin asparagus spears

About 15 hazelnuts

2 petrale or Dover sole fillets (about 5 ounces each)

Kosher salt

Freshly ground white pepper

1 tablespoon finely chopped fresh chives

1 tablespoon unsalted butter

1 tablespoon extra-virgin olive oil

Hazelnuts and asparagus, a Super-Savvy Carb, are a classic combination. Here, the nuts add a crunch to the fish fillets, while the asparagus contributes color as well as texture. Fish is a terrific source of omega-3 fatty acids. If you cannot find thin asparagus spears, you can use thicker ones, but you may need to cook them a bit longer and use fewer so the fillets will wrap around them. You can also use fillets of catfish, flounder, or trout.

1   Bring a large pot of salted water to a boil. Snap or cut off the tough ends of each asparagus spear. If the spears have thick skin, use a vegetable peeler to remove the skin below the tips. Drop the asparagus into the boiling water and cook until the spears are bright green and just begin to bend when picked out of the water with tongs, about 3 minutes. Drain and scatter on a work surface to cool.

2   In a small, dry skillet over medium heat, toast the hazelnuts, stirring constantly, until they just begin to turn light brown, about 5 minutes. Immediately enclose them in a clean kitchen towel and rub vigorously to remove the dark brown skins. Do not worry if tiny pieces of skin remain on the nuts. Pour the nuts into a colander and shake to separate the nuts from the flakes of skin. Coarsely chop the nuts and set them aside.

3   Lay the fillets on a work surface and lightly season both sides with salt and pepper. Sprinkle with the hazelnuts, dividing them evenly, then sprinkle with the chives. Arrange 5 asparagus spears in a neat pile across the center of each fillet. Roll the fillet around the spears and secure with 2 wooden toothpicks. In a large skillet over medium heat, melt the butter with the oil. Add the rolls and cook, turning as needed, until the fish is opaque throughout, 6 to 8 minutes.

4   Transfer the rolls to 2 warmed plates and serve.

GRILLED GROUPER WITH WARM TOMATO SALSA AND ARUGULA SALAD

SERVES 2

WARM TOMATO SALSA

1 tablespoon olive oil

2 tablespoons chopped shallots

½ teaspoon ground cumin

2 tomatoes, chopped and well drained

Kosher salt

Freshly ground white pepper

4 cups baby arugula leaves, rinsed and thoroughly dried

½ small red onion, thinly sliced

Kosher salt

1 to 2 tablespoons extra-virgin olive oil, plus more for brushing

½ teaspoon red wine vinegar or freshly squeezed lemon juice (optional)

Freshly ground white pepper

2 grouper, halibut, or snapper fillets (about 5 ounces each)

Fish recipes are well suited to the Wine and Food Lover's Diet because of their complete protein and supply of omega-3 fatty acids. In this one, the fish is paired with two Super-Savvy Carbs. Remember that eating protein helps you lose weight by initiating a Burning Cascade (see page 20), during which you burn fat instead of storing it (in all the places you don't want it to be). Protein also increases your feeling of satiety, meaning you won't feel hungry for a long time afterward. The arugula salad can be served on its own, but I particularly like it as a bed for fish, or with a chicken paillard (page 140).

1   To make the salsa: In a small saucepan over medium heat, warm the oil until it shimmers. Add the shallots and cook, stirring constantly, until softened, about 2 minutes. Add the cumin and cook, stirring, for 30 seconds. Add the tomatoes and salt and pepper to taste. Continue to cook just until the tomatoes are softened and warmed through, about 2 minutes. Set aside and keep warm.

2   If grilling the fish, prepare an outdoor charcoal or gas grill for cooking over medium heat. Meanwhile, place the arugula and onion in a large bowl. Sprinkle lightly with salt. Toss well with tongs. Add the oil, 1 tablespoon at a time, tossing well after each addition. Add just enough to coat the leaves lightly. Sprinkle with the vinegar (if using) and toss again. Season with pepper and toss again. Set aside.

3   Lay the fillets on a work surface and lightly season both sides with salt and pepper. When the grill is ready, brush the grill rack with oil. Place the fillets on the rack directly over the heat and grill the fillets, without disturbing them, until light to medium brown on the first side, about 3 minutes. Turn and cook until the fish is opaque throughout and flakes easily when tested with a knife, 2 to 3 minutes. Alternatively, brush a grill pan with oil and place over medium heat. When the pan is hot, add the fillets and cook until light brown on the first side, about 3 minutes. Turn and cook on the second side until the fish is opaque throughout, 2 to 3 minutes.

4   To serve, divide the salad between 2 warmed plates. Spoon a little salsa over each portion and then arrange a fillet on the salad. Spoon the remaining salsa over the fillets.

SEARED HALIBUT WITH LEMON-BUTTER SAUCE

SERVES 4

At one time, I was intimidated by cooking fish. That changed when I learned the simple technique of searing fish on top of the stove and then slipping it into the oven to finish cooking. Another advantage is that you are free to prepare an accompanying sauce or a side dish or salad. The sauce here is quickly made from simple ingredients. You will be amazed by the intensity and sophistication of the flavors. Believe it or not, sumptuous butter sauces can be part of the Wine and Food Lover's Diet. The fatty acids in butter are not as damaging to heart health as previously believed and, when not eaten with enablers, can be a part of a healthful diet. Butter, as well as the fish, is a source of omega-3 fatty acids, which help improve cholesterol levels.

1 Preheat the oven to 300°F. Pat the fillets dry with paper towels and lay them on a plate. Lightly season both sides with salt and pepper. In a large skillet over medium-high heat, heat the oil until very hot. Add the fillets and cook until light to medium brown on the first side, 2 to 3 minutes. Turn and cook until light brown on the second side, 2 to 3 minutes. Transfer to warmed plates and put in the oven to finish cooking while you make the sauce.

2 To make the sauce: In a small saucepan over medium-high heat, combine the shallot and white wine. Bring to a boil and cook until the liquid is reduced to about 1 tablespoon, about 3 minutes. Reduce the heat to low and whisk in the butter, 1 or 2 cubes at a time. Adjust the heat if necessary so the butter melts but does not overheat and separate. Strain the sauce into a small bowl and whisk in the lemon juice, parsley, and salt and pepper to taste.

3 Remove the fillets from the oven, drizzle with the sauce, and serve.

---

4 halibut fillets (about 5 ounces each)

Kosher salt

Freshly ground white pepper

3 tablespoons grapeseed oil

LEMON-BUTTER SAUCE

1 shallot, finely chopped

½ cup dry white wine

½ cup cold unsalted butter, cut into cubes

1 teaspoon freshly squeezed lemon juice

1 teaspoon finely chopped fresh flat-leaf parsley

Kosher salt

Freshly ground white pepper

FILLETS OF SOLE WITH CLASSIC BUTTER SAUCE

SERVES 2

2 petrale or Dover sole
fillets, flounder fillets,
or trout fillets (about
5 ounces each)

Kosher salt

Freshly ground white
pepper

5 tablespoons cold
unsalted butter, cut into
cubes

2 tablespoons
grapeseed oil

½ teaspoon finely
chopped fresh thyme

1 shallot, chopped

2 tablespoons white
vinegar

2 tablespoons dry white
wine

½ teaspoon freshly
squeezed lemon juice,
or more to taste

The Wine and Food Lover's Diet is very different from most other regimens. You are encouraged to enjoy sauces, such as this luscious butter sauce. I believe that sauce adds to your feeling of satisfaction at the table. You won't feel deprived and so you will be more motivated to stick with the diet and see results. The butter sauce does more than taste wonderful. It also increases the feeling of satiety and decreases the overall glycemic value of accompanying carbohydrates. This means that the blood sugar does not increase rapidly and thus instigate a Storage Cascade (see page 19) in which the body busily creates fat for storage instead of using it for energy.

1   Preheat the oven to 200°F. Pat the fillets dry with paper towels and lay them on a plate. Lightly season both sides with salt and pepper. In a large skillet over medium-high heat, melt 1 tablespoon of the butter with the oil. When the mixture is hot, add the fish and cook until light to medium brown on the first side, 2 to 3 minutes. Turn and cook until light brown on the second side and the fish is opaque throughout, 4 to 5 minutes. Sprinkle the thyme over the fillets. Transfer to warmed plates and put in the oven to keep warm while you make the sauce.

2   In a small saucepan over medium-high heat, combine the shallot, vinegar, and wine. Bring to a boil and cook until the liquid is reduced to about 1 tablespoon, about 2 minutes. Reduce the heat to low and whisk in the butter, 1 or 2 cubes at a time. Adjust the heat if necessary so the butter melts but does not overheat and separate. Strain the sauce into a small bowl and whisk in the ½ teaspoon lemon juice. Taste for seasoning and adjust with salt, pepper, and more lemon juice, if desired.

3   Remove the fillets from the oven, spoon some of the sauce around and on top of the fillets, and serve.

FLOUNDER WITH LEMON ZEST AND CAPERS

SERVES 2

This recipe has an Italian flair, with its classic flavor combination of lemon, capers, and parsley. It's a simple sauté, and the sauce is made in the pan in under 3 minutes. Pair the fish with Swiss Chard Stuffed with Barley (page 186), a combination that will give you sustained energy. You can substitute skinless, boneless chicken breast halves, about 5 ounces each, pounded thin, for the fish fillets.

1   Preheat the oven to 200°F. Place the fillets and beaten egg in a zippered plastic bag. Close the bag and gently shake it until the fillets are well coated with the egg. Lay the fillets on a plate and lightly season both sides with salt and pepper.

2   In a large skillet over medium-high heat, warm the oil until it shimmers. Add the fillets and cook until light golden brown on the first side, about 2 minutes. Turn and cook until light golden brown on the second side and the fish is opaque throughout, about 2 minutes. Transfer to warmed plates and put in the oven to keep warm while you make the sauce.

3   Melt the butter in the same skillet over medium heat. Add the shallot and cook until softened, about 2 minutes. Working quickly, add the wine, capers, and lemon zest. Stir to combine and scrape any browned bits from the bottom and sides of the pan. Taste for seasoning and adjust with salt and pepper. Stir in the parsley.

4   Remove the fillets from the oven, pour the sauce over the fillets, and serve with the lemon wedges.

---

2 flounder fillets (about 5 ounces each)

1 egg, lightly beaten

Kosher salt

Freshly ground white pepper

2 tablespoons olive oil

2 tablespoons unsalted butter

1 large shallot, finely chopped

¼ cup dry white wine

1½ teaspoons capers, drained and roughly chopped

Zest of ½ lemon

2 tablespoons finely chopped fresh flat-leaf parsley

2 lemon wedges

SPICE-CRUSTED FISH FILLETS WITH ARUGULA-MINT PESTO

SERVES 2

ARUGULA-MINT PESTO

½ cup almonds

1 cup packed stemmed arugula leaves

½ cup packed fresh mint leaves

1 clove garlic, smashed

Grated zest and juice of ½ lime or lemon

⅓ cup walnut oil or extra-virgin olive oil

Kosher salt

Freshly ground pepper

2 teaspoons sesame seeds

1 teaspoon fennel seeds

1 teaspoon cumin seeds

1 teaspoon caraway seeds

1 teaspoon coriander seeds (optional)

2 tablespoons chickpea flour, soy flour, or nut flour such as almond or hazelnut

Grated zest of 1 lime or lemon

Kosher salt

Freshly ground pepper

2 firm, white-fleshed fish fillets such as snapper, catfish, or trout (about 5 ounces each)

2 tablespoons olive oil or grapeseed oil

Crème fraîche

When you eat according to the Wine and Food Lover's Diet, you can enjoy sauces that give dishes rich, satisfying flavors. Pesto, typically a purée of basil and pine nuts with olive oil, makes an ideal Wine and Food Lover's Diet sauce. The herbs are Super-Savvy Carbs, and olive oil and nuts are full of monounsaturated fats that help improve cholesterol levels. I've modified the traditional recipe to create this unusual and equally appealing version. The bright, fresh flavor partners well with these crunchy fillets. The seed coating on the fish is made of all Super-Savvy Carbs. I started finding substitutions for flour-based coatings since flour is among the foods that cause a rapid increase in blood sugar and creates all the conditions for your body to store fat instead of burn it.

1   To make the pesto: In a small, dry skillet over medium heat, toast the almonds, stirring constantly, until they just begin to turn light brown, about 3 minutes. Immediately pour them into a food processor. Add the arugula, mint, garlic, and lime zest and process until a paste forms. Using a rubber spatula, scrape down the sides of the processor bowl. With the motor running, add the lime juice and then the oil. Scrape down the sides of the bowl. Taste for seasoning and adjust with salt and pepper. You should have about 1 cup.

2   Using a spice grinder, lightly crush the sesame, fennel, cumin, caraway, and coriander (if using) seeds. Be careful not to grind them to a powder. In a bowl, combine the crushed seeds, flour, lime zest, and salt and pepper to taste. The mixture will be slightly moist and crumbly. Press the mixture as evenly as possible onto both sides of the fillets. Do not worry if the coating is not uniform.

3   In a skillet over medium heat, warm the oil until it shimmers. Add the fillets and cook until browned and crusty on the first side, about 3 minutes. Turn and cook on the second side until the fish is opaque throughout, about 3 minutes.

4   Transfer the fillets to 2 warmed plates. Top each serving with a dollop of pesto and drizzle with a little crème fraîche.

GARLIC SHRIMP WITH SPAGHETTI SQUASH

SERVES 4

Garlic and shrimp are a nearly irresistible pairing. These shrimp cook very quickly on top of the stove, and the sauce comes together in the same pan—all in the time it takes to cook the squash if using a microwave. If you bake the squash in the oven, you can prepare it a day ahead and reheat it while cooking the shrimp. Spaghetti squash, a Super-Savvy Carb, has a delicate, sweet flavor. The flesh pulls apart into long, thin strands, thus the name.

1   Preheat the oven to 375°F. Pierce the skin of the squash in several places with a knife and put it in a baking dish. Bake until very soft, about 1 hour. (Alternatively, cook in a microwave: Halve the squash and pierce in several places. Scoop out and discard the seeds. Place the halves, cut side down, in a dish. Pour in ¼ cup water. Cover with plastic wrap and cook on high for 10 minutes.) Use a pot holder to grasp the squash and cut in half if still whole. Scoop out the seeds. Then, with a long-handled fork, tease out the strands into a warmed serving bowl. Fluff and separate the strands with the fork. Keep warm while cooking the shrimp.

2   In a skillet over medium-high heat, warm 2 tablespoons of the oil until it shimmers. Add the shrimp and stir and toss until the shrimp are bright pink and opaque throughout, about 4 minutes. Add to the bowl with the squash.

3   Add the garlic to the hot pan and cook until softened, about 30 seconds. Stir in the capers and a pinch of cayenne. Add the remaining 1 tablespoon oil and the parsley and stir well. Remove the pan from the heat, reduce the heat to very low, and whisk in the butter, a few cubes at a time, moving the pan on and off the heat so the butter just melts and emulsifies with the oil. Taste for seasoning and adjust with salt and pepper. Pour over the squash and toss well. Scatter the cheese (if using) over the top, divide among 4 plates or bowls, and serve.

---

1 spaghetti squash (about 3 pounds)

3 tablespoons olive oil

1 pound large shrimp, peeled and deveined

5 cloves garlic, very finely chopped

2 tablespoons capers, drained and roughly chopped

Cayenne pepper

2 tablespoons finely chopped fresh flat-leaf parsley

2 tablespoons cold unsalted butter, cut into cubes

Kosher salt

Freshly ground pepper

½ cup freshly grated Parmesan cheese (optional)

SNAPPER BAKED IN PARCHMENT

SERVES 2

1 small fennel bulb

2 snapper or flounder
fillets (about 5 ounces
each)

Kosher salt

Freshly ground pepper

1 small yellow onion,
chopped

2 teaspoons extra-virgin
olive oil, plus
2 tablespoons

2 tablespoons dry
vermouth

1 tablespoon finely
chopped fresh thyme

1 tablespoon finely
chopped fresh flat-leaf
parsley

1 lemon, thinly sliced

2 green onions, green
parts only, thinly sliced

Cooking in parchment seals in all the flavors and juices. Each diner opens an individual, puffed, browned packet and releases all the delicious aromas trapped inside. This snapper is infused with the delicate anise scent of fennel and the herbal notes of vermouth, thyme, and parsley, accented by lemon. Cooking in parchment may seem complicated and impressive, but it is very easy to do.

1   Preheat the oven to 400°F. Cut off the stems and leaves from the fennel bulb and, if desired, reserve for another use. If the outer layer of the bulb is tough, remove it. Cut the bulb lengthwise into thin slices and then cut each slice into matchsticks. Bring a small pot of salted water to a boil and add the fennel. Reduce the heat to low and cook for 1 minute. Drain and run under cold water to stop the cooking. Drain well.

2   Cut 2 sheets of parchment paper, each large enough to enclose a snapper fillet completely. Fold each sheet in half and then unfold. Lightly season each fillet on both sides with salt and pepper.

3   In a bowl, toss the fennel and onion with the 2 teaspoons oil until lightly coated. Spread half of the fennel mixture on one side of a parchment sheet. Sprinkle lightly with salt and pepper. Top with a fillet. Repeat with the remaining fennel mixture and fillet. Drizzle the fillets with the vermouth and the 2 tablespoons olive oil, dividing evenly. Sprinkle with the thyme and parsley, and lay the lemon slices on top.

4   Fold the parchment over the fish. Starting at one end, fold the paper over itself. Continue folding the parchment along the open ends until you have a completely sealed packet. Place the packets on a large baking sheet. Bake until the packets are puffy and browned on top, about 12 minutes.

5   To serve, place each packet on a warmed plate. Let the diners open the packets at the table and sprinkle each portion with half of the green onions.

PAN-ROASTED SALMON WITH CUCUMBER SALSA

SERVES 2

Outside of a pill, salmon is perhaps the richest source of omega-3 fatty acids, polyunsaturated fatty acids that have been shown to have a positive effect on heart health. Another reason to eat fish is recent research that indicates eating one to two meals of fish per week really does make us smarter and decrease the risk of stroke. But the best reason to eat this salmon is the taste. Searing the fish gives it a crispy, browned skin and rich flavor. The cucumber salsa adds a cool, crunchy contrast.

1   Put the fillets on a plate and generously brush all over with 1½ tablespoons of the oil. Lightly season on both sides with salt and white pepper. Let stand for 30 minutes.

2   Meanwhile, place the cucumber in a colander and sprinkle with a large pinch of salt. Let stand for 15 minutes to release excess water. Rinse quickly and pat dry with paper towels or a clean kitchen towel. Transfer the cucumber to a bowl and add the shallot, avocado, dill, lemon juice, coriander, oregano, and 1 tablespoon olive oil. Toss well. Taste and adjust the seasoning with salt and black pepper. Let stand for 15 minutes. Preheat the oven to 350°F.

3   In an ovenproof skillet over medium-high heat, warm the remaining 1 tablespoon oil until it shimmers. Add the salmon fillets, skin side down, and cook until the skin is browned and crisp, 2 to 3 minutes. Using a wide spatula, carefully turn the fillets and cook until browned on the second side, about 1 minute. Place the skillet in the oven and cook until the salmon is barely opaque throughout, about 7 minutes. It will finish cooking in the few minutes between removing from the oven and serving.

4   Transfer the fillets to 2 warmed plates and top each with about ¼ cup of the cucumber salsa. Serve, passing the remaining salsa at the table.

---

2 skin-on salmon fillets (about 5 ounces each)

3½ tablespoons olive oil

Kosher salt

1 teaspoon freshly ground white pepper

2 cucumbers, peeled, seeded, and cut into ½-inch chunks

1 shallot, finely chopped

1 avocado, cut into ¼-inch cubes

¼ cup finely chopped fresh dill

1 tablespoon freshly squeezed lemon juice

½ teaspoon ground coriander

1 teaspoon dried oregano, crumbled

Freshly ground black pepper

EXCELLENT — NO NEED FOR SHRIMP !

BARLEY PAELLA

SERVES 4 TO 6

5 tablespoons olive oil

1 cup pearl barley

2¾ cups water

Kosher salt

2 uncooked sweet Italian sausages (about 6 ounces each), cut in half lengthwise

6 ounces skinless, boneless chicken thighs, cut into 1-inch cubes

6 ounces pork shoulder, trimmed of fat, cut into ¾-inch cubes

Freshly ground pepper

½ cup dry white wine

1 large yellow onion, chopped

8 cloves garlic, finely chopped

One 8-ounce jar pimientos, drained and cut into ⅓-inch-wide strips

One 14.5-ounce can diced tomatoes

1 teaspoon red pepper flakes

¼ teaspoon saffron threads or powder

1 pound large shrimp, peeled, with tails intact, and deveined

This is my adaptation of a recipe developed by my friend Thom Winslow. Paella is a Spanish rice dish that includes a variety of meats and seafood. It is ideal for parties since it can be assembled ahead and baked just before serving. Thom uses barley instead of the traditional rice. Rice converts rapidly to sugar, triggering a Storage Cascade (see page 19) during which the body stores fat instead of burning it for fuel. Barley, because of its high-fiber content, gives a sustained energy release. Look for sausages without fillers such as bread and without sweeteners. A good source is a butcher shop that makes its own sausages.

1   In a large saucepan over medium heat, warm 1 tablespoon of the oil until it shimmers. Add the barley and cook, stirring frequently, until thoroughly coated with the oil and lightly toasted, about 5 minutes. Lower the heat, if needed, to prevent scorching. Add the water and a large pinch of salt and bring to a boil. Reduce the heat to low, cover, and simmer until the barley is tender but still slightly chewy, about 45 minutes. Add more water, ¼ cup at a time, if the barley becomes too dry. Do not drown the barley; all the water should be absorbed just as the barley is done. Drain the barley, if necessary. You should have about 3 cups. Set aside.

2   Preheat the oven to 350°F. In a large skillet over medium heat, warm 1 tablespoon of oil until it shimmers. Place the sausage halves, cut side down, in the pan. Cook until browned on the first side, about 3 minutes. Turn and cook until browned on the second side, about 3 minutes. Remove to a cutting board. When the sausages are cool enough to handle, cut each half crosswise into ¼-inch-thick half moons.

3   Place the same pan over medium-high heat and add the chicken and pork. Cook, stirring frequently, until browned on all sides, about 5 minutes. Season to taste with salt and pepper. Remove to a plate and set aside.

4   Discard all but 1 tablespoon of the fat in the pan. Place over medium heat and add the wine. Stir and scrape any browned bits from the bottom and sides of the pan. Cook until the pan is nearly dry.

? leave some wine

5   Add the remaining 3 tablespoons oil, raise the heat to medium-high, and heat the oil until it shimmers. Add the onion, garlic, and pimientos and cook until the onion is softened, about 5 minutes. Add the tomatoes and their juice, the red pepper flakes, and the saffron. Cook until the flavors are melded, about 5 minutes. Season to taste with salt and pepper.

6   Spread the cooked barley in a large paella pan or ovenproof skillet. Scatter the sausage and chicken and pork mixture evenly over the top. Pour the tomato mixture over the meat. Bake until the paella is hot and bubbling, 20 to 30 minutes. Arrange the shrimp on top and cook just until the shrimp are bright pink and opaque throughout, about 5 minutes. Serve directly from the pan.

GRILLED SHRIMP WITH ROMESCO SAUCE

SERVES 4

1 red bell pepper

¼ cup blanched almonds

¼ cup hazelnuts

4 cloves garlic

2 plum tomatoes (about 4 ounces each), peeled, seeded, and chopped

1 tablespoon red wine vinegar

¼ teaspoon cayenne

¼ cup extra-virgin olive oil

Kosher salt

Freshly ground black pepper

1¼ pounds large (16–20 per pound) shrimp, peeled, with tails intact, and deveined

2 teaspoons pure olive oil, plus more for brushing

2 red onions, quartered lengthwise

Spanish in origin, romesco sauce is a delicious combination of roasted red peppers, fresh tomatoes, and toasted nuts. It complements grilled and roasted seafood, meat, and vegetables and can be prepared well ahead of time. Best of all, perhaps, the nuts and olive oil are high in healthy monounsaturated fats and keep you feeling full longer. Plus, the nuts and shrimp are both good sources of healthy fats, which tend to improve cholesterol levels. Serve the shrimp with steamed green beans. The sauce will make them taste like party fare.

1   Arrange the broiler rack about 5 inches from the heat source and preheat the broiler. Place the bell pepper on the broiler pan and broil, turning as needed, until charred all over, about 10 minutes. Place the roasted pepper in a bowl, cover, and set aside until cool enough to handle.

2   Working over a bowl to catch the juices, pull the blackened skins from the pepper and discard. Pull out the stem and remove the seeds and ribs. Tear the pepper into strips and set aside. Strain any juices into a jar and reserve for use in salad dressings.

3   In a small, dry skillet over medium heat, toast the almonds, stirring constantly, until they just begin to turn light brown, about 3 minutes. Immediately pour them into a small bowl to cool.

4   Return the pan to medium heat, add the hazelnuts, and toast, stirring constantly, until they just begin to turn light brown, about 5 minutes. Immediately enclose them in a clean kitchen towel and rub vigorously to remove the dark brown skins. Do not worry if tiny pieces of skin remain on the nuts. Pour the nuts into a colander and shake to separate the nuts from the flakes of skin.

5   In a food processor, pulse the almonds and hazelnuts. Add the garlic, tomatoes, vinegar, cayenne, and roasted pepper and process to a smooth paste. With the machine running, add the ¼ cup extra-virgin olive oil in a thin stream until completely incorporated. The mixture should be the consistency of a thick, creamy sauce. Add warm water, if needed, to make a sauce the texture of thickened cream. Taste and adjust the seasoning with salt and pepper. Transfer the sauce to a bowl and set aside at room temperature for up to 1 hour, or cover and chill until ready to serve. You should have about 1½ cups. The sauce may be made a day ahead of time.

6   If grilling the shrimp, prepare an outdoor charcoal or gas grill for cooking over medium heat. In a bowl, toss the shrimp with the 2 teaspoons pure olive oil and season lightly with salt and pepper. Brush the onions with oil and season with salt and pepper.

7   When the grill is ready, brush the grill rack with oil. Place the shrimp on the rack directly over the heat and grill the shrimp, without disturbing them, until they begin to turn pink and opaque on the first side, about 2 minutes. Turn and cook until the shrimp are pink and opaque throughout, about 2 minutes. Remove to a plate and keep warm. Grill the onions, turning as needed, until browned on all sides and cooked through, about 5 minutes total. Alternatively, brush a grill pan with oil and place over medium-high heat. When the pan is hot, add the shrimp and cook until they begin to turn pink and opaque on the first side, about 2 minutes. Turn and cook on the second side until opaque throughout, about 2 minutes. Remove to a plate and keep warm. Add the onions to the pan and cook over medium-high heat, turning as needed, until browned on all sides and cooked through, about 5 minutes total.

8   Divide the shrimp and onions among 4 warmed plates. Spoon some of the romesco sauce over each portion and serve.

SEAFOOD CAKES WITH LEMON CRÈME FRAÎCHE

SERVES 4

Most crab cakes are bound together with bread crumbs or cracker crumbs, foods not on the Wine and Food Lover's Diet. As a substitute, I use an egg, and I blend the ingredients in a food processor to make a thick mixture that holds together while the cakes cook. Including shrimp and scallops along with crabmeat gives the cakes a particularly robust flavor accented with a little hot chile.

1 Using your fingers or a small, sharp knife, remove the muscle from the side of each scallop. In a food processor, combine the scallops, shrimp, Parmesan, egg, mustard, and salt and pepper to taste. Process until a smooth paste forms. Using a rubber spatula, scrape the mixture into a bowl. Fold in the jalapeño, the cilantro, and the zest of 1 lemon. Fold in the crabmeat, being careful not to break up the chunks of crab. Cover and refrigerate until ready to cook.

2 In a small bowl, stir together the remaining lemon zest, the lemon juice, and the crème fraîche. Set aside.

3 In a skillet over medium heat, warm the oil until it shimmers. Spoon the seafood mixture, ¼ cup at a time, into the pan, being careful not to be spattered by the hot oil. You should have 8 cakes. Cook until light golden brown on the first side, about 3 minutes. Using a spatula, carefully turn the cakes and cook until golden brown on the second side, about 3 minutes. Remove the cakes to paper towels to drain briefly.

4 Arrange 2 cakes on each plate. Drizzle basil oil around the cakes (if using). Spoon some of the lemon crème fraîche on top of the cakes and serve.

---

2 ounces sea scallops

4 ounces large shrimp, peeled and deveined

½ cup freshly grated Parmesan cheese

1 egg

1 tablespoon Dijon mustard

Kosher salt

Freshly ground white pepper

1 jalapeño chile, seeds removed, finely chopped

2 tablespoons coarsely chopped fresh cilantro

Freshly grated zest of 2 lemons

5 to 6 ounces cooked crabmeat, picked over and shells removed

Juice of 1 lemon

½ cup crème fraîche

2 tablespoons grapeseed oil

About 2 tablespoons basil-flavored olive oil or other flavored olive oil (optional)

CHICKEN BREASTS STUFFED WITH CHEESE AND SPINACH

SERVES 2

2 skinless, boneless chicken breast halves (about 5 ounces each)

Kosher salt

Freshly ground pepper

4 cups stemmed and well-rinsed baby spinach leaves

2½ ounces Boursin cheese

1 tablespoon olive oil

½ cup canned reduced-sodium chicken broth

Instead of enclosing a stuffing in a pasta such as ravioli, I use it as a filling, along with spinach, in chicken breast rolls. Boursin, a triple-cream cheese seasoned with herbs and sometimes garlic, is one of my favorites for this recipe and other stuffings. An equal amount of fresh goat cheese or ricotta combined with garlic, your favorite herbs, and salt and pepper to taste may be substituted. As an alternative stuffing, you could try ¼ cup each finely chopped fresh flat-leaf parsley and basil, and two slices of prosciutto, dividing them between the two breast halves. The chicken is pounded flat so that it can be rolled. This is easy to do and takes just a minute or so.

1	Place each breast half between sheets of plastic wrap. Using a meat mallet or rubber hammer, lightly pound the chicken to a uniform thickness of about ¼ inch. Lightly season on both sides with salt and pepper. Set aside.

2	Place the spinach in a saucepan with just the rinsing water clinging to the leaves. Cover and cook over medium heat until wilted, about 2 minutes. Scatter the spinach on a work surface to cool. Gather the spinach into a ball and squeeze with your hands to remove the excess moisture. Coarsely chop the spinach.

3	Spread half of the cheese over each breast half. Pat half of the spinach over the cheese. Roll the chicken around the filling and secure each roll with 2 wooden toothpicks.

4	In a large skillet over medium heat, warm the oil until it shimmers. Add the chicken rolls and cook, turning as needed, until browned, about 12 minutes. Remove to warmed plates and keep warm. Add the broth to the pan and stir and scrape any browned bits from the bottom and sides of the pan. Cook until the liquid is reduced by half, about 2 minutes. Pour the pan sauce over the chicken and serve.

MEDITERRANEAN SPICED CHICKEN WITH OLIVES AND ALMONDS

SERVES 4

8 skinless, boneless chicken thighs (about 4 ounces each)

Kosher salt

Freshly ground pepper

¼ cup chickpea flour or soy flour

1 tablespoon olive oil

1 yellow onion, coarsely chopped

4 cloves garlic, very finely chopped

2 tablespoons peeled and minced fresh ginger

1½ teaspoons ground coriander

1½ teaspoons ground cumin

1 cup dry white wine

2 cups canned reduced-sodium chicken broth

1 cup blanched almonds

1 cup brine-cured green olives, pitted

This is a terrific, saucy chicken dish full of spice and savor. After only a few minutes of initial cooking, the chicken simmers in a flavorful broth, allowing time for you to prepare an accompanying dish, perhaps the Quinoa Pilaf with Sunflower and Pumpkin Seeds (page 197), to absorb the sauce. The pilaf ingredients are Savvy Carbs that help you stay off the insulin rollercoaster of rapidly rising and falling blood sugar.

1 Lightly season the chicken thighs on both sides with salt and pepper. Place in a bowl, sprinkle with the flour, and toss to coat evenly. Gently shake off any excess flour. In a large skillet over high heat, warm the oil until it shimmers. Add the thighs and cook, turning, until browned on all sides, about 2 minutes per side. Remove to a plate.

2 Reduce the heat to medium-low, add the onion, garlic, and ginger, and cook, stirring frequently, until the onions are soft, about 5 minutes. Stir in the coriander and cumin and cook, stirring, until the mixture is aromatic, about 30 seconds. Pour in the wine, raise the heat to high, bring to a boil, and cook until the wine is reduced by half, about 3 minutes. Add the chicken broth, almonds, and olives.

3 Bring to a simmer, reduce the heat to low, cover, and cook until the thighs are opaque throughout, about 45 minutes. The cooking liquid should be about the thickness of heavy cream. If it is not, remove the chicken to a deep serving platter or to 4 warmed plates and keep warm. Bring the liquid in the pan to a rapid boil and cook, uncovered, until thickened. Taste for seasoning and adjust with salt and pepper. Pour the sauce over the chicken and serve.

CHICKEN WITH CRAB, ASPARAGUS, AND LEMON-CRÈME FRAÎCHE SAUCE

SERVES 2

Yes, sauces made with butter and crème fraîche, like the simple but elegant lemon sauce here, are allowed on the Wine and Food Lover's Diet. The trick is to enjoy the sauce in moderation and serve it with protein and Super-Savvy Carbs only, such as Spinach with Toasted Garlic and Pine Nuts (page 176). It's important not to eat foods containing saturated fat like butter and cream with enablers such as potatoes. Eating saturated fat with Super-Savvy accompaniments, however, encourages the body to burn the fat as energy instead of storing it.

1   To make the sauce: In a small saucepan over low heat, melt the butter. Add the shallot and cook, stirring frequently, until softened, about 2 minutes. Add the lemon juice and cook until reduced by about half, about 1 minute. Whisk in the crème fraîche until smooth. Stir in the chives. Taste for seasoning and adjust with salt and pepper. Keep the sauce warm until ready to serve. The sauce can be reheated over very low heat while stirring constantly with a whisk.

2   Preheat the oven to 200°F. Bring a large pot of salted water to a boil. Snap or cut off the tough ends of each asparagus spear. If the spears have thick skin, use a vegetable peeler to remove the skin below the tips. Drop the asparagus into the boiling water and cook until the spears are bright green and just begin to bend when picked out of the water with tongs, about 3 minutes. Drain, transfer to a plate, and put in the oven to keep warm.

3   Place each breast half between sheets of plastic wrap. Using a meat mallet or rubber hammer, lightly pound the chicken to a uniform thickness of about ¼ inch. Lightly season on both sides with salt and pepper. Place in a bowl, sprinkle with the flour, and turn to coat evenly. Gently shake off any excess flour.

CONTINUED

LEMON-CRÈME FRAÎCHE SAUCE

1 tablespoon unsalted butter

1 tablespoon finely chopped shallot

2 tablespoons freshly squeezed lemon juice

5 tablespoons crème fraîche

1 tablespoon finely chopped fresh chives

Kosher salt

Freshly ground white pepper

10 thin asparagus spears

2 skinless, boneless chicken breast halves (about 5 ounces each)

Kosher salt

Freshly ground pepper

2 tablespoons chickpea flour, soy flour, or nut flour such as almond or hazelnut

1 teaspoon unsalted butter

1 tablespoon olive oil

½ small red onion, chopped

1 small tomato, chopped

3 ounces cooked crabmeat, picked over and shells removed

4 cherry tomatoes, quartered

CHICKEN WITH CRAB, ASPARAGUS, AND LEMON–CRÈME FRAÎCHE SAUCE CONTINUED

4   In a skillet over medium heat, melt the butter with the oil. Add the breast halves and cook until browned on the first side, about 3 minutes. Turn and cook on the second side until browned and opaque throughout, about 3 minutes. Remove to individual plates and keep warm in the oven until ready to serve.

5   Return the skillet to medium heat and add the onion. Cook, stirring frequently, until softened, about 5 minutes. Raise the heat to high, add the tomato, and cook until most of the liquid evaporates, about 2 minutes. Reduce the heat to low and add the crabmeat. Stir gently to avoid breaking up any lumps of crab. Cook just until heated through, about 1 minute.

6   To serve, arrange 5 asparagus spears on top of each chicken breast half and top with the crab mixture. Drizzle with the sauce and garnish the plates with the cherry tomatoes.

PECAN-CRUSTED CHICKEN BREASTS

SERVES 4

Remembering the pecan-crusted catfish I ate while working in Oklahoma one summer inspired me to make this dish. It appealed to my roots in the South, where pecans are grown and used in many dishes. The pecan coating added a crunchy texture and wonderful toasted flavor to the delicate flesh of the fish, as it does to these chicken breasts. Nuts are an excellent source of protein as well as healthy monounsaturated fats, which help improve cholesterol levels. They have another advantage: a little goes a long way to satisfying hunger, because fat is a flavor enhancer and increases feelings of satiety. Serve with Roasted Eggplant, Bell Pepper, and Tomato Salad (page 98).

1   Preheat the oven to 375°F. In a food processor, pulse the pecans until finely ground. Watch carefully so the pecans do not turn into pecan butter. Add the cream, flour, cayenne, cumin, and cinnamon. Alternatively, finely chop the pecans with a knife and mix them in a bowl with the cream, flour, cayenne, cumin, and cinnamon. Season to taste with salt and pepper.

2   Lightly season both sides of the chicken with salt and pepper. Arrange in a small baking dish. Pat a thin layer of the pecan mixture all over the tops of the breasts. Bake until the crust is golden brown and the chicken is opaque throughout but still juicy, about 30 minutes. Arrange on 4 warmed plates and serve.

½ cup pecans

1 tablespoon heavy cream

3 tablespoons chickpea flour, soy flour, or nut flour such as almond or hazelnut

½ teaspoon cayenne pepper

⅛ teaspoon ground cumin

⅛ teaspoon ground cinnamon

Kosher salt

Freshly ground black pepper

4 skinless, boneless chicken breast halves (about 5 ounces each)

GRILLED CHICKEN WITH CLINTON'S HERB-YOGURT SAUCE

SERVES 4 OR 5

HERB-YOGURT SAUCE

1 small cucumber, peeled

Kosher salt

½ teaspoon cumin seeds

1 cup plain yogurt

1 tablespoon finely chopped fresh cilantro

1 tablespoon finely chopped fresh mint

1½ teaspoons finely chopped fresh dill

Freshly ground black pepper

GRILLED CHICKEN

1 chicken (about 4 pounds), cut into 8 pieces (2 drumsticks, 2 thighs, 2 breasts, and 2 wings)

½ yellow onion, finely chopped

2 cloves garlic, very finely chopped

2 tablespoons olive oil, plus oil for brushing

1½ teaspoons celery seeds

1 teaspoon ground cumin (optional)

Kosher salt

Freshly ground white pepper

Freshly ground black pepper

For this Wine and Food Lover's Diet version of barbecued chicken, I marinate the chicken in olive oil and spices and serve it with a chilled cucumber-yogurt sauce made for me by my friend Dr. Clinton Pinto. Marinating the chicken results in a clean, spicy flavor, and the grilling provides an ample dose of smokiness. The yogurt sauce is a good alternative to barbecue sauce, which contains sugar, an enabler, sometimes in several forms, such as molasses, honey, and brown sugar. Salting and draining the cucumber removes excess water so it does not dilute the sauce. The sauce is good with a variety of grilled foods and is a soothing accompaniment to spicy-hot dishes.

1 To make the sauce: Cut the cucumber in half lengthwise and scoop out the seeds with a spoon. Sprinkle the halves lightly with salt and leave them in a colander to drain for 10 to 15 minutes. Rinse quickly under cold running water. Press the halves firmly between a clean kitchen towel. Finely chop the cucumber.

2 In a small, dry skillet over medium heat, toast the cumin seeds until very lightly browned and fragrant, about 1 minute. Immediately pour them onto a plate. Grind the seeds in a spice mill or with a mortar and pestle.

3 In a bowl, stir the yogurt with a fork or whisk. Stir in the cucumber, toasted cumin, cilantro, mint, and dill. Taste for seasoning and adjust with salt and black pepper. Serve immediately, or cover and refrigerate for several hours. Stir well before serving.

4 To make the chicken: Put the chicken pieces in a large bowl and add the onion, garlic, 2 tablespoons oil, celery seeds, and cumin (if using). Toss well. Season with salt, white pepper, and black pepper and toss well. Cover and let stand for 15 to 30 minutes. Refrigerate if setting aside for longer than 30 minutes.

5 Meanwhile, prepare an outdoor charcoal or gas grill for cooking over medium heat. When the grill is ready, brush the grill rack with oil. Place the chicken pieces, skin side down, on the rack directly over the heat, cover the grill, and grill until browned on the first side, about 5 minutes. Turn, re-cover the grill, and cook on the second side until browned, about 5 minutes. Continue to cook the chicken, covered, turning as needed, until an instant-read thermometer inserted into the thickest part of each breast and thigh away from the bone reads 160°F for white meat and 165°F for dark meat, 10 to 20 minutes longer. If the chicken appears to be cooking too rapidly, move the pieces to a cooler part of the grill. As they are done, remove to a platter and keep warm. Serve hot with the cucumber sauce on the side.

DR. PHILLIP'S ROAST CHICKEN WITH TARRAGON SAUCE

SERVES 4

1 chicken (about
4 pounds), quartered

About 2 tablespoons
olive oil

Kosher salt

Freshly ground pepper

2 teaspoons herbes de
Provence (optional)

1 shallot, finely chopped

¾ cup dry white wine

1 tablespoon freshly
squeezed lemon juice

3 tablespoons crème
fraîche or unsalted
butter

2 tablespoons finely
chopped fresh tarragon

When I was actively losing weight, I made this recipe for dinner several times a week and never tired of its taste. And I lost weight quickly. Many diets tell you to stay away from dark meat and to avoid the tasty, crispy browned poultry skin. On the Wine and Food Lover's Diet, you can eat both. The saturated fats in chicken are not as bad for our hearts as previously believed as long as they aren't eaten with enablers. The combination of tarragon and chicken is a classic French pairing. The delicious sauce, made in the pan used to cook the chicken, goes together in minutes and is enriched at the end with a dollop of crème fraîche or butter. For a complete Meal-Planning Trilogy meal, serve with Button Mushrooms with Thyme, Rosemary, and Basil (page 180) and Spinach with Toasted Garlic and Pine Nuts (page 176).

1   Preheat the oven to 375°F. Brush the chicken with the oil and then season lightly with salt and pepper and the herbes de Provence (if using). Arrange the chicken pieces in a single layer in a roasting pan. Roast until an instant-read thermometer inserted into the thickest part of each breast and thigh away from the bone reads 160°F for white meat and 165°F for dark meat, about 50 minutes to 1 hour.

2   Remove the chicken to a warmed serving platter and keep warm while making the sauce. Discard the fat in the roasting pan. Set the pan over low heat on the stove top. Add the shallot and wine. Stir to combine and scrape any browned bits from the bottom and sides of the pan. Cook until reduced by about half, about 5 minutes. Add the lemon juice and stir in the crème fraîche. Simmer until thickened slightly, about 1 minute. Stir in the tarragon.

3   Pass the chicken and sauce at the table, or divide the chicken among 4 warmed plates and top with the sauce.

STUFFED CHICKEN BREASTS WITH CASCADE FALLS SAUCE

SERVES 2

Nearly every evening before dinner, I go on a walk. My walks frequently take me past Cascade Falls, where I came up with the idea for this dish. The bacon-and-herb stuffing gives the chicken a mouthwatering smoky savor. The pan sauce—a quick reduction of vermouth—adds an extra taste fillip. It's fine to have bacon on the Wine and Food Lover's Diet. While I don't advise eating several slices with your breakfast eggs, I do like to use a modest amount of nitrite-free bacon as a flavoring. The intensity of very smoky bacon goes a long way, so you don't need much. I frequently cook chicken, as well as turkey, that has been pounded to a thickness of about ¼ inch. The cooking time of a flattened breast is half that of a regular breast. Plus, I can roll the flattened breasts around stuffings, an easy way to make an impressive presentation.

2 skinless, boneless chicken breast halves (about 5 ounces each)

Kosher salt

Freshly ground pepper

2 slices nitrite-free bacon, cut crosswise into ¼-inch pieces

¼ cup finely chopped fresh basil or flat-leaf parsley

3 tablespoons plus 2 teaspoons finely chopped fresh flat-leaf parsley

2 tablespoons olive oil

1 clove garlic, very finely chopped

1 shallot, chopped

¼ cup dry vermouth

2 tablespoons crème fraîche (optional)

1   Preheat the oven to 200°F. Place each breast half between sheets of plastic wrap. Using a meat mallet or rubber hammer, lightly pound the chicken to a uniform thickness of about ¼ inch. Lightly season both sides with salt and pepper.

2   In a skillet over medium heat, cook the bacon, stirring occasionally, until very lightly browned but not completely cooked and crisp, about 5 minutes. Remove to paper towels to drain. In a bowl, mix together the bacon, basil, 3 tablespoons parsley, 1 tablespoon of the oil, and garlic. Spoon the mixture onto the chicken breasts, dividing evenly. Roll the chicken around the filling and secure each roll with 2 wooden toothpicks.

3   In a large skillet over medium heat, warm the remaining 1 tablespoon oil until it shimmers. Add the chicken rolls and cook, turning as needed, until each side is browned and an instant-read thermometer inserted into the thickest part of each roll reads 160°F, about 12 minutes. Remove to a plate and keep warm in the oven while you make the sauce.

4   Add the shallot to the same skillet over medium heat and cook until softened, about 2 minutes. Add the vermouth, bring to a boil, and cook until reduced to about 2 tablespoons, about 1 minute. Stir in the crème fraîche (if using). Season to taste with salt and pepper.

5   To serve, cut the chicken rolls crosswise into thick slices and arrange on 2 warmed plates. Drizzle each serving with the sauce and sprinkle with the remaining 2 teaspoons parsley.

SPICED CHICKEN BURGERS

SERVES 4

1 pound ground chicken

1 yellow onion, finely chopped

3 cloves garlic, very finely chopped

2 tablespoons fresh cilantro, chopped

1 tablespoon peeled and grated fresh ginger

1 teaspoon curry powder, preferably East Indian

1 extra-large egg

Kosher salt

Freshly ground pepper

Olive oil for brushing

1 avocado, pitted, peeled, and sliced

1 small red onion, thinly sliced

The idea for these burgers with an Indian accent is from my friend Dr. Clinton Pinto, a New Zealand transplant whose family originally came from India. These flavorful chicken burgers stay juicy on the grill. I add an egg, which keeps them moist and acts as a binding agent. Flour or bread crumbs are often used as a binding agent but tend to cause a rapid rise in blood sugar, which initiates a Storage Cascade (see page 19). By avoiding these enablers, we experience a sustained energy release and prevent rapid changes in blood sugar. So hold the bun and, instead, serve the burgers with Clinton's Herb-Yogurt Sauce (page 134), steamed green beans, and Quinoa-Chile Skillet Bread (page 199).

1   In a large bowl, knead together the chicken, yellow onion, garlic, cilantro, ginger, curry powder, egg, and salt and pepper to taste. Form the mixture into 4 equal patties and place between sheets of waxed paper. The mixture will be sticky but becomes very moist when grilled. Refrigerate for at least 1 hour before grilling.

2   Prepare an outdoor charcoal or gas grill for cooking over medium-hot heat. When the grill is ready, brush the grill rack with oil. Place the burgers on the rack directly over the heat, cover the grill, and grill until browned on the first side, 3 to 5 minutes. Turn the burgers, re-cover the grill, and grill on the second side until cooked through but still juicy, 3 to 5 minutes. Check the burgers to make sure they are not cooking too rapidly. If they are, move them to a cooler part of the grill. Serve with the sliced avocado and red onion.

GRILLED CHICKEN THIGHS WITH ROASTED RED PEPPER AND TOMATO SAUCE

SERVES 4

Argentineans and Brazilians have a special way of preparing grilled meats. This is my interpretation of the seasonings used in the grilled poultry I had at a South American restaurant. I use both coriander and cayenne. The former has a complex, highly aromatic flavor that partners well with chicken. Grilling brings out the sweetness of this spice which balances the heat of the cayenne. The deep red sauce enhances the spices rubbed on the chicken and is also terrific with pork, lamb, and even steamed green beans. Serve the chicken with Roasted Broccoli with Pecorino and Pecans (page 167) or Sweet Pea Shoots with Garlic (page 172).

1 Prepare an outdoor charcoal or gas grill for cooking over medium heat. In a small bowl, mix together the coriander, ½ teaspoon salt, and cayenne. Rub the spice mixture all over the chicken thighs. Cover and let stand for 30 minutes. Refrigerate if setting aside for longer than 30 minutes.

2 When the grill is ready, brush the grill rack with oil. Brush the peppers all over with oil and place on the rack directly over the heat. Roast, turning as needed, until charred all over, about 10 minutes. Place the peppers in a bowl, cover, and set aside until cool enough to handle. Working over a bowl to catch the juices, pull the blackened skins from each pepper and discard. Pull out the stems and remove the seeds and ribs. Set the peppers and juices aside separately.

3 Place the chicken thighs on the rack directly over the heat, cover the grill, and grill until browned, about 5 minutes. Turn the chicken, re-cover the grill, and grill on the second side until browned, about 5 minutes. Check the thighs to make sure they are not cooking too rapidly. If they are, move them to a cooler part of the grill. Continue to cook the thighs, turning as needed and re-covering the grill, until an instant-read thermometer inserted into the thickest part of each thigh away from the bone reads 165°F, about 15 minutes longer.

4 While the chicken is cooking, make the sauce: Place the roasted peppers, tomatoes, onion, garlic, cilantro, pinch of salt, and pinch of pepper into a blender or food processor. Process until smooth. Pour into a saucepan over low heat and heat just until hot. Taste and adjust the seasoning with salt and pepper. Thin, if necessary, with the reserved roasted pepper juices.

5 To serve, divide the sauce among 4 warmed plates and arrange the chicken thighs on top. Garnish each plate with the avocado slices and dollops of crème fraîche.

1 teaspoon ground coriander

½ teaspoon kosher salt, plus a pinch

¼ teaspoon cayenne pepper

8 skinless, bone-in chicken thighs (about 5 ounces each)

4 red bell peppers

Olive oil for brushing

2 tomatoes, coarsely chopped

1 small red onion, coarsely chopped

1 clove garlic, coarsely chopped

¼ cup coarsely chopped fresh cilantro

Freshly ground pepper

1 avocado, pitted, peeled, and sliced

¼ cup crème fraîche or sour cream

CHICKEN PAILLARDS AND CAESAR SALAD

SERVES 4

CAESAR DRESSING

1 egg (see head note)

2 oil-packed anchovy fillets

1 tablespoon plus 1½ teaspoons Dijon mustard

1 clove garlic, very finely chopped

1½ teaspoons freshly squeezed lemon juice

1 teaspoon red wine vinegar

¾ teaspoon Worcestershire sauce

¼ teaspoon Tabasco sauce

1 tablespoon plus 1½ teaspoons freshly grated Parmesan cheese

1 cup olive oil, preferably extra-virgin

Kosher salt

Freshly ground pepper

1 large head romaine lettuce, trimmed, rinsed, thoroughly dried, and chopped or torn into bite-sized pieces

Kosher salt

4 skinless, boneless chicken breast halves (about 5 ounces each)

Freshly ground pepper

1 tablespoon finely chopped fresh thyme

1 to 2 tablespoons olive oil

Freshly grated Parmesan cheese

This recipe offers a great way to enjoy a delicious meal combining lean protein, healthy fats, and Super-Savvy Carbs. The Caesar dressing comes from Douglas Katz, chef at Fire restaurant in Cleveland, Ohio. Most dieters would avoid Caesar salad, but fat consumed without enablers such as white flour, corn, and potatoes does not cause you to gain weight. In the right company—protein and Savvy or Super-Savvy Carbs—fat is burned for current energy needs. The anchovies in the dressing, as well as contributing their wonderful pungent flavor, are a source of omega-3 fatty acids, polyunsaturated oils that help improve cholesterol levels and enhance brain function. "Paillard" is a fancy word for a thin slice of meat created by pounding a thicker piece. Originally it referred to veal, but is now used to describe any type of meat. I often microwave the egg for the Caesar dressing in a small cup for 15 seconds on high so it is not completely raw. An alternative is to use a pasteurized egg product available in supermarkets.

1   To make the dressing: Put the egg, anchovy fillets, mustard, garlic, lemon juice, vinegar, Worcestershire sauce, Tabasco, and Parmesan in a blender or food processor. Process until well blended. With the machine running, add the oil drop by drop until an emulsion forms. Slowly add the remaining oil in a thin, steady stream. Taste for seasoning and adjust with salt and pepper. Add a splash of water to thin the dressing, if needed.

2   Place the lettuce in a large bowl and sprinkle lightly with salt. Toss well with tongs. Add some of the dressing and toss well. Add more dressing, tossing well after each addition, until the leaves are lightly coated. Refrigerate until ready to serve.

3   Place each breast half between sheets of plastic wrap. Using a meat mallet or rubber hammer, lightly pound the chicken to a uniform thickness of about ¼ inch. Lightly season both sides with salt and pepper and the thyme.

4   In a large skillet over medium-high heat, warm 1 tablespoon oil until it shimmers. Add the chicken and cook, turning once, until opaque throughout, about 3 minutes per side. Add more oil if needed. Remove the paillards to a platter as they are cooked and keep warm.

5   Divide the paillards among 4 individual plates and top with the salad. Sprinkle each serving with Parmesan and serve.

CHICKEN GUMBO

SERVES 6 TO 8

3 tablespoons olive oil

1¼ cups pearl barley

3½ cups water

Kosher salt

4 skinless, bone-in chicken thighs (about 5 ounces each)

2 skinless, bone-in chicken drumsticks (about 4 ounces each)

2 skinless, boneless chicken breast halves (about 5 ounces each), cut into bite-sized pieces

1 large yellow onion, chopped

2 stalks celery, chopped

1 large green bell pepper, seeds and ribs removed, chopped

1 teaspoon freshly ground black pepper

1 tomato, peeled, seeded, and chopped

5 cloves garlic, very finely chopped

1 tablespoon hot paprika

1 pound fresh or frozen okra, cut into ½-inch pieces

½ pound fully cooked andouille sausage, cut into ¼-inch-thick slices

8 cups canned reduced-sodium chicken broth

½ teaspoon hot sauce such as Tabasco or Crystal, plus more for serving

4 bay leaves

1 teaspoon finely chopped fresh oregano

1 teaspoon finely chopped fresh thyme

1 tablespoon filé powder

1 teaspoon cayenne pepper (optional)

¼ cup finely chopped fresh flat-leaf parsley

Recipes for gumbo usually begin with a roux, a mixture of equal amounts of flour and fat, used to thicken the gumbo and give it a rich flavor. In this flourless version, the okra and the filé powder (ground sassafras leaves) act as thickeners. Filé, an essential ingredient in Louisiana Creole cooking, adds a grassy, almost tealike flavor that is easiest to imagine by thinking of root beer, also derived from sassafras. The gumbo has an abundance of protein plus Super-Savvy Carbs including okra, onions, celery, tomato, and bell pepper. And I've used the Savvy Carb barley instead of the traditional rice. Andouille, another essential ingredient of southern Louisiana cookery, is a richly smoked, spicy pork sausage seasoned with garlic, black pepper, and cayenne.

1   In a large saucepan over medium heat, warm 1 tablespoon of the oil until it shimmers. Add the barley and cook, stirring frequently, until thoroughly coated with the oil and lightly toasted, about 5 minutes. Add the water and a large pinch of salt and bring to a boil. Reduce the heat to low, cover, and simmer until the barley is tender but still slightly chewy, about 45 minutes. Add more water, ¼ cup at a time, if the barley becomes too dry. Do not drown the barley; all the water should be absorbed just as the barley is done. Drain the barley, if necessary, and keep warm while making the gumbo.

2   In a large Dutch oven over medium-high heat, warm the remaining 2 tablespoons oil until it shimmers. Add the chicken and cook, stirring occasionally, until lightly browned, about 5 minutes. Add the onion, celery, and bell pepper and cook, stirring occasionally, until softened, about 5 minutes. Season to taste with salt and add the black pepper. Add the tomato, garlic, and paprika and cook, stirring constantly, until the tomato has begun to break down, about 2 minutes. Add the okra and cook, stirring frequently, until the vegetables are soft, about 5 minutes.

3   Add the sausage and stir in the broth, the ½ teaspoon hot sauce, the bay leaves, the oregano, and the thyme. Bring to a boil, reduce the heat to low, and simmer, occasionally skimming any foam from the top, until the chicken is cooked through and the flavors have melded, about 20 minutes. Raise the heat to medium high, bring to a rapid simmer, and cook until the gumbo is slightly thickened, about 5 minutes. Add the filé powder and continue to simmer rapidly until the gumbo is thickened and aromatic, about 5 minutes. Stir in the cayenne (if using). Taste for seasoning and adjust with salt and pepper.

4   Ladle the gumbo into warmed bowls and splash each with hot sauce. Top with the barley, sprinkle with the parsley, and serve.

PUMPKIN-SEED TURKEY TENDERLOINS

SERVES 4

1½ pounds skinless, boneless turkey breast tenderloins, cut into 4 equal portions

Kosher salt

Freshly ground pepper

⅓ cup chickpea flour, soy flour, or nut flour such as almond or hazelnut

2 eggs

½ cup pumpkin seeds, coarsely ground

3 tablespoons grapeseed or peanut oil

1 lemon, cut into wedges

Pumpkin seeds and pumpkin seed oil are specialties of Graz, Austria, where I travel for an annual medical conference. There, cooks make a pumpkin seed version of schnitzel, which I have adapted to the Wine and Food Lover's Diet style of eating. Instead of the traditional veal, I've substituted turkey breast, which is lean, and given it a crunchy coating of pumpkin seeds. A quick turn in a hot skillet toasts the coating and retains all the natural juiciness of the meat.

1   Place each piece of turkey between sheets of plastic wrap. Using a meat mallet or rubber hammer, lightly pound the turkey to a uniform thickness of about ¼ inch. Lightly season both sides with salt and pepper.

2   In pie pan or shallow baking dish, mix together the chickpea flour, ½ teaspoon salt, and ¼ teaspoon pepper. In a second pie pan or dish, beat the eggs lightly. In a third pie pan or dish, place the ground pumpkin seeds.

3   Dip each piece of turkey into the flour mixture, coating it thoroughly and gently shaking off any excess flour. Next dip the turkey into the egg, covering it completely. Finally, turn the turkey in the pumpkin seeds until evenly coated. As each piece is coated, set it aside on a large plate or baking sheet.

4   In large skillet over medium heat, warm the oil until it is hot. Add the turkey and cook until browned on the first side, about 3 minutes. Turn and cook on the second side until browned and opaque throughout, about 3 minutes. Remove to paper towels to drain. Divide the turkey among warmed plates. Accompany each serving with a lemon wedge.

DOUBLE-CUT PORK CHOPS WITH GREEN PEPPERCORNS

SERVES 4

Green peppercorns, the unripe version of black peppercorns, make a crunchy coating for meat, poultry, and flavorful fish such as salmon. They are less pungent that the fully ripe peppercorns, so they add some heat but not too much. You might wonder why pork plays such a prominent role in the Wine and Food Lover's Diet recipes. Pork is now bred to be very lean. I do not trim it obsessively since I believe that the fat adds both flavor and moisture to the meat. I am fussy, however, about the quality of the pork I buy, choosing organically or naturally raised animals fed a good diet and allowed plenty of space to roam. Such animals take longer to reach marketable weight, but the rewards are meat with real savor and a low level of saturated fat. Serve the chops with Saffron-Braised Leeks (page 177) and Barley Risotto with Garlic and Almonds (page 194).

¼ cup dried green peppercorns

4 center-cut boneless loin pork chops (about 5 ounces each)

Kosher salt

Freshly ground pepper

1 tablespoon unsalted butter

2 tablespoons olive oil

1 shallot, finely chopped

¼ cup dry vermouth

1 cup canned reduced-sodium chicken broth

1 tablespoon Dijon mustard

1　Enclose the peppercorns in a clean kitchen towel. Crush them with the flat side of a meat mallet or a rubber hammer. Shake the crushed peppercorns into a bowl.

2　Preheat the oven to 400°F. Lightly season the chops on both sides with salt and pepper. Firmly press the crushed peppercorns onto both sides of the chops. Place on a plate and set aside for 5 to 10 minutes.

3　In a large ovenproof skillet over medium-high heat, melt the butter with the oil and heat until shimmering. Add the chops and cook until browned, about 5 minutes per side. Place in the oven and cook until an instant-read thermometer inserted into the thickest part of the chops away from the bone reads 145°F for medium, about 10 minutes. Remove the chops to a warmed platter and let rest while you prepare the sauce.

4　Discard the fat from the pan. Place the pan over medium heat, add the shallot, and cook until softened, about 2 minutes. Add the vermouth and cook until reduced to about 2 tablespoons, about 1 minute. Add the broth, bring to a boil over medium-high heat, and cook until reduced to about ½ cup, about 7 minutes. Whisk in the mustard. Pour the sauce through a sieve into a small bowl.

5　To serve, spoon a little of the sauce onto 4 warmed plates. Top with the chops and drizzle with the remaining sauce.

GRILLED PORK CHOPS WITH MERLOT-SHALLOT SAUCE

SERVES 4

Four 1½-inch-thick, bone-in rib pork chops (about 8 ounces each)

1 tablespoon olive oil, plus more for brushing

Kosher salt

Freshly ground pepper

1 shallot, finely chopped

1 cup Merlot or other full-bodied red wine

3 cups canned reduced-sodium beef broth

1 tablespoon crème fraîche or unsalted butter (optional)

The lean, flavorful pork produced today is quick and easy to cook and can be complemented by many different herbs and quick sauces, such as the one here. Grilling underscores the delicate succulence of the meat. The sauce offers deep, rich, complex flavors, yet is easy to make and can be prepared ahead of time. Accompany the chops with a Savvy Carb such as Barley Risotto with Tomatoes and Lemon (page 193) or Quinoa Pilaf with Sunflower and Pumpkin Seeds (page 197) and a Super-Savvy Carb such as the Collard Greens with Garlic (page 182).

1   Prepare an outdoor charcoal or gas grill for cooking over medium heat. Place the pork chops on a plate and brush both sides with oil. Lightly season both sides with salt and pepper.

2   In a saucepan over medium heat, warm the 1 tablespoon oil. Add the shallot and cook, stirring frequently, until softened, about 2 minutes. Add the wine, raise the heat to high, bring to a boil, and cook until reduced to about ¼ cup, about 5 minutes. Add the broth, bring to a boil, and cook until reduced to about 1 cup, about 10 minutes. Taste for seasoning and adjust with salt and pepper. Keep warm over low heat while grilling the chops.

3   Brush the grill rack with oil. Place the chops on the rack directly over the heat, cover the grill, and grill until browned on the first side, about 6 minutes. Check the chops after a few minutes to make sure they are not cooking too rapidly. If they are, move them to a cooler part of the grill. Turn the chops, re-cover the grill, and cook until browned on the second side and an instant-read thermometer inserted in the center of a chop away from the bone reads 145°F for medium, about 3 minutes. The chops will continue to cook as they rest a few minutes while your prepare the plates.

4   To serve, swirl the crème fraîche (if using) into the sauce. Ladle a little sauce onto each warmed plate and arrange a chop on top. Drizzle with a little more sauce.

PORK CUTLETS WITH LEMON SAUCE AND HAZELNUTS

SERVES 2

One of the best things about the Wine and Food Lover's Diet is that you do not have to be afraid of food. I firmly believe, from personal experience, that if a dieter feels deprived, a diet regimen is not going to last. The primary goal of the Wine and Food Lover's Diet is to attain and then to maintain a healthy weight while eating a wide variety of delicious foods, exemplified by the flavors in this recipe. Slices of pork loin are pounded until they are thin, then coated with a little chickpea flour, which adds crunch and protects the delicate meat while it cooks. The lemon in the accompanying pan sauce sets off the richness of the pork. The finished dish is garnished with toasted hazelnuts and Parmesan.

1 In a small, dry skillet over medium heat, toast the hazelnuts, stirring constantly, until they just begin to turn light brown, about 5 minutes. Immediately enclose them in a clean kitchen towel and rub vigorously to remove the dark brown skins. Do not worry if tiny pieces of skin remain on the nuts. Pour the nuts into a colander and shake to separate the nuts from the skins. Coarsely chop the nuts and set aside.

2 In a small saucepan over high heat, bring the broth to a boil and cook until reduced by about half, about 7 minutes. Set aside.

3 Place each slice of pork between sheets of plastic wrap. Using a meat mallet or rubber hammer, lightly pound the pork to a uniform thickness of about ⅓ inch. Lightly season both sides with salt and pepper. Place on a large plate, sprinkle with the flour, and turn to coat evenly. Gently shake off any excess flour.

4 In a large skillet over medium heat, warm the oil until it shimmers. Add the sage leaves and cook, stirring constantly, until crispy, about 30 seconds. Using a slotted spoon, remove to a paper towel to drain.

5 Add the pork and cook until lightly browned on the first side, about 1 minute. Turn and cook on the second side until the pork is browned, firm, and cooked through, about 2 minutes. Remove the cutlets to a warmed platter and keep warm.

6 Place the same skillet over medium-high heat and add the lemon juice. Stir and scrape any browned bits from the bottom and sides of the pan. Add the reserved broth, bring to a boil, and cook until the flavors have melded. Taste for seasoning and adjust with salt and pepper.

7 Pour the sauce over the cutlets. Sprinkle with the nuts and Parmesan, scatter the fried sage leaves around the platter, and serve.

¼ cup hazelnuts

1 cup canned reduced-sodium chicken broth

1 boneless pork loin (about 1 pound), cut crosswise into 2 uniform slices

Kosher salt

Freshly ground pepper

½ cup chickpea flour, soy flour, or nut flour such as almond or hazelnut

2 tablespoons olive oil

4 fresh sage leaves

Juice of ½ lemon

¼ cup freshly grated Parmesan cheese

ROAST PORK WITH A WALNUT CRUST

SERVES 6

Here a crust of toasted walnuts and sesame seeds flavored with herbes de Provence and mustard seasons a pork loin as it roasts and adds a crunchy texture. When accompanied with Super-Savvy Carbs such as Roasted Eggplant, Bell Pepper, and Tomato Salad (page 98) and Roasted Asparagus with Pecorino Romano and Hazlenuts (page 170), the meal will be burned for immediate energy instead of stored for later use as fat.

1   In a small, dry skillet over medium heat, toast the walnuts, stirring constantly, until they just begin to turn light brown, about 3 minutes. Immediately pour them into a small bowl to cool. In the same pan over medium heat, toast the sesame seeds, stirring constantly, until they just begin to turn light brown, 1 to 2 minutes. Pour into the bowl with the walnuts to cool.

2   Preheat the oven to 350°F. Place a rack in a roasting pan just large enough to hold the pork. Trim any fat from the pork. Season all over with salt and pepper and spread evenly with the mustard. In a food processor, combine the walnuts, sesame seeds, herbes de Provence, and shallot. Pulse until finely chopped. Pat the walnut mixture evenly over the pork.

3   Place the pork on the rack in the pan. Roast until the crust is lightly browned and an instant-read thermometer inserted into the center of the pork reads 145°F for medium, 1 to 1½ hours. Remove the pork to a carving board and let rest for 5 to 10 minutes. During this resting time, the meat will continue to cook a little. Carve and serve on warmed plates.

½ cup walnuts

¼ cup sesame seeds

1 boneless, center-cut pork loin roast (about 3 pounds)

Kosher salt

Freshly ground pepper

2 to 3 tablespoons Dijon mustard

1 teaspoon herbes de Provence

1 shallot, coarsely chopped

PORK CHOPS WITH GREEK HERBS AND CABBAGE

SERVES 4

Four 1½-inch-thick, bone-in, rib pork chops (about 8 ounces each)

1 tablespoon olive oil, plus more for brushing

Kosher salt

Freshly ground pepper

½ teaspoon dried mint

½ teaspoon dried oregano

1 teaspoon dried parsley

Grated zest of 1 lemon

1 head green cabbage (about 1½ pounds), cored and finely shredded

1 tablespoon finely chopped fresh oregano

½ cup dry white wine

2 tablespoons crème fraîche

Pork roasted with oregano, mint, and lemon is a common mouthwatering combination in Greece, where the meat might be cooked in an outdoor oven fueled with olive wood. Using herb blends is a great way to add variety to your cooking. Changing only the seasonings in a recipe can transform it into a new dish—a strategy that will inspire you to continue on a diet and reap the rewards. I've combined the pork with cabbage, an often overlooked Super-Savvy Carb that deserves more attention. When briefly cooked, it has a subtle flavor that enhances the sweetness of pork. Crumbling the herbs with your fingers as you add them to food helps release their distinctive flavor and aroma.

1   Preheat the oven to 350°F. Place a rack in a roasting pan just large enough to hold the chops in a single layer. Brush the chops all over with oil and lightly season both sides with salt and pepper. In a small bowl, mix the dried mint, oregano, and parsley and the lemon zest with your fingers. Rub the mixture all over the chops. Place the chops on the rack in the pan.

2   Roast until an instant-read thermometer inserted into the thickest part of the chops away from the bone reads 145°F for medium, about 30 minutes. Remove to a warmed platter and let rest while you cook the cabbage.

3   Discard the fat from the roasting pan and add the 1 tablespoon oil. Place the pan over medium heat and add the cabbage and fresh oregano. Stir and toss until the cabbage begins to wilt, about 1 minute. Add the wine and stir to combine and scrape any browned bits from the bottom and sides of the pan. Cook the cabbage just until crisp-tender, about 3 minutes. Stir in the crème fraîche and season to taste with salt and pepper.

4   Divide the cabbage among 4 warmed plates, top with the pork chops, and serve.

SPICY GRILLED BABY BACK RIBS

SERVES 4

When I pass a barbecue house, the aroma of slow-roasting meat sets off a nearly overwhelming desire for a plate of ribs. Luckily, ribs fit the Wine and Food Lover's Diet if you forgo the sweet barbecue sauce. While I generally recommend eating lean cuts of meat for general good health, occasionally you need to forget the rules. Normally, I will order smoked, dry-rubbed ribs and ask the proprietor to hold the sauce. The flavor of the rub here is so robust that you won't miss the sugar-laden barbecue sauce. In the South, where I grew up, onion and garlic powders are often used in dry rubs. They give a particular flavor that I like very much. Team the ribs with Super-Savvy Carbs, for example, Napa Cabbage Slaw with Pumpkin Seeds (page 183) and a platter of sliced garden tomatoes.

1   Preheat the oven to 300°F. Place a rack in a roasting pan just large enough to hold the ribs in a single layer. In a small bowl, stir together the onion powder, garlic powder, oregano, black pepper, cayenne, celery seeds, and salt to taste. Place the ribs on a cutting board, bone side up. Insert a small sharp knife under the shiny membrane that covers the bones. Pry the membrane up and off the bones. Since it can be slippery, grasp it with a kitchen towel or paper towels. Removing the membrane allows the flavors to penetrate the ribs and makes them easier to separate later, but don't worry if removing it proves too difficult.

2   Rub the spice mixture over both sides of the ribs and place them on the rack in the pan. Pour the beer (if using) or water into the pan to reach a depth of ½ inch. Tightly cover the pan with aluminum foil. Bake until the ribs are tender, about 1¾ hours.

3   Meanwhile, prepare an outdoor charcoal or gas grill for cooking over medium-hot heat. When the grill is ready, brush the rack with oil. Arrange the ribs on the rack directly over the heat and grill until crusty and brown, 3 to 5 minutes per side. Cut into 1- or 2-rib pieces and serve.

---

1 tablespoon onion powder, or 1 yellow onion, finely chopped

2 teaspoons garlic powder, or 8 cloves garlic, very finely chopped

2 tablespoons finely chopped fresh oregano

2 tablespoons freshly ground black pepper

1 tablespoon cayenne pepper

1 teaspoon celery seeds

Kosher salt

2 slabs baby back ribs (1½ to 2 pounds each)

Two 12-ounce bottles premium dark beer, or as needed (optional)

Olive oil for brushing

BEEF TENDERLOIN WITH RED WINE AND SHALLOT SAUCE

SERVES 4

A roasted beef tenderloin always arrives at table to a chorus of anticipatory *oohs* and *aahs*. Yet, it is one of the easiest cuts of meat to prepare. For a naturally lean and tender result, buy the very best beef. I try to find grass-fed beef. Beef finished in feedlots on a grain diet put on weight quickly, most of it saturated fat. Grass-fed cattle are leaner, and their fat composition is, I believe, friendlier to heart health, having a higher percentage of omega-3 fatty acids. Ask the butcher to prepare the tenderloin for roasting by removing the fat, chain muscle, and silver skin, and tying the tenderloin every 2 inches so it retains its shape while cooking. I drape the meat with strips of nitrite-free bacon. During roasting, the bacon bastes the meat and keeps it moist.

1 Preheat the oven to 350°F. Place a rack in a roasting pan just large enough to hold the tenderloin. Lightly season both sides of the tenderloin with salt and pepper. In a large skillet over medium-high heat, warm the oil until it shimmers. Add the tenderloin and cook on all sides until browned, about 10 minutes total. Remove to a platter and let rest until cool enough to handle.

2 Rub the meat all over with the garlic and place it on the rack in the pan. Lay the bacon slices crosswise over the top. Roast until an instant-read thermometer inserted into the thickest part of the meat reads 125°F for rare, 45 to 60 minutes. Start checking for doneness earlier rather than later, to avoid overcooking the meat. Transfer the tenderloin to a carving board, tent with aluminum foil, and let rest while you make the sauce.

3 Discard all but 1 tablespoon fat from the roasting pan. Place the pan over medium heat on the stove top, add the shallot and thyme, and cook, stirring constantly, until the shallot has softened, about 2 minutes. Add the wine and beef broth, raise the heat to high, and bring to a boil while stirring and scraping up the browned bits on the bottom and sides of the pan. Cook until the sauce is reduced to ½ to ¾ cup, about 5 minutes.

4 Discard the bacon from the meat and carve into ½-inch-thick slices. Pour any accumulated juices into the sauce. Add the butter (if using) and swirl the pan to melt it into the sauce. Pour a little of the sauce on the bottom of a warmed platter and arrange the slices on top. Top with the rest of the sauce and serve.

---

1 beef tenderloin (about 2 pounds)

Kosher salt

Freshly ground pepper

1 tablespoon olive oil

3 cloves garlic, very finely chopped

2 slices nitrite-free bacon

1 shallot, finely chopped

1 tablespoon finely chopped fresh thyme

½ cup full-bodied red wine such as Merlot

½ cup canned reduced-sodium beef broth

2 tablespoons unsalted butter (optional)

HERBED LAMB CHOPS WITH CUCUMBER, TOMATO, AND MINT SALSA

SERVES 4

CUCUMBER, TOMATO, AND MINT SALSA

1 large cucumber, peeled

Kosher salt

3 tablespoons hazelnuts

Grated zest of 1 small lime

1 teaspoon freshly squeezed lime juice

8 cherry tomatoes, chopped

1 small tomatillo, husk removed, chopped

3 tablespoons finely chopped fresh cilantro

3 tablespoons finely chopped fresh mint

Freshly ground pepper

2 tablespoons crème fraîche

LAMB CHOPS

8 bone-in, single-rib lamb loin chops (about 1½ pounds total), well trimmed of fat

Kosher salt

Freshly ground pepper

½ cup each finely chopped fresh mint and flat-leaf parsley

2 tablespoons finely chopped fresh rosemary

Olive oil for brushing

Grilling brings out the best in lamb, making it deliciously succulent. Here, I give the chops a coating of fresh herbs and team them with an unusual fresh and crunchy salsa that includes toasted hazelnuts and crème fraîche. Lamb is fairly lean when trimmed, though I recommend pairing the chops with Super-Savvy Carbs such as the salsa to prevent any fat in the meat from turning directly into fat on your body. The salsa pairs well with fish such as sole, chicken, and asparagus as well as grilled lamb.

1 To make the salsa: Cut the cucumber in half lengthwise and scoop out the seeds with a spoon. Sprinkle the halves lightly with salt and leave them in a colander to release excess water for 10 to 15 minutes. Rinse briefly under cold running water. Press the halves firmly between paper towels or with a kitchen towel. Cut the cucumber into ¼-inch dice. Set aside.

2 In a small, dry skillet over medium heat, toast the nuts, stirring constantly, until they just begin to turn light brown, about 5 minutes. Immediately enclose them in a clean kitchen towel and rub vigorously to remove the dark brown skins. Do not worry if tiny pieces of skin remain on the nuts. Pour the nuts into a colander and shake to separate the nuts from the flakes of skin. Coarsely chop the nuts and set aside.

3 In a bowl, combine the cucumber, lime zest and juice, tomatoes, tomatillo, cilantro, and mint and mix well. Taste for seasoning and adjust with salt and pepper. Fold in the crème fraîche. Cover and refrigerate until ready to serve. Just before serving, add the reserved nuts and mix well.

4 To make the chops: Prepare an outdoor charcoal or gas grill for cooking over medium-high heat. Arrange the lamb chops on a cutting board and lightly season both sides with salt and pepper. In a small bowl, mix together the mint, parsley, and rosemary. Pat the herb mixture evenly over both sides of the chops.

5 When the grill is ready, brush the grill rack with oil. Arrange the chops on the rack directly over the heat, cover the grill, and grill, carefully turning the chops once to avoid disturbing the herb coating, until an instant-read thermometer inserted into the thickest part of the chops away from the bone reads 120°F for medium-rare, about 2 minutes per side. Check the chops occasionally to make sure they are not cooking too rapidly. If they are, move them to a cooler part of the grill. Remove the chops to a platter as they are cooked. Spoon the salsa over the chops and serve, or pass the salsa at the table.

SEARED TOFU POCKETS WITH TAHINI-LEMON SAUCE

SERVES 2

10 fresh basil leaves

2 tablespoons sesame seeds, preferably a mixture of black and white

2 green onions, white and light green parts, thinly sliced on the diagonal

2 tablespoons chopped fresh chives

1 tablespoon chopped fresh flat-leaf parsley

1 teaspoon grated lemon zest (about ½ lemon)

½ teaspoon red pepper flakes

8 ounces firm tofu, drained

⅓ cup tahini

½ cup water, or more as needed

1 tablespoon plus 1 teaspoon freshly squeezed lemon juice

2 cloves garlic, very finely chopped

Kosher salt

Freshly ground black pepper

Cayenne pepper (optional)

1 tablespoon olive oil

Tofu soaks up the flavors of the ingredients cooked with it and is a great cholesterol-free source of protein. Here, triangles of tofu are stuffed with an herb and sesame seed mixture and are served with a sauce that also contains sesame seeds—in ground form as tahini. More than three-fourths of the fat content of sesame seeds is mono- and polyunsaturated. The seeds are also good sources of calcium, magnesium, and other important minerals. Serve the tofu with a Super-Savvy Carb such as Ratatouille with Chile (page 185). The tahini sauce would also taste great with fish or chicken.

1   Stack half the basil leaves on top of one another and roll into a tight cylinder. Cut the rolled leaves crosswise to make thin strips. Repeat with the remaining leaves. Set aside.

2   In a small skillet over medium heat, toast the sesame seeds, stirring constantly, just until light brown, 1 to 2 minutes. Immediately pour them into a bowl to cool. Add the green onions, chives, parsley, lemon zest, red pepper flakes, and reserved basil. Mix well and set aside.

3   Rinse the tofu under cold running water and drain again. Cut the tofu in half horizontally, then cut each piece in half again vertically to make 4 equal rectangles. Cut each rectangle on the diagonal to form 2 triangles. You will have a total of 8 triangles. Starting at the apex, insert a thin sharp knife halfway through the thickness and slice a pocket into each triangle, making sure not to cut through the long side. Place the tofu on paper towels to drain. Very carefully stuff the pockets with the sesame-seed mixture, dividing it evenly. Set aside.

4   Place the tahini, ½ cup water, lemon juice, and garlic in a blender. Process on high until a creamy sauce forms, adding more water if the sauce is too thick. Taste for seasoning and adjust with salt, black pepper, and cayenne (if using). Pour the sauce into a small pan and warm over low heat.

5   In a large skillet over medium-high heat, warm the oil until it shimmers. Add the tofu and cook until golden, about 2 minutes. Using a spatula, carefully turn and cook on the second side until golden, about 2 minutes.

6   Divide the tofu pockets among warmed plates, pour the sauce over and around them, and serve.

SPICY TOFU WITH TOMATO SAUCE

SERVES 2

This dish takes inspiration from Italy and its wealth of simple tomato sauces, but uses tofu instead of pasta. Tofu does not need to be cooked, but I like to sauté it to firm the tofu further and give it a slight caramelized flavor. I prefer plain firm tofu, but you can substitute any one of a variety of marinated tofu products. Make sure to read the label carefully and choose tofu free of fillers and sugar. This is a substantial dish combining a protein and a Super-Savvy Carb tomato sauce. To make a complete Meal-Planning Trilogy meal, serve with Mushrooms Stuffed with Parmesan Cheese and Almonds (page 169) or Roasted Asparagus with Pecorino Romano and Hazelnuts (page 170).

10 ounces firm tofu, cut into 1-inch cubes

½ teaspoon kosher salt

½ teaspoon cayenne pepper

2 to 3 tablespoons olive oil

½ yellow onion, thinly sliced

3 tomatoes, chopped (about 1 cup)

½ cup dry white wine

2 cloves garlic, finely chopped

1 teaspoon finely chopped fresh oregano

10 fresh basil leaves

2 tablespoons finely chopped fresh flat-leaf parsley

1   In a bowl, gently toss the tofu, salt, and cayenne. In a large skillet over medium-high heat, warm 2 tablespoons of the oil until it shimmers. Add the tofu and cook until lightly browned all over, about 5 minutes. Using a slotted spoon, remove the tofu to a bowl and set aside.

2   Place the same pan over medium heat and add the remaining 1 tablespoon oil if the pan seems dry. Add the onion and cook, stirring frequently, until softened, about 5 minutes. Add the tomatoes, wine, garlic, and oregano. Bring to a boil and cook, stirring occasionally, until the sauce thickens slightly, about 5 minutes.

3   While the sauce is cooking, prepare the basil: Stack half of the basil leaves on top of one another and roll into a tight cylinder. Cut the rolled leaves crosswise to make thin strips. Repeat with the remaining leaves. Set aside.

4   Add the tofu to the tomato sauce and toss to coat well. Reduce the heat to low and simmer gently until heated through, about 1 minute. Stir in the basil and parsley, divide among warmed plates, and serve.

EGGPLANT ROLLS STUFFED WITH THREE CHEESES

SERVES 4

Eggplant, a Super-Savvy Carb, has a robust taste and texture that even meat lovers find satisfying. When grilled, as here, eggplant takes on an irresistible caramelized sweetness. Maybe this is because eggplant is botanically a fruit and is closely related to tomatoes, another fruit used as a vegetable. The grilled eggplant slices are rolled around a combination of three cheeses seasoned with herbs and studded with pine nuts. Each cheese contributes a distinctive flavor. Together, they increase the protein value of the dish. Canned tomatoes qualify as a Super-Savvy Carb. Look for tomatoes without sugar. I usually buy tomatoes without added salt, as I prefer to season while I cook. In place of the ricotta or Brie, I often use a favorite cheese, Teleme, a luscious, soft-ripening cheese similar to Brie, made in Point Reyes, California. Brie makes a creamy filling while ricotta gives a lighter result. Serve the rolls with Roasted Broccoli with Pecorino and Pecans (page 167) or Leeks and Pattypan Squash with Tarragon and Crème Fraîche (page 163).

1 To make the tomato sauce: In a large saucepan over medium heat, warm the oil until it shimmers. Add the shallot and garlic and cook, stirring frequently, until softened, about 2 minutes. Add the bay leaf and celery and season to taste with salt and pepper. Cook until the vegetables are very soft, about 5 minutes. Add the tomatoes, bring to a boil, cover, reduce the heat to low, and simmer until the flavors meld, about 20 minutes. Uncover and simmer, stirring frequently to prevent scorching, until the sauce is thick, about 10 minutes. Remove and discard the bay leaf. Taste for seasoning and adjust with salt and pepper.

2 While the tomato sauce is cooking, prepare the eggplant. Trim the eggplant and cut lengthwise into ½-inch-thick slices. Discard the slices that are mostly skin. You will need 2 slices per serving. Place the slices in a single layer on a baking sheet. Sprinkle with salt and let stand for 15 minutes to remove any bitterness. Briefly rinse the slices under cold running water. Dry by pressing the slices firmly between paper towels.

3 Place a grill pan over medium heat. Brush both sides of the eggplant slices with olive oil. Working in batches, cook the slices, turning once, until lightly browned and cooked through, about 12 minutes total. Let cool.

CONTINUED

TOMATO SAUCE

2 tablespoons olive oil

1 large shallot, finely chopped

4 cloves garlic, very finely chopped

1 bay leaf

One 3-inch piece celery, finely chopped

Kosher salt

Freshly ground pepper

One 28-ounce can chopped or diced tomatoes

1 large globe eggplant (at least 1 pound)

Kosher salt

Olive oil for brushing

6 fresh basil leaves

1 egg, lightly beaten

½ cup ricotta or softened Brie cheese

½ cup freshly grated Parmesan cheese

¼ cup Boursin or fresh goat cheese

2 tablespoons pine nuts

Freshly ground pepper

1 tablespoon finely chopped fresh oregano

4   Preheat the oven to 350°F. Stack the basil leaves on top of one another and roll into a tight cylinder. Cut the rolled leaves crosswise to make thin strips. In a large bowl, using a large fork, mix together the egg and ricotta. Add half of the Parmesan, the Boursin, and the pine nuts and stir gently to combine. Fold in the basil. Season with pepper.

5   Lightly oil an 8- or 9-inch square baking dish. Spoon a thin layer of tomato sauce over the bottom of the dish. Place about 2 tablespoons of the cheese mixture on each eggplant slice and spread evenly to within about ½ inch of each end. Beginning at a narrow end, tightly roll the slice around the cheese mixture. Place, seam side down, in the prepared dish. Evenly spoon the remaining tomato sauce over the rolls. Sprinkle with the remaining Parmesan and the oregano. Bake until bubbling, about 20 minutes. Serve hot.

SWISS CHARD WITH BACON

SERVES 4 TO 6

Chard has become one of my favorite vegetables. Cooked on its own or with chopped onion, it tastes great, but when you add bacon, as I have here, the chard becomes an indulgence. The earthiness and slight bitterness of these dark, leafy greens have a special affinity for the deep smoky sweetness of bacon. The bacon is cooked crisp, then drained, and most of the fat is discarded, leaving just enough to flavor the chard. You can use the colorful rainbow chard found increasingly on the market. In a single bunch you will have stalks with red stems, others with yellow stems, and still others with white stems. I cook the stems as well as the leaves because they provide both texture and bright color. You can substitute any leafy green vegetable, such as kale, spinach, collards, or mustard greens. Adjust the cooking time to the toughness of the leaves, cooking tender leaves less and tougher greens, such as kale, longer.

2 bunches Swiss chard (about 2½ pounds total)

3 slices nitrite-free bacon, cut crosswise into ¼-inch pieces

1½ tablespoons olive oil

1 small yellow onion, coarsely chopped

½ cup canned reduced-sodium chicken broth

Kosher salt

Freshly ground pepper

1   Remove the stems from the chard and chop into small pieces. Stack several leaves on top of one another and roll into a cylinder. Cut the rolled leaves crosswise to make strips about ⅓ inch wide. Repeat with the remaining leaves. Set aside.

2   In a large Dutch oven over medium heat, cook the bacon, stirring occasionally, until browned and crisp, about 7 minutes. Remove to paper towels to drain. Discard the fat in the pan and place the pan over medium-high heat. Add the oil, onion, and chard stems and cook until the onions begin to soften, about 2 minutes. Add the chard, 1 large handful at a time, stirring and tossing after each addition, then adding another handful as the first wilts.

3   Add the stock and the bacon and bring to a boil over high heat. Reduce the heat to low and simmer just until the chard is cooked through but still bright green, about 2 minutes. Season to taste with salt and pepper and serve.

LEEKS AND PATTYPAN SQUASH WITH TARRAGON AND CRÈME FRAÎCHE

SERVES 4

The plump, sunny-yellow, ruffled disks that are pattypan squash are at their peak of delicate sweetness in the summer. Tarragon, one of my favorite herbs and a classic of French cooking, is also at its best in the summer. Its distinctive anise flavor sets off the sweet earthiness of cooked leeks and of the squash as well. Take care in your use of tarragon. Particularly when it is fresh, a little goes a long way. This is an easy, all-purpose way to cook vegetables that you can adapt to whatever is in season, especially yellow or green zucchini. The little bit of crème fraîche adds a touch of luxury to this otherwise simple dish.

2 large leeks (about 1½ pounds total), white and light green parts only

1½ tablespoons olive oil

1 tablespoon dry white wine or canned reduced-sodium chicken broth

10 baby pattypan squash (about 1 pound total), cut into ½-inch pieces

1 teaspoon finely chopped fresh tarragon

½ teaspoon kosher salt

½ teaspoon freshly ground pepper

2 tablespoons crème fraîche or sour cream

1   Lay the leeks on a cutting board. Starting just above the root end, insert a sharp knife all the way through each leek. Then pull the knife along the length of the leek, cutting it in half while keeping it attached at the root end. Rotate the leek 90 degrees and repeat. Slice the leeks crosswise into 1-inch lengths, discarding the root ends. Put the leeks in a colander and rinse thoroughly. Drain well.

2   In a large skillet over medium heat, warm the oil until it shimmers. Add the leeks and cook, stirring constantly, just until they begin to soften, 1 to 2 minutes. Add the wine, reduce the heat to low, cover, and cook gently until the leeks are very soft, about 6 minutes.

3   Add the squash, raise the heat to medium, and cook until the squash just begins to soften, about 4 minutes. Add the tarragon, salt, pepper, and crème fraîche. Stir and toss until well mixed and hot, about 2 minutes. Taste for seasoning and adjust if necessary. Put the vegetables in a warmed serving bowl and serve.

CAULIFLOWER WITH SMOKED MOZZARELLA

SERVES 4

1 head cauliflower (1½ to 2 pounds), cut into florets

1 clove garlic

2 teaspoons crème fraîche

1 teaspoon unsalted butter

4 ounces smoked mozzarella or smoked Gouda, shredded

Kosher salt

Freshly ground pepper

I enjoy cauliflower on its own, but I also like it puréed, as it reminds me of eating potatoes. For this reason, I make this recipe to serve with Beef Tenderloin with Red Wine and Shallot Sauce (page 153). In my experience, people who otherwise avoid cauliflower are fond of this dish because the cheese gives the vegetable an irresistible smokiness. And, like potatoes, a cauliflower purée can be varied according to your whim and the contents of your refrigerator. For instance, you can make an especially suave purée by mixing in 2 tablespoons unsalted butter and 1 tablespoon sour cream or crème fraîche. Or you might add several slices of bacon, cooked crisp and crumbled, or 2 tablespoons minced fresh chives and/or fresh parsley.

1   Put the cauliflower florets and garlic in a saucepan and add just enough water to cover. Bring to a boil over high heat, reduce the heat to low, and simmer, uncovered, until cauliflower is just tender, about 5 minutes. Drain well.

2   Transfer the cauliflower and garlic to a food processor and add the crème fraîche, butter, cheese, and salt and pepper to taste. Pulse in short bursts just to blend the ingredients and produce a fine-grained texture. Do not overprocess; cauliflower easily liquefies, and you want to retain some texture. Taste and adjust the seasoning with salt and pepper, if necessary.

3   Place the cauliflower purée in a warmed serving dish and serve.

BROCCOLINI WITH PESTO

SERVES 4

Restrictive diet programs often call for eating plain steamed vegetables, perhaps drizzled with a squeeze or two of lemon juice. Simply cooked vegetables are fine, but I insist on enhancing them with seasonings that burst with flavor, such as the classic Italian herb sauce here. The more satisfying and appealing Super-Savvy Carbs are, the more you will enjoy them and the less you will miss bread, pasta, potatoes, and rice. Broccolini, a newly developed, dark green vegetable, is a cross between broccoli and Chinese kale. It looks like a slimmed-down version of broccoli and has a similar flavor, a balance of slightly sweet and bitter. The long slender stems blossom with small flowering buds. Broccolini is edible from bud to stem and needs just a little trimming, and the stems do not need to be peeled.

PESTO

2 cloves garlic, coarsely chopped

1 cup packed fresh basil leaves

1 tablespoon coarsely chopped fresh flat-leaf parsley

3 tablespoons extra-virgin olive oil

¼ cup freshly grated Parmesan cheese

Freshly ground pepper

2 bunches broccolini (about 1 pound total)

2 tablespoons freshly grated Parmesan cheese

1   To make the pesto: Place the garlic, basil, and parsley in a food processor and process until very well chopped. Scrape down the sides of the work bowl and add the oil. Process again until well mixed and smooth, scraping down the sides as needed. Add the ¼ cup Parmesan and pulse to incorporate. Taste for seasoning and adjust with pepper.

2   Remove damaged or discolored leaves from the broccolini. Cut off any tough ends from the stalks. Bring a large pot of salted water to a boil and prepare a bowl of ice water. Add the broccolini and cook until it is just bright green and crisp-tender, about 2 minutes. Drain the broccolini and plunge into the ice water to stop the cooking. Drain well.

3   Heat a skillet over medium heat. Add the broccolini and pesto and stir well to combine. Cook, stirring and tossing, until the broccolini is well coated and hot, about 3 minutes. Transfer to a serving dish, sprinkle with the 2 tablespoons Parmesan, and serve.

FENNEL WITH SHALLOTS AND WHITE WINE

SERVES 4

2 large fennel bulbs

2 tablespoons olive oil

1 shallot, finely chopped

1 clove garlic, chopped

½ cup dry white wine

1½ teaspoons freshly squeezed lemon juice

Kosher salt

Freshly ground pepper

When I go out to a new restaurant, I tend to judge its quality by the variety of vegetable dishes. Serving different vegetables with each main course is a challenge. To meet that challenge, I shop every other day, buying what is freshest at my local market. The preparation must be quick and straightforward since I arrive home from work late in the day, and the results must be tasty. This fennel dish meets all of these qualifications. It has a light, sweet licorice flavor that I especially enjoy with fish. This same cooking method can be applied to leeks, using aromatic seasonings and a combination of wine and citrus.

1   Cut off the stems and leaves from each fennel bulb and, if desired, reserve for another use. If the outer layer of the bulb is tough, remove it. Cut the bulb in half lengthwise and remove the core if it is tough. Cut each half lengthwise into 2 or 3 wedges.

2   In a skillet over medium heat, warm the oil until it shimmers. Add the shallot and garlic and cook, stirring constantly, until softened, about 2 minutes. Add the fennel and toss well to combine with the shallot and garlic. Pour in the wine and lemon juice and season lightly with salt and pepper. Cover, reduce the heat to low, and cook until the fennel is tender when pierced with a thin, sharp knife, about 15 minutes.

3   Uncover and cook until the liquid has reduced slightly and the fennel is beginning to caramelize and brown around the edges, about 5 minutes. Taste for seasoning, adjust with salt and pepper, and serve hot.

ROASTED BROCCOLI WITH PECORINO AND PECANS

SERVES 4

Everyone knows that broccoli is good for you. But that is not reason enough to eat it. It has to taste delicious. Roasting brings out the sweetness in broccoli. The vegetable also has an earthiness that goes particularly well with the nutty character of pecorino cheese. Adding nuts contributes another layer of toasty flavor, along with a crunchy texture and a small boost of protein and healthy fat. Any one of several types of pecorino, a sheep's milk cheese, would be good in this dish: pecorino sardo, a moist, fresh cheese; pecorino romano, which is somewhat firm; pecorino pepato, which contains black peppercorns; or pecorino toscano, which is an aged variety with a nutty flavor.

1   Preheat the oven to 400°F. Separate the florets from the broccoli stems, making sure to keep the florets fairly large so they will not overcook. Peel the tough skin from the stems. Cut the stems into pieces about 1½ inches long and ½ inch wide.

2   In a shallow baking dish, toss the broccoli florets and stems with salt and pepper to taste and the shallot, thyme, and pecans. Drizzle with the oil and toss well again. Roast, stirring once or twice, until the broccoli is crisp-tender and the nuts are fragrant, about 15 minutes. Spoon into a warmed serving bowl, sprinkle with the cheese, and serve.

---

1 bunch broccoli (about 1 pound)

Kosher salt

Freshly ground pepper

1 shallot, finely chopped

1 tablespoon finely chopped fresh thyme

¼ cup pecans, broken into fairly large pieces

2 tablespoons olive oil

¼ cup coarsely grated pecorino cheese

MUSHROOMS STUFFED WITH PARMESAN CHEESE AND ALMONDS

SERVES 4

Mushrooms are a wonderful, all-you-can-eat Super-Savvy Carb packed with nutrients. They are one of my favorite foods, especially when roasted or grilled, which adds caramelized flavors. The high fiber content of mushrooms makes them filling and gives them a big rich taste. In this recipe, I stuff them with a filling of onion, another Super-Savvy Carb, and nuts. Parmesan cheese adds protein and an intense nutty flavor. The mushrooms are easy to make in abundance to serve as a party appetizer.

⅓ cup almonds, finely chopped

1½ teaspoons olive oil, plus more for brushing

¼ cup chopped yellow onion

1 egg

½ cup freshly grated Parmesan cheese

1 tablespoon Dijon mustard

½ teaspoon freshly grated nutmeg

Kosher salt

Freshly ground pepper

8 large button or cremini mushrooms (about ½ pound total), stems removed

1   Preheat the oven to 350°F. Lightly oil a baking sheet. In a small, dry skillet over medium heat, toast the almonds, stirring constantly, until they just begin to turn light brown, about 3 minutes. Immediately pour them into a small bowl to cool. Chop the almonds finely and set aside.

2   In a skillet over medium-high heat, warm the 1½ teaspoons oil until it shimmers. Add the onion and cook, stirring constantly, until softened and slightly brown around the edges, about 5 minutes. Remove to a bowl. Stir in the almonds, egg, Parmesan, mustard, and nutmeg until well combined. Season to taste with salt and pepper.

3   Brush the mushroom caps all over with oil. Spoon the cheese mixture into the caps, dividing evenly. Arrange the stuffed mushrooms, filling side up, on the prepared sheet. Bake until the filling is lightly browned and the mushrooms are tender, about 20 minutes. Serve warm.

ROASTED ASPARAGUS WITH PECORINO ROMANO AND HAZELNUTS

SERVES 4

¼ cup hazelnuts

1 bunch asparagus
(about 1 pound)

2 tablespoons olive oil

Kosher salt

Freshly ground pepper

½ cup freshly grated
pecorino romano cheese

This dish tastes sweet, salty, toasty, and earthy all at once. I'll take my asparagus thick or thin and steamed, blanched, grilled, or roasted, but I admit a preference for roasting and grilling, which boost the sweetness of the long, elegant spears. Asparagus pairs very well with many nuts, but its flavor is particularly enhanced by the richness of toasted hazelnuts. The pungent, sharp, salty flavor of the pecorino, sheep's milk cheese, creates a vibrant contrast with the nuts and asparagus.

1   In a small, dry skillet over medium heat, toast the hazelnuts, stirring constantly, until they just begin to turn light brown, about 5 minutes. Immediately enclose the nuts in a clean kitchen towel and rub vigorously to remove the dark brown skins. Do not worry if tiny pieces of skin remain on the nuts. Pour the nuts into a colander and shake to separate the nuts from the skins. Coarsely chop the nuts and set aside.

2   Preheat the oven to 400°F. Snap or cut off the tough ends of each asparagus spear. If the spears have thick skin, use a vegetable peeler to remove the skin below the tips. Put the spears in a baking dish, drizzle with the olive oil, and turn to coat. Season to taste with salt and pepper and spread the spears in an even layer. Roast the spears, turning once or twice, until crisp-tender, 15 to 20 minutes. Transfer to a warmed platter and sprinkle with the cheese. Scatter the hazelnuts over the top and serve.

SPAGHETTI SQUASH WITH SUMMER-RIPE TOMATO SAUCE

SERVES 4

Spaghetti squash is wonderful with all the sauces you would normally eat with pasta. This sauce is cooked so briefly that the tomatoes still have their fresh flavor. Therefore, you'll want to make the sauce using the season's best garden-ripe tomatoes. I prefer not to peel tomatoes, as most of the beneficial antioxidants are in the skin.

1 Preheat the oven to 375°F. Pierce the skin of the squash in several places with a knife and put it in a baking dish. Bake until very soft, about 1 hour. (Alternatively, cook in a microwave: Halve the squash, scoop out and discard the seeds, and pierce in several places. Place the halves, cut side down, in a dish. Pour in ¼ cup water. Cover with plastic wrap and cook on high for 10 minutes.)

2 Meanwhile, in a saucepan over medium heat, warm the oil until it shimmers. Add the garlic and shallot and cook until softened, about 2 minutes. Add the tomatoes, half of the basil, and salt and pepper to taste. Bring to a boil, reduce the heat to low, and simmer just until the tomatoes are softened, about 3 minutes.

3 Use a pot holder to grasp the squash and halve, if still whole. Scoop out the seeds. Then, with a long-handled fork, tease out the strands of the squash into a warmed serving bowl. Fluff and separate the strands with the fork. Add the remaining basil and the tomato sauce. Toss very well. Taste for seasoning and adjust with salt and pepper. Top with the Parmesan and serve.

1 spaghetti squash (about 3 pounds)

2 tablespoons olive oil

5 cloves garlic, very finely chopped

2 shallots, finely chopped

5 or 6 tomatoes (about 2 pounds total), seeded, finely chopped, and well drained

¼ cup chopped fresh basil

Kosher salt

Freshly ground pepper

¼ cup freshly grated Parmesan cheese

SWEET PEA SHOOTS WITH GARLIC

SERVES 4

1 tablespoon plus 1½ teaspoons olive oil

5 to 7 cloves garlic, very finely chopped

½ pound pea shoots or sunflower sprouts

½ teaspoon freshly ground white pepper

Kosher salt

After my children and I discovered this quick, garlicky sauté of fresh sweet pea shoots in a local Asian restaurant, they wanted me to cook it for them nearly every night. The pea shoots are the growing tips of sweet pea vines. Originally the shoots were harvested as a by-product of cultivating sweet peas and showed up on menus for a very brief season. But they are so delicious—bright green and full of snap and sweetness—that demand grew, and soon farmers began growing the pea shoots as a vegetable crop. Sunflower sprouts, another Super-Savvy Carb, are large sprouts with a fleshy, crisp stem and two broad, rounded green leaves. They have a slightly spicy taste.

In a large skillet over medium heat, warm the oil until it shimmers. Add the garlic and cook, stirring constantly, until it softens, about 1 minute. Add the pea shoots and mix well with the garlic. Raise the heat to medium-high and stir and toss constantly until the shoots soften but are still slightly crunchy, 2 to 3 minutes. Add the pepper and season to taste with salt. Remove to a warmed serving bowl and serve.

BRUSSELS SPROUTS WITH PANCETTA

SERVES 4

¾ pound brussels sprouts

2 slices pancetta or nitrite-free bacon, cut crosswise into ¼-inch pieces

1 small yellow onion, finely chopped

1 tablespoon finely chopped fresh thyme

Kosher salt

Freshly ground pepper

⅛ teaspoon freshly grated nutmeg

The presence of young brussels sprouts in the market announces that fall has arrived. If you don't like sprouts, you have probably eaten only overcooked specimens with their unappealing strong taste and aroma. You'll be surprised when you prepare this dish, a knockout combination of sprouts, pancetta, nutmeg, and thyme. Separating the individual leaves of the sprouts hastens the cooking time. The color brightens and the fresh flavor is retained. Brussels sprouts and other members of the cabbage family have a natural affinity for pork, especially cured pork such as pancetta, an Italian unsmoked bacon. It comes in a long, fat roll and is usually sold in thin slices. You unroll the slices and cut them into small pieces to flavor meat and vegetables. Serve this Super-Savvy Carb with Grilled Pork Chops with Merlot-Shallot Sauce (page 146), Beef Tenderloin with Red Wine and Shallot Sauce (page 153), or Dr. Phillip's Roast Chicken with Tarragon Sauce (page 136).

1   Bring a saucepan of salted water to a boil and prepare a large bowl of ice water. Halve and core the brussels sprouts. Add the sprouts to the boiling water and cook until the color brightens and the sprouts are just beginning to soften, about 3 minutes. Drain the sprouts and plunge into the ice water to stop the cooking. Drain well. Separate as many of the large, outer leaves from each sprout as will come off easily. Leave the smaller, inner leaves attached to each other.

2   In a large skillet over medium heat, cook the pancetta until soft but not yet crisp, about 2 minutes. Add the onion and cook, stirring constantly, until softened, about 5 minutes. Add the thyme, brussels sprouts and leaves, and salt and pepper to taste. Stir and toss until heated through, about 1 minute. Add the nutmeg and toss well. Remove to a warmed serving dish and serve.

SPINACH WITH TOASTED GARLIC AND PINE NUTS

SERVES 2

2 tablespoons pine nuts

1 tablespoon olive oil

3 cloves garlic, thinly sliced

5 cups stemmed and well-rinsed baby spinach leaves

Kosher salt

Freshly ground pepper

Early on, when I was developing the Wine and Food Lover's Diet, I ate spinach cooked different ways nearly every day. I still never tire of eating it. Prepared simply as here, the spinach takes on a velvety texture because it cooks so quickly that it hardly does more than wilt. Toasted garlic has, to me, a nearly addictive caramelized flavor. It is cooked first and reserved, then added to the spinach at the last second so the garlic retains its texture and intense flavor. Pine nuts are usually avoided by dieters because of their high fat content, but most of it is heart-healthy mono- and polyunsaturated fat. Plus, they have the highest protein content of any nut, 7 grams in a 1-ounce portion. In this dish, it's their flavor—at once sweet and rich and delicately nutty—that stands out.

1   In a small, dry skillet over medium heat, toast the pine nuts, stirring constantly, until they just begin to turn light brown, about 1 minute. Immediately pour them into a small bowl to cool. Set aside.

2   In a large skillet over medium heat, warm the oil until it shimmers. Add the garlic and cook, stirring frequently, until it softens and just begins to color, about 1½ minutes. Be careful that it does not burn. Using a slotted spoon, remove the garlic to a small dish and reserve.

3   Add the spinach to the hot pan and cook, stirring, until it is wilted and cooked through, about 2 minutes. Add the toasted garlic and season to taste with salt and pepper. Toss well. Transfer to a warmed serving bowl, scatter the nuts over the top, and serve.

SAFFRON-BRAISED LEEKS

SERVES 4

My brother, Claude Tirman, inspired this Super-Savvy Carb dish. He braised some leeks in a little butter and vermouth. I was taken with the slightly sweet, earthy character of the leeks. I like to add saffron, which imparts a yellow-orange color and a distinctive aromatic flavor. I first discovered saffron when I was in medical school in Arkansas. I used to eat at a vegetarian restaurant run by a native of India who served saffron milk each day. The saffron gave the milk a richness and reminded me of the before-bed warmed milk my mother sometimes made. You can cook whole heads of endive this same way with delicious results. Serve the leeks with Seared Halibut with Lemon-Butter Sauce (page 115) or Flounder with Lemon Zest and Capers (page 117).

8 small leeks (about 1 pound), white parts only

1 tablespoon unsalted butter

Pinch of saffron threads

1 tablespoon dry vermouth

1 tablespoon finely chopped fresh flat-leaf parsley

1   Lay the leeks on a cutting board. Starting about ½ inch above the root end, insert a sharp knife all the way through each leek. Then pull the knife along the length of the leek, cutting it in half while keeping it attached at the root end. Rinse the leeks carefully between the layers and drain.

2   In a skillet over medium heat, melt the butter. Add the leeks and roll them around in the butter until coated. Crumble the saffron between your fingers and add to the pan. Add the vermouth, stir briefly, cover, reduce the heat to low, and simmer until the leeks are very tender, 5 to 7 minutes. Stir in the parsley, transfer the leeks to warmed serving dish, and serve.

GREEN BEANS WITH CHILE-LIME MAYONNAISE

SERVES 6

CHILE-LIME MAYONNAISE

1 extra-large egg

2 tablespoons plus
1 teaspoon freshly
squeezed lime juice

1 teaspoon Dijon
mustard

⅔ cup pure olive oil

2 tablespoons extra-
virgin olive oil

Kosher salt

Freshly ground pepper

1 red jalapeño or serrano
chile, seeds removed,
finely chopped

3 tablespoons finely
chopped fresh cilantro

1½ pounds green beans

Steaming green beans retains their nutrients and is the best way to maintain their color and cook them to just the right degree of crispness. You can use any green bean, including Blue Lake beans, romano beans, and the small, thin French beans called haricots verts. This tangy-spicy mayonnaise gives the beans the luxurious appeal of a party dish. You can also serve the mayonnaise with steamed asparagus or broccoli, or with hard-boiled eggs. I often microwave the egg in a small cup for 15 seconds on high so it is not completely raw. An alternative is to use a pasteurized egg product available in supermarkets.

1   To make the mayonnaise: Put the egg, lime juice, and mustard in a food processor or blender. Process until smooth. With the machine running, add the pure olive oil drop by drop until an emulsion forms. Slowly add the remaining oil in a thin, steady stream and then add the extra-virgin olive oil. Taste for seasoning and adjust with salt and pepper. Scrape the mayonnaise into a bowl and fold in the chile and cilantro. You should have about 1 cup mayonnaise. The mayonnaise can be stored for up to 5 days in an airtight plastic container in the refrigerator.

2   Fit a steaming basket into a large saucepan and pour water into the pan to reach a depth of 1 inch. Bring the water to a boil, place the green beans in the basket, cover, and cook until crisp-tender, about 8 minutes. Remove to a colander and rinse with cold running water to stop the cooking. Drain the beans well and transfer to a serving bowl. Toss the warm beans with the mayonnaise until well mixed and serve while still warm. To make ahead, let the beans cool to room temperature or refrigerate them, and serve on a platter with the mayonnaise dolloped on top.

ROASTED VEGETABLES WITH ARUGULA PESTO

SERVES 4

Roasting gives all sorts of vegetables, including the Super-Savvy Carbs here, a hearty, satisfying flavor. They taste wonderful hot, at room temperature, or cold. For this reason, you can make this dish regularly and have the vegetables on hand in the refrigerator for quick salads and snacks. I've given traditional basil pesto a twist by using arugula with its assertive bite. The robust flavor partners well with the rich taste of the vegetables. Herb purées like pesto coat the vegetables easily and well so the seasonings are evenly distributed.

1   Preheat the oven to 400°F.

2   To make the pesto: Put the arugula, garlic, and oregano in a food processor. Process until well blended. With the machine running, add the oil drop by drop until an emulsion forms. Slowly add the remaining oil in a thin, steady stream. Taste for seasoning and adjust with salt and pepper. You should have about 1 cup pesto.

3   Put the broccoli, bell pepper, eggplant, onion, mushrooms, and garlic in a large bowl. Drizzle three-fourths of the pesto over the vegetables and toss to coat evenly. Evenly spread the vegetables on a baking sheet. Roast, tossing occasionally, until cooked through, 15 to 20 minutes. Transfer to a warmed serving bowl and toss with the remaining pesto. Dust lightly with the Parmesan (if using) and serve.

ARUGULA PESTO

2 packed cups well-rinsed baby arugula leaves

1 clove garlic, smashed

1 tablespoon finely chopped fresh oregano

½ cup extra-virgin olive oil

Kosher salt

Freshly ground pepper

1 cup broccoli florets

1 red bell pepper, cut lengthwise into quarters, seeds and ribs removed

1 Japanese eggplant, cut crosswise into ⅓-inch-thick slices

1 yellow onion, quartered

12 button mushrooms (about ¾ pound total), halved

6 cloves garlic

2 tablespoons freshly grated Parmesan cheese (optional)

✓ good

BUTTON MUSHROOMS WITH THYME, ROSEMARY, AND BASIL

SERVES 2

- 2 tablespoons unsalted butter or olive oil
- 15 large button mushrooms (about 1 pound total), halved
- 1 shallot, finely chopped
- 1 teaspoon finely chopped fresh thyme
- ½ teaspoon finely chopped fresh rosemary
- 1 tablespoon finely chopped fresh basil or oregano
- ¼ cup canned reduced-sodium chicken broth
- Kosher salt
- Freshly ground pepper

This is such an appetizing dish, you may not believe it is as easy to cook as it is. The trio of herbs I've used, all essential to French and Mediterranean cooking, add layers of flavor to the mushrooms. Although the combination is quite light, the mushrooms are filling and very satisfying. They make a versatile accompaniment, suitable for fish, chicken, or meat.

1   In a large skillet over medium-high heat, melt the butter. Add the mushrooms, cut side down. Do not crowd the pan. Cook the mushrooms, undisturbed, until browned, 1 to 2 minutes. Add the shallot, thyme, and rosemary and cook until the shallot softens, about 2 minutes.

2   Sprinkle the basil over the mushrooms and add the chicken broth. Quickly stir and toss the mushrooms and season lightly with salt and pepper. Reduce the heat to low, cover, and simmer until the mushrooms are tender, about 5 minutes. Transfer to a warmed serving dish and serve.

KALE TWO WAYS

SERVES 4

Everyone needs a few tried-and-true cooking methods for leafy greens. I've written these two recipes for kale, a nutritional powerhouse, because it deserves greater popularity in the kitchen and at the table. The first recipe, a simple sauté, flavors the vegetable with garlic and lemon. Serve this with dishes that have a sauce. The second braises the kale briefly in broth, which gives a richer, smoother flavor. I cook kale this way to serve with chicken, fish, or meat without a sauce. When very fresh, kale has a light cabbage flavor. The flavor tends to get stronger and more bitter with time, so it should be cooked within a day or two of purchase. Any of the several kale varieties on the market is suitable for this dish. If the kale you purchase has tough stems, fold each leaf in half lengthwise, with the stem out, and cut out the stem. If the stems are tender, chop them and add with the leaves to the pot. Swiss chard or spinach can be substituted for the kale in either recipe. When sautéing spinach, you do not need to add extra water and cook the tender leaves for less time than the kale.

KALE WITH GARLIC AND LEMON

In a large saucepan over medium heat, melt the butter (if using) with the oil. Add the garlic and cook, stirring frequently, until softened, about 1 minute. Add the kale and water. Toss well to combine. Cover and cook for 5 minutes. Uncover and continue to cook, stirring, until the liquid has evaporated and the kale is tender, about 5 minutes. Season to taste with salt and pepper and add the lemon juice. Mix well, transfer to a warmed serving bowl, and serve.

BRAISED GREENS

In a large saucepan over medium heat, warm the oil until it shimmers. Add the garlic and cook, stirring frequently until softened, about 1 minute. Add the kale and chicken broth, cover, and cook until the kale is very tender, about 10 minutes. Add the nutmeg and salt and pepper to taste and mix well. Transfer to a warmed serving bowl and serve.

KALE WITH GARLIC AND LEMON

1 tablespoon unsalted butter (optional)

2 tablespoons olive oil

4 cloves garlic, thinly sliced

1 bunch kale (about 1½ pounds), leaves and stems coarsely chopped (see head note)

¼ cup water

Kosher salt

Freshly ground pepper

½ teaspoon freshly squeezed lemon juice

SERVES 4

BRAISED GREENS

2 tablespoons olive oil

4 cloves garlic, minced

1 bunch kale (about 1½ pounds), leaves and stems coarsely chopped (see head note)

¾ cup canned reduced-sodium chicken broth

⅛ teaspoon freshly grated nutmeg

Kosher salt

Freshly ground pepper

COLLARD GREENS WITH GARLIC

SERVES 4

2 bunches collard greens (about 2 pounds total), stems removed (see head note)

2 tablespoons olive oil

5 large cloves garlic, finely chopped

Kosher salt

Freshly ground pepper

Since I grew up in the South, collard greens are part of my heritage. I was often served them after they had been stewed for what seemed like hours with a ham hock, so this quick and simple way of cooking them came as a revelation. It's my take on the Brazilian approach to cooking collards. Collard greens, like kale, are a member of the cabbage family, and their taste is similar to that of kale but with more bite. Also like kale, collards are a good source of vitamin C, calcium, and iron. The broad, deep green leaves are cut into shreds. If the stems are tender, they can be chopped and added to the pot with the leaves.

1   Stack several leaves of collard on top of one another and roll them into a cylinder. Cut the rolled leaves crosswise to make strips about ¼ inch wide. Repeat with the remaining leaves.

2   In a large skillet over medium heat, warm the oil until it shimmers. Add the garlic and cook, stirring frequently, until softened, about 1 minute. Add the collards, 1 large handful at a time, stirring and tossing after each addition, then adding another handful. Season to taste with salt and pepper. Stir well, cover, and cook until the collards are tender, about 5 minutes. Remove to a warmed serving dish and serve.

NAPA CABBAGE SLAW WITH PUMPKIN SEEDS

SERVES 6

In the South, where I come from, every family believes that its version of cole slaw is the best. The competition can be fierce, but I would enter this version in any contest. It's a colorful, crunchy medley of cabbage, roasted red pepper, and toasted pumpkin seeds with a dressing enriched by crème fraîche. In my opinion, napa cabbage makes the crispest slaw. The cabbage has a long head of very pale green leaves with a crinkly texture. Serve with Spiced Chicken Burgers (page 138) or Spicy Grilled Baby Back Ribs (page 151).

1 red bell pepper

½ cup pumpkin seeds

1 head napa cabbage, trimmed and finely shredded (about 9 cups cut)

1 tablespoon freshly squeezed lime juice

1 tablespoon celery seeds

3 tablespoons high-quality mayonnaise

2 tablespoons crème fraîche

Kosher salt

Freshly ground pepper

1   Arrange the broiler rack about 5 inches from the heat source and preheat the broiler. Place the bell pepper on the broiler pan and broil, turning as needed, until charred all over, about 10 minutes. Place the roasted pepper in a bowl, cover, and set aside until cool enough to handle. Working over a bowl to catch the juices, pull the blackened skins from the pepper and discard. Pull out the stem and remove the seeds and ribs. Cut the pepper into very fine strips and set aside. Strain any pepper juices into a bowl or jar and reserve for use in salad dressings.

2   While the bell pepper is cooling, in a small, dry skillet over medium heat, toast the pumpkin seeds, stirring constantly, until they just begin to turn light brown, about 2 minutes. Immediately pour them into a small bowl to cool. Set aside.

3   In a large bowl, toss the cabbage with the roasted pepper strips. Add the lime juice, celery seeds, mayonnaise, and crème fraîche. Toss well again. Taste for seasoning and adjust with salt and pepper. Let stand at room temperature for at least 5 to 10 minutes, or in the refrigerator for up to a day, to let the flavors develop. Toss well and divide among individual plates or bowls. Sprinkle each portion with some of the toasted pumpkin seeds and serve.

RATATOUILLE WITH CHILE

SERVES 10 TO 12

My friend Douglas Katz, chef of Fire Restaurant in Cleveland, Ohio, gave me this recipe, his version of the classic French dish. He's pepped it up with poblano chile, which contributes a little bit of spice. When preparing ratatouille, I like to make a generous quantity. It keeps well in the refrigerator for several days and tastes great hot, at room temperature, or cold. I serve it as a side dish and also enjoy it as a snack or for lunch.

1   Put the eggplant in a colander, sprinkle with salt, toss, and let stand for 20 minutes to remove any bitterness. Rinse well under cold running water and drain. Dry by pressing the cubes firmly between paper towels or in a clean kitchen towel.

2   In a large skillet over medium-high heat, warm 1 tablespoon of the oil until it shimmers. Add the onion and cook, stirring and tossing, until softened and lightly browned, about 6 minutes. Add the garlic and cook, stirring frequently, until softened, about 1 minute. Season lightly with salt and pepper and remove to a baking sheet to cool.

3   Return the pan to medium-high heat and warm 1 tablespoon oil until hot. Add the poblano chile and bell pepper and cook, stirring constantly, until lightly browned and cooked through, about 5 minutes. Season lightly with salt and pepper and transfer to the baking sheet. Repeat with the eggplant, seasoning it only with pepper and adding more oil as needed. Then repeat with the zucchini and the yellow squash. When the vegetables have cooled to room temperature, transfer them to a large bowl, add the tomatoes, oregano, and basil, and toss well. Taste for seasoning and adjust with salt and pepper. Toss well again.

4   To serve the ratatouille at room temperature, top each portion with a dollop of fresh ricotta cheese (if using). To serve it hot, preheat the oven to 375°F. Place the ratatouille in a baking dish and cook until bubbling, 30 to 45 minutes. Dust with Parmesan (if using) just before serving.

One 1-pound eggplant, cut into ½-inch cubes

Kosher salt

5 to 8 tablespoons olive oil

1 red onion, cut into ¼-inch dice

3 cloves garlic, very finely chopped

Freshly ground pepper

1 poblano chile, seeded and cut into ½-inch pieces

1 red bell pepper, seeds and ribs removed, cut into ½-inch pieces

2 zucchini, cut into ½-inch cubes

2 yellow crookneck squash, cut into ½-inch cubes

1 pint cherry tomatoes, halved, or quartered if large

1 tablespoon finely chopped fresh oregano

1 tablespoon finely chopped fresh basil

About ¾ cup ricotta cheese or about ¼ cup freshly grated Parmesan cheese (optional)

SWISS CHARD STUFFED WITH BARLEY

SERVES 4

2 tablespoons olive oil, plus more for brushing

¾ cup pearl barley

2½ cups water

Kosher salt

1 bunch Swiss chard (about 1 pound)

2 shallots, finely chopped

1 clove garlic, very finely chopped

1 tablespoon finely chopped fresh thyme

½ cup coarsely shredded mozzarella cheese, Gruyère, or Jarlsberg cheese, plus 2 tablespoons

2 tablespoons freshly grated Parmesan cheese

Freshly ground pepper

½ cup canned reduced-sodium chicken or vegetable broth

These rolls, an adaptation of Mediterranean stuffed grape leaves, make a substantial side dish. I use barley instead of rice because barley does not cause a rapid rise in blood sugar, as rice does, and so therefore doesn't initiate a strong Storage Cascade (see page 19). I wrap the stuffing in large chard leaves, a Super-Savvy Carb, instead of grape leaves, but feel free to use grape leaves too if you wish. The barley is flavored with fresh herbs, aromatic vegetables, and two cheeses, which melt as the rolls heat to give the filling an almost creamy texture. The rolls could easily be served as a main dish with the addition of some shredded, cooked chicken or diced tofu to the filling.

1   In a large saucepan over medium heat, warm 1 tablespoon of the oil until it shimmers. Add the barley and cook, stirring frequently, until thoroughly coated with the oil and lightly toasted, about 5 minutes. Lower the heat, if needed, to prevent scorching. Add the water and a large pinch of salt and bring to a boil. Reduce the heat to low, cover, and simmer until the barley is tender but still slightly chewy, about 45 minutes. Add more water, ¼ cup at a time, if the barley becomes too dry. Do not drown the barley; all the water should be absorbed just as the barley is done. Drain the barley, if necessary. Set aside.

2   Preheat the oven to 375°F. Bring a large pot of salted water to a boil and prepare a large bowl of ice water.

3   Remove the stems from the chard leaves and chop the stems into small pieces. Set aside. Plunge the chard leaves into the boiling water and stir so they all wilt as quickly and uniformly as possible. Cook just until wilted, about 30 seconds. Immediately drain the leaves and plunge into the ice water to stop the cooking. Working carefully to keep the leaves whole, remove them from the water and lay them out on paper towels. Dry them gently and lay them out on a work surface.

4   Heat the remaining 1 tablespoon oil in a large skillet over medium heat. Add the shallots, garlic, and reserved chard stems and cook, stirring constantly, until lightly browned, about 3 minutes. Turn off the heat and stir in the barley and thyme. Stir in the ½ cup mozzarella and the Parmesan and season to taste with salt and pepper.

5   Use the largest leaves first. Place a heaping tablespoonful of the barley mixture in the center of each leaf. Roll the leaf around the filling and tuck the edges under to make a neat package. The packages may be of different sizes because the leaves vary in size. Arrange the rolls in an 8-inch square baking pan, fitting them snugly against each other. Brush the rolls with olive oil and sprinkle lightly with salt and the 2 tablespoons mozzarella.

6   Pour the broth around the rolls and bake until the rolls are hot throughout, about 10 minutes. Serve hot or at room temperature.

CANNELLINI BEAN SALAD WITH FETA CHEESE AND MINT

SERVES 4

This salad looks almost like a bowl of confetti. Sweet green peas, red and yellow peppers, and fresh herbs all add zesty flavors and vibrant color. The combination of crumbled feta and chopped mint gives a Mediterranean flair to the white beans. I always keep cans of cannellini beans in the pantry. The beans are a good source of protein and fiber, but what I like best about them is how well they absorb flavors and can be turned into any number of delicious salads and side dishes just by varying the seasonings.

1   If using fresh peas, put about an inch of water in a small saucepan. Add a pinch of salt and bring to a boil. Add the peas and simmer, uncovered, until bright green and just tender, about 3 minutes.

2   In a large serving bowl, toss together the peas, beans, mint, red and yellow bell pepper, garlic, oil, vinegar, oregano (if using), and feta. Taste for seasoning and adjust with salt and pepper. Let the salad stand for 30 minutes. Toss again gently before serving.

½ cup fresh baby green peas or thawed frozen green peas

One 15-ounce can cannellini beans, drained

½ cup packed fresh mint leaves, chopped

½ red bell pepper, ribs and seeds removed, chopped

½ yellow bell pepper, ribs and seeds removed, chopped

1 clove garlic, very finely chopped

2 tablespoons extra-virgin olive oil

½ teaspoon red wine vinegar

1½ teaspoons finely chopped fresh oregano (optional)

¼ cup crumbled feta cheese

Kosher salt

Freshly ground pepper

WHITE BEANS WITH BASIL, OREGANO, AND LEMON

SERVES 4

One 15-ounce can small white beans such as navy or cannellini

½ small red onion, thinly sliced

2 tablespoons plus 1½ teaspoons extra-virgin olive oil

Grated zest and juice of 1 lemon

1 tablespoon chopped fresh basil

1 tablespoon chopped fresh flat-leaf parsley

1 teaspoon finely chopped fresh oregano

Kosher salt

Freshly ground pepper

This easy side dish, with its bright and bracing flavors of fresh herbs and lemon, can be paired with lamb, chicken, or fish. If you prefer to serve the beans hot, heat them in a saucepan over medium-low heat until hot, then pour them into a bowl, add the remaining ingredients, toss well, and serve immediately. In addition to their culinary versatility, beans are a good source of protein and fiber.

In a serving bowl, combine the beans, onion, oil, lemon zest and juice, basil, parsley, and oregano. Toss well. Taste for seasoning and adjust with salt and pepper. Toss again. Serve at room temperature, or refrigerate and serve cold.

TOMATO, CUCUMBER, AND BARLEY SALAD WITH LIME AND MINT

SERVES 6

This is a terrific dish to make at the height of summer when tomatoes and cucumbers are at their most flavorful. The combination of chewy barley, crunchy cucumbers, sun-ripened tomatoes, and bracing lime and mint are sure to perk up appetites that might be flagging in the heat. The salad doesn't even need oil, but you can drizzle a bit of olive oil on the finished dish if you wish. It travels well, making it a great choice to take on a picnic.

1   In a large saucepan over medium heat, warm the oil until it shimmers. Add the barley and cook, stirring frequently, until thoroughly coated with the oil and lightly toasted, about 5 minutes. Lower the heat, if needed, to prevent scorching. Add the water and a large pinch of salt and bring to a boil. Reduce the heat to low, cover, and simmer until the barley is tender but still slightly chewy, about 45 minutes. Add more water, ¼ cup at a time, if the barley becomes too dry. Do not drown the barley; all the water should be absorbed just as the barley is done. Drain the barley, if necessary.

2   In a large bowl, combine the barley, green onions, bell pepper, tomato, cucumber, lime juice, mint, parsley and almonds. Toss well. Taste for seasoning and adjust with salt and pepper. Toss well again and serve. The salad may be prepared up to a day ahead of time. Cover and refrigerate; return to room temperature before serving.

1 tablespoon extra-virgin olive oil

1 cup pearl barley

2¾ cups water

Kosher salt

2 green onions, white and light green parts, thinly sliced

1 small bell pepper, seeds and ribs removed, finely chopped

1 small tomato, finely chopped

1 cup peeled, seeded, and diced cucumber (¼-inch dice)

¼ cup freshly squeezed lime juice

2 tablespoons roughly chopped fresh mint

1 tablespoon roughly chopped fresh parsley

¼ cup finely chopped toasted almonds

Freshly ground pepper

CAJUN BARLEY

SERVES 4

1 small yellow onion, chopped

½ red bell pepper, ribs and seeds removed, chopped

1 stalk celery, chopped

1 cup pearl barley

½ teaspoon hot paprika

3 cups canned reduced-sodium chicken broth

Kosher salt

Freshly ground pepper

1 bay leaf

2 green onions, white and light green parts, thinly sliced

¼ cup finely chopped fresh flat-leaf parsley

Here is my version of a classic Cajun dish called Dirty Rice. Traditionally it includes meat such as chopped chicken gizzards, which give the rice a "dirty" look. This is a "cleaner" version, based on vegetables and hot paprika for spice, and substituting barley for rice. You begin the recipe with the Cajun holy trinity of cooking—onion, bell pepper, and celery. Classic French recipes would start with onion, celery, and carrot as the aromatics. Bell pepper, instead of carrot, provides the distinctive Cajun flavor. Serve Cajun Barley with any main dish you would normally accompany with rice.

1   Preheat the oven to 350°F. In a large bowl, combine the yellow onion, bell pepper, celery, barley, paprika, broth, a large pinch of salt, and pepper to taste and mix well. Spoon into a 9-inch square baking dish. Add the bay leaf and cover tightly with aluminum foil.

2   Bake until the barley is tender but still slightly chewy, about 1¼ hours. Discard the bay leaf. Scatter the green onions and parsley over the top. Serve hot.

BARLEY RISOTTO WITH TOMATOES AND LEMON

SERVES 4

The tomatoes, lemon, and fresh herbs combine to create a refreshing and satisfying first course. There is very little, in my opinion, that tastes more delicious and comforting than risotto. On my way to becoming overweight, I often ate a large portion of risotto as a main dish rather than how it is traditionally served in Italy: in a small portion as a first course. As my ideas for the Wine and Food Lover's Diet took shape, I discovered that I was eating too large a portion, and the rice quickly turned to blood sugar, causing my body to store fat. To re-create the flavors and texture I so enjoyed in risotto, I learned to substitute barley and to serve a small portion as a first course or side dish with meat, fish, and chicken.

1   In large saucepan over medium heat, warm the oil until it shimmers. Add the shallots and cook, stirring frequently, until softened, about 2 minutes. Add the barley and cook, stirring constantly, until thoroughly coated with oil and lightly toasted, about 5 minutes. Lower the heat, if needed, to prevent scorching.

2   Add the wine (if using) and thyme and stir until the pan is nearly dry. Add the broth, the salt, and pepper to taste. Bring to a very slow simmer, cover, and cook until the broth is absorbed and the barley is tender but still slightly chewy, 45 minutes to 1 hour.

3   Add the tomatoes, lemon zest and juice, and parsley and stir until heated through and well combined. Stir in the crème fraîche (if using). Taste for seasoning and
adjust with salt and pepper. Divide among 4 warmed soup plates and sprinkle each serving with a little of the cheese. Serve immediately.

1 tablespoon olive oil

2 shallots, finely chopped

1 cup pearl barley

¼ cup dry white wine (optional)

1 tablespoon finely chopped fresh thyme

About 3 cups canned low-sodium vegetable or chicken broth, or water, simmering

¾ teaspoon kosher salt

Freshly ground pepper

1 pint cherry tomatoes, halved, or quartered if large

1½ teaspoons freshly grated lemon zest

1 tablespoon freshly squeezed lemon juice

2 tablespoons finely chopped fresh flat-leaf parsley

2 tablespoons crème fraîche (optional)

¼ cup freshly grated Parmesan cheese

★ A# 1 — AWESOME

BARLEY RISOTTO WITH GARLIC AND ALMONDS

SERVES 4

½ cup almonds

2 tablespoons olive oil

1 small yellow onion, finely chopped

2 stalks celery, finely chopped

2 cloves garlic, very finely chopped

1 cup pearl barley

½ cup dry vermouth

1 tablespoon finely chopped fresh thyme

3 cups canned reduced-sodium chicken or vegetable broth, simmering

¾ teaspoon kosher salt

Freshly ground pepper

4 tablespoons unsalted butter or crème fraîche

½ cup freshly grated Parmesan cheese

This risotto builds on a pair of classic Spanish flavors, garlic and almonds. The butter or crème fraîche stirred in at the end of cooking with the cheese adds an appealing creaminess in contrast to the crunchy texture of the almonds. If you follow my advice and make a large batch of barley in the beginning of the week, this dish comes together in a flash. Follow the recipe below, making these few adjustments: Cook the aromatics and then add the vermouth and thyme. Cook the wine down as the recipe instructs and then add the broth. Simmer it rapidly until reduced by about half. Then add the cooked barley and stir and toss until hot. Finish with the butter, almonds, and cheese, and season to taste.

1   In a small, dry skillet over medium heat, toast the almonds, stirring constantly, until they just begin to turn light brown, about 3 minutes. Immediately pour them into a small bowl to cool. Coarsely chop the nuts and set aside.

2   In a large saucepan over medium heat, warm the oil until it shimmers. Add the onion, celery, and garlic and cook, stirring frequently until softened, about 5 minutes. Add the barley and cook, stirring constantly, until thoroughly coated with oil and lightly toasted, about 5 minutes. Lower the heat, if needed, to prevent scorching.

3   Add the vermouth and thyme and stir until the pan is nearly dry. Add the broth, the salt, and pepper to taste. Bring to a very slow simmer, cover, and cook until the broth is absorbed and the barley is tender but still slightly chewy, 45 minutes to 1 hour.

4   Add the butter and almonds and stir until evenly distributed. Add the cheese and stir well. Taste for seasoning and adjust with salt and pepper. Divide among 4 warmed plates and serve immediately.

— ADD PUMPKIN SEEDS & SUNFLOWER SEEDS

— USE ½ WHITE WINE ½ CHX BROTH

LENTILS WITH SHALLOT AND HERBS

SERVES 4

1 cup French lentils

1 bay leaf

Kosher salt

1 tablespoon olive oil

1 large shallot, finely chopped

3 tablespoons finely chopped mixed fresh herbs such as thyme, basil, mint, oregano, parsley, and marjoram

Cayenne pepper (optional)

½ teaspoon freshly grated lemon zest (optional)

Freshly ground black pepper

A friend in Chicago, Dr. Mickey Jester, gave me this recipe that heightens the earthy character of lentils with an abundance of fresh herbs. Lentils are a good source of protein and iron on their own, but I enjoy them as a side dish for fish and chicken. For this recipe, use the French or European green lentils. Their intact seed coat gives them an attractive dark green and black mottled appearance. They also remain separate and firm even when cooked until tender, whereas the larger brown and red lentils tend to turn mushy when cooked. This characteristic makes green lentils a good choice for salads such as this, when looks matter. For variety, add 2 slices of nitrite-free bacon, chopped, to the lentils at the start of cooking.

1   Put the lentils and bay leaf in a saucepan and pour in water to reach about 1 inch above the lentils. Bring to a boil, reduce the heat to low, cover, and simmer until tender, about 30 minutes. After 15 minutes, add a pinch of salt. Add more water if the lentils become too dry. Discard the bay leaf. Drain the lentils, if necessary, and transfer to a warmed serving bowl.

2   In a small skillet over medium heat, warm the oil until it shimmers. Add the shallot and cook, stirring frequently, until softened, about 2 minutes. Add the herbs, cayenne (if using), and lemon zest (if using), stir well, and add to the lentils. Stir well. Taste for seasoning and adjust with salt and pepper. Serve warm.

QUINOA PILAF WITH SUNFLOWER AND PUMPKIN SEEDS

SERVES 6 TO 8

Quinoa, a staple crop in South America and available in many North American markets, is packed with high-quality protein, more than any plant protein source other than soybeans. It has an appealing earthy, nutty flavor enhanced in this recipe with toasted sunflower and sesame seeds. The seeds add great texture and healthy mono- and polyunsaturated fats, along with more protein. Quinoa ranks low on the glycemic index (see page 26), meaning it does not cause a rapid rise in blood sugar and thereby cause the body to manufacture fat instead of use the food consumed for immediate energy needs.

½ cup sunflower seeds, roughly chopped

½ cup pumpkin seeds, roughly chopped

2 cups quinoa

1 tablespoon unsalted butter

4 cups water

Kosher salt

Freshly ground pepper

1   In a small, dry skillet over medium heat, toast the sunflower and pumpkin seeds, stirring constantly, until they just begin to turn light brown, about 2 minutes. Immediately pour them onto a plate to cool.

2   Thoroughly rinse the quinoa in a fine sieve under cold running water and drain well. In a saucepan over medium heat, melt the butter. Add the quinoa and cook, stirring occasionally, until lightly toasted, about 3 minutes. Lower the heat, if needed, to prevent scorching. Add the water and ¾ teaspoon salt, bring to a boil, cover, reduce the heat to low, and cook until the quinoa is nearly tender, about 10 minutes.

3   Using a fork, fluff the quinoa grains, stirring from the bottom of the pan. Cover and continue to cook until very tender, about 5 minutes longer. The quinoa will look partly translucent, and the little white corkscrew germs will have lifted from the grains. Stir in the toasted seeds. Taste for seasoning and adjust with salt and pepper. Serve warm or at room temperature.

QUINOA-CHILE SKILLET BREAD

SERVES 6 TO 8

Cornbread was a staple food in the South, where I come from, and was served in many households at breakfast with molasses and at dinner especially with barbecue. This recipe is a spicy cornbread replacement, made with high-protein, gluten-free quinoa. It has lots of toasted nuts and sunflower seeds for crunch and flavor and Cheddar cheese for savory richness. Serve the bread as a side dish for Spicy Grilled Baby Back Ribs (page 151). You can also make it ahead, let it cool, and cut it into bite-size pieces. Brush the pieces with oil and toast in a heavy skillet to make an excellent appetizer or snack.

½ cup hazelnuts or almonds

2 cups quinoa

4 cups water

Kosher salt

½ cup sunflower seeds, chopped

3 eggs, lightly beaten

2 tablespoons olive oil

Freshly ground pepper

1 tablespoon canola oil

3 jalapeño chiles, seeds removed, finely chopped

½ cup shredded sharp white Cheddar cheese

1   In a small, dry skillet over medium heat, toast the hazelnuts, stirring constantly, until they just begin to turn light brown, about 5 minutes. Immediately enclose them in a clean kitchen towel and rub vigorously to remove the dark brown skins. Do not worry if tiny pieces of skin remain on the nuts. Pour the nuts into a colander and shake to separate the nuts from the flakes of skin. Coarsely chop the nuts and set aside.

2   Preheat the oven to 450°F. Thoroughly rinse the quinoa in a fine sieve under cold running water and drain well. In a saucepan over medium-high heat, combine the quinoa, water, and ¾ teaspoon salt. Bring to a boil, cover, reduce the heat to low, and cook until the quinoa is nearly tender, about 10 minutes.

3   Using a fork, fluff the quinoa grains, stirring from the bottom of the pan. Cover and continue to cook until very tender, about 5 minutes longer. The quinoa will look partly translucent, and the little white corkscrew germs will have lifted from the grains. Stir in the reserved hazelnuts, the sunflower seeds, the eggs, and the olive oil. Season to taste with salt and pepper.

4   In a large, ovenproof skillet (preferably cast iron) over medium heat, warm the canola oil until it shimmers. Pour in half of the quinoa mixture and cook until the edges firm up a bit and some bubbles appear in the center, about 3 minutes. Evenly sprinkle the chiles and half of the Cheddar over the top. Spread the remaining quinoa mixture over the top and out to the edges of the pan. Place the pan in the oven and bake until the bread is firm and hot throughout, about 10 minutes. Invert onto a serving plate so the crisp side is up. Sprinkle with the remaining Cheddar. The cheese should melt; return to the oven, if necessary, until it melts. Cut into wedges and serve hot.

SAUTÉ

— Mix all together —
Save Cheddar for top
some

SOUTH AMERICAN TABBOULEH

SERVES 6 TO 8

2 cups quinoa

4 cups water

Kosher salt

¼ cup chopped red onion

½ cup chopped fresh cilantro

½ cup chopped fresh mint

½ cup finely chopped fresh flat-leaf parsley

⅓ cup extra-virgin olive oil

3 tablespoons freshly squeezed lime juice

2 tablespoons freshly squeezed lemon juice

4 tomatoes, peeled, seeded, and diced

1 avocado, pitted, peeled, and cut into ¼-inch cubes

Freshly ground pepper

Tabbouleh, a Mediterranean grain salad with ripe tomatoes and fresh mint, is usually made with bulghur, cooked wheat berries that are then roughly crushed. The Wine and Food Lover's Diet omits wheat in all forms so this version is based on South American quinoa. Bernard Guillas, executive chef at La Jolla Beach & Tennis Club in La Jolla, California, adds cilantro, lime juice, and avocado to the customary mix. He garnishes his version with melon and serves it with spiced diver scallops. It's also delicious as a side dish with grilled fish or chicken such as Spiced Chicken Burgers (page 138).

1   Thoroughly rinse the quinoa in a fine sieve under cold running water and drain well. In a saucepan over medium-high heat, combine the quinoa, water, and ¾ teaspoon salt. Bring to a boil, cover, reduce the heat to low, and cook until the quinoa is nearly tender, about 10 minutes.

2   Using a fork, fluff the quinoa grains, stirring from the bottom of the pan. Cover and continue to cook until very tender, about 5 minutes longer. The quinoa will look partly translucent, and the little white corkscrew germs will have lifted from the grains. Transfer the quinoa to a large bowl and let cool.

3   In another bowl, toss together the onion, cilantro, mint, parsley, oil, lime juice, and lemon juice. Add to the quinoa with the tomatoes and avocado and toss gently until well mixed. Taste for seasoning, adjust with salt and pepper, and serve.

ITALIAN BUTTER BEANS

SERVES 6

Dan Baker, chef at Marché aux Fleurs restaurant in Ross, California, showed me this unusual way to cook fresh shelling beans. After they simmer until tender, they are drained and then sautéed in butter until lightly browned, giving them an irresistible sweetness and a slight crispness. Fresh shelling beans like Italian butter beans, picked while the beans are relatively small and tender and before the pods have dried, are more flavorful than the dried versions, have a higher vitamin content, and cook more quickly. The season for fresh shelling beans is very short, but they are well worth seeking out in specialty markets and farmers' markets. Butter bean is the common name in the South for a flat, meaty bean that is light green under a thin, beige skin. Many people equate butter beans with lima beans, but butter beans are more tender and delicately flavored than limas. Either can be used in this recipe, as can fresh soybeans (also sold as edamame) or cannellini or cranberry beans.

1 Gather together the onion, celery, carrot, garlic, thyme, bay leaf, and peppercorns and tie them in a piece of cheesecloth. Put the bundle in a large pot with the broth and water and bring to a boil. Meanwhile, shell the beans.

2 Add the beans to the pot, reduce the heat to low, and simmer gently, uncovered and stirring occasionally, until tender, about 25 minutes. After about 15 minutes, add a large pinch of salt. Do not overcook the beans; you want the beans to remain whole. Drain the beans and spread on a baking sheet to cool. Discard the cheesecloth bundle. The skins of the beans will have puffed out and loosened. It is not necessary to remove them, as they are tender to the bite.

3 In a large skillet over medium-high heat, melt the butter. Add the beans and cook, stirring and tossing, until slightly brown and crisp, about 5 minutes. Season to taste with salt and pepper. Serve hot.

---

1 small yellow onion, quartered

1 small stalk celery, cut crosswise into several pieces

1 small carrot, cut crosswise into several pieces

6 cloves garlic

2 fresh thyme sprigs

1 bay leaf

½ teaspoon black peppercorns

2 cups canned reduced-sodium chicken broth

2 cups water

1½ pounds Italian butter beans

Kosher salt

2 tablespoons unsalted butter

Freshly ground pepper

ROSEMARY ROASTED NUTS

MAKES 2 CUPS

2 cups walnuts, pecans, almonds, or hazelnuts

1 tablespoon grapeseed oil or canola oil

2 teaspoons finely chopped fresh rosemary

Kosher salt

½ teaspoon cayenne pepper

Every diet needs an approved list of snacks. This nut mix, roasted with fragrant fresh rosemary, not only satisfies hunger pangs but makes a positive contribution to your health and nutrition. The nuts are full of healthy mono- and polyunsaturated fats that have a positive effect on cholesterol levels and help you feel full. Enjoy a small handful of eight to ten nuts. Eat them slowly, and by the time you are done, you will no longer feel hungry.

Preheat the oven to 350°F. Put the nuts in a large bowl and drizzle with the oil. Sprinkle with the rosemary, ½ teaspoon salt, and the cayenne and toss well to distribute the seasonings evenly. Spread the nuts on a rimmed baking sheet. Roast, stirring and tossing once or twice, until fragrant and lightly browned, 10 to 12 minutes. Remove to a bowl to cool. Taste and adjust the seasoning with salt. Serve warm or at room temperature. The nuts can be stored in an airtight container in a cool, dark place for about 1 week.

SPICED CHICKPEAS

MAKES ABOUT 1⅓ CUPS

When you just have to eat something fried, reach for a small handful of these nutty chickpeas. The sweet spices and quick turn in hot oil make them as irresistible and crunchy as popcorn, but they do not initiate the rapid rise in blood sugar that popcorn does. The high protein and fiber content makes the chickpeas a filling and satisfying snack.

1   Put the chickpeas in a zippered plastic bag and add the chickpea flour, cinnamon, coriander, and salt and pepper to taste. Seal the bag and shake very well until the chickpeas are evenly coated. Transfer the chickpeas to a strainer and gently shake off any excess seasonings.

2   In a large skillet over medium-high heat, warm the oil until it shimmers and is hot. Add the chickpeas and cook, stirring constantly, until lightly browned all over, about 2 minutes. Remove to paper towels to drain. Let cool. Store in an airtight container in the refrigerator for up to 5 days.

One 15-ounce can chickpeas, well drained

½ cup chickpea flour, soy flour, or nut flour such as almond or hazelnut

¼ teaspoon ground cinnamon

¼ teaspoon ground coriander

Kosher salt

Freshly ground pepper

½ cup grapeseed oil or olive oil

JALAPEÑO JACK CHEESE MELT WITH TOASTED PUMPKIN SEEDS

SERVES 2

This is one of my favorite snacks. The combination of melted cheese, ground cumin, and pumpkin seeds reminds me of Texas, where I did my residency training. The same three flavors appear together in many Tex-Mex dishes. You can use any cheese that melts easily into a smooth mass. Alternatives to the spicy chile-flecked cheese here include fontina and Port Salut. For more authenticity, substitute queso fresco, a fresh Mexican cheese.

2 heaping tablespoons pumpkin seeds

4 ounces jalapeño Jack cheese, shredded or cut into small cubes

Ground cumin

1   Preheat the oven to 250°F. In a small, dry skillet over medium heat, toast the pumpkin seeds, stirring constantly, until they just begin to turn light brown, 2 to 5 minutes. Immediately pour them into a small bowl to cool.

2   Divide the cheese evenly between 2 small ovenproof ramekins or bowls. Place in the oven and cook until the cheese melts, about 3 minutes. (Alternatively, place the bowls in a microwave on high for about 30 seconds.) Sprinkle the pumpkin seeds on the cheese, dividing evenly, and dust with cumin. Serve warm.

TURKEY ROLLS WITH ROASTED BELL PEPPER AND HUMMUS

SERVES 2

HUMMUS

3 cloves garlic

One 15-ounce can chickpeas, drained, rinsed, and drained again

¼ cup tahini

2 tablespoons freshly squeezed lemon juice, or more to taste

2 tablespoon extra-virgin olive oil

1 teaspoon ground cumin

½ teaspoon paprika

Kosher salt

Freshly ground pepper

TURKEY ROLLS

1 large red bell pepper

6 slices turkey breast (about 1½ ounces each)

Ground cumin

Cayenne

Imagine finding a healthful snack at an airport. But that is exactly where I discovered this one. An airport buffet provided all the fixings for this super-easy, flavorful, and satisfying snack. All of the oils in hummus—olive oil and the sesame seed oil in the tahini—are heart healthy. Hummus, a seasoned purée of chickpeas, is a good protein source. You can make it as spicy as you like. If I have fresh cilantro on hand, I purée the chickpeas with a few sprigs, which add a fresh flavor and a little color. The recipe makes more hummus than you will need for the rolls. The remainder will keep well in the refrigerator for up to a week and can be enjoyed as a great dip for raw vegetables.

1   To make the hummus: In a food processor, chop the garlic. Add the chickpeas and process again until the mixture is as smooth as possible. Add the tahini, 2 tablespoons lemon juice, the oil, cumin, paprika, and salt and pepper to taste. Process again until well blended. With the machine running, add just enough warm water to make a thick paste. Taste and adjust the seasoning with lemon juice, salt, and pepper. Scrape the hummus into a shallow bowl. You should have about 2 cups. The hummus can be made ahead and stored in a covered container in the refrigerator for up to 1 week.

2   To make the rolls: Arrange the broiler rack about 5 inches from the heat source and preheat the broiler. Place the bell pepper on the broiler pan and broil, turning as needed, until charred all over, about 10 minutes. Place the roasted pepper in a bowl, cover, and set aside until cool enough to handle. Working over a bowl to catch the juices, pull the blackened skins from the pepper and discard. Pull out the stem and remove the seeds and ribs. Tear the pepper into strips about ¼ inch wide. Set aside. Strain any juices into a jar and reserve for use in salad dressings.

3   Arrange the turkey slices on a work surface. Spread each slice with about 1 tablespoon of hummus and dust with a pinch of cumin and/or cayenne. Top with a few strips of bell pepper. Roll each turkey slice around the filling. Secure the rolls with toothpicks, if necessary. Refrigerate until serving.

DEVILED EGGS

SERVES 8

When I was growing up in Arkansas, deviled eggs were served at nearly every family gathering. Not long afterward, many people avoided eating eggs because of their cholesterol content. Now that we know more about various types of fat and their effect on the body, I consider eggs a very healthful food and eat them nearly every day. Eggs stimulate secretion of a substance that helps the digestion of fat and protein and also suppresses hunger. So when we eat an egg—perhaps a perfect combination of protein and fat—we feel full.

1 In a skillet over medium heat, cook the bacon, stirring occasionally, until crisp, about 6 minutes. Remove to paper towels to drain. Peel the eggs. Carefully cut them in half lengthwise. Using a spoon, scoop out the yolks and place in a bowl. Set the whites aside.

2 Mash the yolks with a fork. Stir in the mayonnaise, mustard, salt, black and white peppers, and a few splashes of hot sauce to taste. Fold in the pickle and bacon. If the filling is too thick, thin with a little pickle juice or oil. Spoon the filling into the hollowed-out whites, dividing evenly. Dust lightly with paprika. The eggs can be prepared several hours ahead. For longer storage, cover them well with plastic wrap or seal in a container and store in the refrigerator for up to 2 days.

2 or 3 slices nitrite-free bacon, chopped

12 eggs, hard-boiled

⅔ cup high-quality mayonnaise

2 tablespoons Dijon mustard

½ teaspoon salt

½ teaspoon freshly ground black pepper

¼ teaspoon ground white pepper

Hot pepper sauce such as Tabasco or Crystal

½ cup finely chopped dill pickle

Pickle juice or extra-virgin olive oil (optional)

Hot paprika

BERRIES WITH TOASTED NUTS AND SPICED WHIPPED CREAM

SERVES 2

2 tablespoons hazelnuts, almonds, or pecans

1 cup raspberries, blueberries, or strawberries, or a mix of berries

¼ cup heavy cream

⅛ teaspoon vanilla extract

Ground cinnamon

Ground mace

Every dieter needs something to look forward to and dessert can be the motivation needed to stick to a diet. This simple dessert takes advantage of the natural sweetness of berries. Especially when in season, they hardly need adornment to taste like a treat. Adhering to the Wine and Food Lover's Diet will improve your ability to enjoy the natural sugar in berries and will lessen your desire to add extra sugar. To give the dessert a little heft and make it more filling, each portion is garnished with toasted nuts and a dollop of whipped cream flavored with vanilla and sweet spices. Whipped cream—without the sugar—gives you a feeling of indulgence.

1   In a small, dry skillet over medium heat, toast the nuts, stirring constantly, until they just begin to turn light brown, about 5 minutes. Immediately pour them into a small bowl to cool. (If using hazelnuts, enclose them in a clean kitchen towel and rub vigorously to remove the dark brown skins. Do not worry if tiny pieces of skin remain on the nuts. Pour the nuts into a colander and shake to separate skins from nuts.) Chop the nuts and set aside.

2   Divide the berries between 2 dessert bowls. In a small bowl, whisk the cream and vanilla until soft peaks form. Spoon onto the berries, dividing evenly. Dust with a small pinch of cinnamon and a small pinch of mace. Scatter the nuts on top and serve.

BARLEY CUSTARD WITH FRESH BERRIES

SERVES 8

This recipe from my friend Thom Winslow is the Wine and Food Lover's Diet version of rice pudding, substituting barley for the rice, with creamy and luscious results. The barley makes the dessert substantial, so diners need only a small portion. I recommend avoiding milk on the Wine and Food Lover's Diet because lactose, or milk sugar, can interfere with weight loss. Therefore, enjoy this custard when you are no longer working to lose weight rapidly. The custard works well for entertaining since it should be made several hours ahead of time. It also can be served for breakfast. If you do not care for Splenda, use half sugar and half Splenda.

1 In a large saucepan over medium-high heat, combine the barley, water, and a pinch of salt. Bring to a boil, reduce the heat to low, cover, and simmer until the barley is tender but still slightly chewy, about 45 minutes. Add more water, ¼ cup at a time, if the barley becomes too dry. Do not drown the barley; all the water should be absorbed just as the barley is done. Drain the barley, if necessary, and let cool to room temperature.

2 Meanwhile, if using the walnuts, in a small, dry skillet over medium heat, toast the nuts, stirring constantly, until they just begin to turn light brown, about 3 minutes. Immediately pour them into a small bowl to cool. Coarsely chop the nuts and set aside.

3 In a saucepan over medium heat, combine the cream and half-and-half and warm just until bubbles form around the edges of the pan. In a bowl, beat the eggs well. Continuing to beat the eggs, pour in a little of the hot cream. Then pour the eggs into the saucepan and place over low heat. Cook, whisking constantly and making sure to scrape the bottom and edges of the pan, until the custard thickens enough to coat the back of a spoon, about 15 minutes. Remove from the heat and whisk in the Splenda, vanilla, and cinnamon (if using). Immediately pour the custard into a serving bowl.

4 Stir the barley into the warm custard. Cover and refrigerate for at least 2 hours or for as long as overnight. The custard will thicken as it chills. Divide the custard among dessert bowls and top with the berries and the nuts (if using).

Scant ¾ cup pearl barley

2½ cups water

Kosher salt

¼ cup walnuts (optional)

1¼ cups heavy cream

1½ cups half-and-half

3 eggs

½ cup Splenda

1 tablespoon vanilla extract

1 teaspoon ground cinnamon (optional)

1½ cups strawberries, raspberries, or blueberries, or a mixture

PEANUT BUTTER SOUFFLÉS WITH CHOCOLATE SAUCE

SERVES 6

Soufflés are a great choice for dessert on the Wine and Food Lover's Diet because they can be made without flour and with very little sugar. This one is simple to prepare and also light and delicious. I use natural or organic peanut butter without added sugar or oil (check the label) and dark chocolate. While many health claims are being made for dark chocolate, I prefer it because of its flavor intensity. In addition, the darker the chocolate, the less sugar it contains. The old standby categories of bittersweet and semisweet no longer define a precise type of chocolate. A more reliable way of choosing chocolate is by cacao (also spelled as cocoa) content, often stated right on the label. Any product that has at least 60 percent cacao will work in these recipes. If you use one with 70 percent cacao, you might need to add a bit of sugar and/or cream to smooth out the flavors.

1   In a small saucepan over very low heat, melt the peanut butter with the butter, stirring occasionally, until smooth. Stir in 3 tablespoons of the cream until well blended. Transfer to a bowl and set aside to cool to room temperature.

2   Preheat the oven to 350°F. Whisk the egg yolks into the cooled peanut butter mixture until smooth. In a very large bowl and using a handheld mixer, or in the bowl of a stand mixer fitted with the whisk attachment, mix together the 8 egg whites and the cream of tartar. Start beating on medium speed. When the whites are foamy, begin adding the 2 tablespoons sugar, little by little, while beating. Beat on high until stiff peaks form.

3   Using a large rubber spatula, gently stir one-fourth of the beaten whites into the peanut butter mixture to lighten it. Then fold the peanut butter mixture into the whites, one-fourth at a time, until well blended. Divide the mixture among six 1-cup ramekins, filling them about three-fourths full. Dust the tops with sugar (if using). Bake until the soufflés rise and are slightly browned on top, 11 to 13 minutes.

4   Meanwhile, in a heatproof bowl suspended over, but not touching, barely simmering water in a saucepan, combine the chocolate and 3 tablespoons of the cream. Let the chocolate soften and melt and then stir until smooth. The sauce may be made ahead and refrigerated for up to 1 week. Reheat over simmering water until just warm or in the microwave for 20 seconds. In a small bowl, whip the remaining 6 tablespoons cream with the vanilla (if using) until soft peaks form.

5   To serve, use a spoon to poke a hole in the top of each soufflé. Spoon some chocolate sauce into the soufflé and then top with a dollop of whipped cream.

⅓ cup smooth or chunky natural peanut butter

2 tablespoons unsalted butter, cut into small cubes

12 tablespoons (¾ cup) heavy cream

4 eggs, at room temperature, separated, plus 4 egg whites, at room temperature

⅛ teaspoon cream of tartar

2 tablespoons sugar, plus more for dusting (optional)

2½ ounces dark chocolate (at least 60 percent cacao), coarsely chopped

⅛ teaspoon vanilla extract (optional)

TRAIL BARK

SERVES 8

½ cup pumpkin seeds

½ cup unsalted pistachios

½ cup hazelnuts

1 pound dark chocolate (at least 60 percent cacao), coarsely chopped

Crossing trail mix with dark chocolate bark, this treat also marries antioxidant-rich dark chocolate and the healthful oils of nuts and seeds. Dark chocolate has very little sugar, and the flavor is so intense that you are satisfied by eating a small portion. Especially in recipes using very few ingredients, quality is important. High-quality chocolate will have stronger flavor and rely less on sugar and other additives for that flavor. And the darker the chocolate, the more beneficial antioxidants it contains.

1   In a small, dry skillet over medium heat, toast the pumpkin seeds, stirring constantly, until they just begin to turn light brown, about 2 minutes. Immediately pour them into a small bowl to cool. Return the pan to medium heat, add the pistachios, and toast, stirring constantly, until they just begin to turn light brown, about 3 minutes. Immediately pour into a separate bowl. Return the pan again to medium heat, add the hazelnuts, and toast, stirring constantly, until they just begin to turn light brown, about 5 minutes. Immediately enclose the nuts in a clean kitchen towel and rub vigorously to remove the dark brown skins. Do not worry if tiny pieces of skin remain on the nuts. Pour the nuts into a colander and shake to separate the skins from the nuts. Coarsely chop the pistachios and hazelnuts and set aside.

2   Line a baking sheet with parchment paper. In a heatproof bowl suspended over, but not touching, barely simmering water in a saucepan, melt the chocolate, stirring frequently until smooth. Remove from the heat and, working quickly, stir in the seeds and nuts until well coated with the chocolate. Pour onto the prepared baking sheet and spread the mixture as thinly as possible. Refrigerate until firm, at least 30 minutes. Break into medium-sized pieces and store in an airtight container in the refrigerator for up to 2 weeks.

HAZELNUT SWIRL CHOCOLATE BROWNIES

SERVES 6

1 cup hazelnuts

Kosher salt

2 teaspoons Splenda, plus ¼ cup

2 to 4 tablespoons toasted hazelnut oil or canola oil

8 ounces dark chocolate (at least 60 percent cacao), coarsely chopped

6 tablespoons unsalted butter

4 large eggs, at room temperature, separated

¼ cup sugar

Whipped cream (optional)

Anyone who likes Nutella, the chocolate-hazelnut spread, will enjoy these brownies, one of my favorite desserts to serve when celebrating. To make them, I've combined toasted hazelnuts with dark chocolate to produce a richly nutty chocolate confection with swirls of dark brown and tan. Once you have toasted the nuts, the recipe goes together in a flash and can be made a day ahead. The brownies won't dry out.

1   In a small, dry skillet over medium heat, toast the nuts, stirring constantly, until they just begin to turn light brown, about 5 minutes. Immediately enclose them in a clean kitchen towel and rub vigorously to remove the dark brown skins. Do not worry if tiny pieces of skin remain on the nuts. Pour the nuts into a colander and shake to separate the nuts from the flakes of skin. Coarsely chop half the nuts and pour them into a small bowl. Season to taste with a small pinch of salt and set aside.

2   Place the remaining hazelnuts in a food processor with the 2 teaspoons Splenda and process to a fine texture. Add a pinch of salt and 2 tablespoons of the hazelnut oil. Continue to process, scraping down the sides of the bowl occasionally, until the mixture forms a paste, about 5 minutes. If the hazelnuts do not seem to be releasing enough oil and are turning into a stiff butter, add the remaining 2 tablespoons hazelnut oil, 1 tablespoon at a time, and process after each addition. Process until the consistency is fairly loose and spreadable. Scrape the hazelnut butter into a bowl and set aside. The butter can be made ahead and stored in a covered container in the refrigerator for up to 3 months. Bring to room temperature before using.

3   Preheat the oven to 375°F. Butter an 8-inch square baking pan with 2-inch sides. Line the bottom with parchment paper and butter the parchment.

4   In a bowl suspended over, but not touching, barely simmering water in a saucepan, melt the chocolate with the 6 tablespoons butter, stirring occasionally until smooth. Set aside to cool to room temperature.

5   In a bowl, using a handheld mixer, beat the egg yolks with the ¼ cup Splenda until thick and pale yellow. Using a rubber spatula or wooden spoon, stir the chocolate mixture into the egg yolks.

6   In another bowl, using clean beaters, beat the egg whites on medium speed until soft peaks form. Add the sugar, little by little, continuing to beat at medium speed. Increase the speed to high and continue beating until stiff peaks form. Using a large rubber spatula, fold one-fourth of the whites into the chocolate mixture to lighten it. Then carefully fold the chocolate mixture into the whites until evenly blended. Pour the batter into the prepared pan and smooth into an even layer.

7   Using a spoon, swirl the nut butter into the chocolate batter, cutting through the batter with a butter knife to create a swirl pattern. Bake until a toothpick inserted in the center comes out clean, 20 to 25 minutes. Let cool in the pan; the brownies will deflate somewhat as they cool. Invert onto a plate and peel off the parchment. Cut into 12 squares.

8   To serve, arrange 2 brownies on each plate and top with a dollop of whipped cream (if using). Sprinkle with some of the reserved hazelnuts.

FLOURLESS CHOCOLATE CAKES

SERVES 5

The original recipe for this cake—a favorite dessert of mine from a local restaurant, Marché aux Fleurs—uses a little flour. My Wine and Food Lover's Diet version substitutes almond meal, which gives the cake a light almond flavor and a rich texture and taste. Also called almond flour, almond meal is simply very finely ground raw almonds. I buy it at a local specialty-food shop. It can also be found online. Almonds offer great nutritional benefits. They are good sources of many nutrients and have more fiber per gram than any other nut. Two-thirds of the fat in almonds is mono-unsaturated, the kind that helps control cholesterol levels. Depending on your preference, you can use all sugar or all Splenda, or half and half as called for here.

¼ cup hazelnuts

½ pound dark chocolate (at least 60 percent cacao), coarsely chopped

½ cup unsalted butter

¼ cup Splenda, plus more for whipping cream (optional)

¼ cup sugar

¼ cup almond meal

3 eggs

¼ cup heavy cream

⅛ teaspoon vanilla extract (optional)

1   In a small, dry skillet over medium heat, toast the hazelnuts, stirring constantly, until they just begin to turn light brown, about 5 minutes. Immediately enclose the nuts in a clean kitchen towel and rub vigorously to remove the dark brown skins. Do not worry if tiny pieces of skin remain on the nuts. Pour the nuts into a colander and shake to separate the skins from the nuts. Coarsely chop the nuts and set aside.

2   Preheat the oven to 375°F. In a bowl suspended over, but not touching, barely simmering water in a saucepan, melt the chocolate with the butter, stirring occasionally until smooth. Set aside to cool to room temperature.

3   In the bowl of a stand mixer fitted with the whisk attachment or in a large mixing bowl with a hand-held mixer, whisk together the ¼ cup Splenda, the sugar, and the almond meal. Add the eggs, one at a time, beating well after each addition. On low speed, whisk in the cooled chocolate mixture.

4   Divide the mixture among five 1-cup ramekins, filling them three-fourths full. Bake until the cakes begin to crack slightly on top, 18 to 22 minutes. While the cakes are baking, in a small bowl, whip the cream with the vanilla and a pinch of Splenda (if using) until soft peaks form.

5   Run a small, sharp knife around the sides of each cake and invert onto a dessert plate. Top with a dollop of whipped cream and a scattering of hazelnuts. Serve warm.

CHOCOLATE SOUFFLÉS

SERVES 6

7 ounces dark chocolate (at least 60 percent cacao), coarsely chopped

2 tablespoons unsalted butter, cut into cubes

12 tablespoons heavy cream

4 large eggs, at room temperature, separated, plus 4 large egg whites, at room temperature

⅛ teaspoon cream of tartar

2 tablespoons sugar, plus more for dusting (optional)

⅛ teaspoon vanilla extract (optional)

Ideal for entertaining, decadent soufflés always impress. On the Wine and Food Lover's Diet, chocolate desserts can be served as a treat. There is no flour and very little sugar in this recipe. If you want to avoid sugar altogether, you can substitute Splenda. Dark chocolate fits the description of a low-glycemic food—it does not cause a rapid rise in blood sugar.

1   In a heatproof bowl suspended over, but not touching, barely simmering water in a saucepan, melt the chocolate with the butter, stirring occasionally until smooth. Stir in 3 tablespoons of the cream until smooth. Set aside to cool to room temperature.

2   Preheat the oven to 350°F. Whisk the egg yolks into the cooled chocolate mixture until smooth. In a very large bowl and using a handheld mixer, or in the bowl of a stand mixer fitted with the whisk attachment, mix together the 8 egg whites and cream of tartar. Start beating on medium speed. When the whites are foamy, begin adding the 2 tablespoons sugar, little by little, while beating. Beat on high until stiff peaks form.

3   Using a large rubber spatula, gently stir one-fourth of the beaten whites into the chocolate mixture to lighten it. Then fold the chocolate mixture into the egg whites, one-fourth at a time, until well blended. Divide the mixture among six 1-cup ramekins, filling them about three-fourths full. Dust the tops with sugar (if using). Bake until the soufflés rise, 11 to 13 minutes.

4   Meanwhile, in a small bowl, whip the remaining 9 tablespoons cream with the vanilla (if using) until soft peaks form. Top each soufflé with a large dollop of whipped cream and serve while still warm.

BIBLIOGRAPHY

Agatston, Arthur. *The South Beach Diet: The Delicious, Doctor-Designed, Foolproof Plan for Fast and Healthy Weight Loss.* Emmaus, NJ: St. Martin's Press, 2003.

Atkins, Robert C. Dr. *Atkins' New Diet Revolution.* New York: M. Evans, 1992.

Brand-Miller, Jennie. *The New Glucose Revolution: The Authoritative Guide to the Glycemic Index—The Dietary Solution for Lifelong Health.* New York: Marlowe and Co., 2003.

Brand-Miller, Jennie. *The Glucose Revolution: The Authoritative Guide to the Glycemic Index— The Groundbreaking Medical Discovery.* New York: Marlowe and Co., 1999.

Critser, Greg. *Fat Land: How Americans Became the Fattest People in the World.* Boston: Mariner Books, 2004.

DesMaisons, Kathleen. *Potatoes Not Prozac: A Natural Seven-Step Dietary Plan to Control Your Cravings and Lose Weight, Recognize How Foods Affect the Way You Feel, and Stabilize the Level of Sugar in your Blood.* New York: Simon & Schuster, 1999.

Gallop, Rick. *Living the GI (Glycemic Index) Diet: Delicious Recipes and Real-Life Strategies to Lose Weight and Keep It Off.* New York: Workman, 2004.

Hill, James O., John C. Peters, and Bonnie T. Jortberg. *The Step Diet Book: Count Steps, Not Calories, to Lose Weight and Keep It Off Forever.* New York: Workman, 2004.

Katahn, Martin. *The T-Factor Diet.* New York: Bantam, 1994.

Mercola, Joseph, with Alison Rose Levy. *The No-Grain Diet: Conquer Carbohydrate Addiction and Stay Slim for Life.* New York: Dutton, 2003.

Rosedale, Ron, and Carol Colman. *The Rosedale Diet.* New York: Harper Resource, 2004.

Sears, Barry. *The Soy Zone.* New York: Regan Books, 2000.

Sears, Barry, with Bill Lawren. *The Zone: A Dietary Road Map.* New York: Regan Books, 1995.

Weight Watchers, Inc. *The Weight Watchers Complete Cookbook & Program Basics.* New York: Macmillan, 1994.

INDEX

TABLE OF EQUIVALENTS

The exact equivalents in
the following tables have been
rounded for convenience.

Liquid/Dry Measures

U.S.	METRIC
¼ teaspoon	1.25 milliliters
½ teaspoon	2.5 milliliters
1 teaspoon	5 milliliters
1 tablespoon (3 teaspoons)	15 milliliters
1 fluid ounce (2 tablespoons)	30 milliliters
¼ cup	60 milliliters
⅓ cup	80 milliliters
½ cup	120 milliliters
1 cup	240 milliliters
1 pint (2 cups)	480 milliliters
1 quart (4 cups, 32 ounces)	960 milliliters
1 gallon (4 quarts)	3.84 liters
1 ounce (by weight)	28 grams
1 pound	448 grams
2.2 pounds	1 kilogram

Lengths

U.S.	METRIC
⅛ inch	3 millimeters
¼ inch	6 millimeters
½ inch	12 millimeters
1 inch	2.5 centimeters

Oven Temperatures

FAHRENHEIT	CELSIUS	GAS
250	120	½
275	140	1
300	150	2
325	160	3
350	180	4
375	190	5
400	200	6
425	220	7
450	230	8
475	240	9
500	260	10